Collins · *do brilliantly !*

RevisionGuide

KS3 Maths

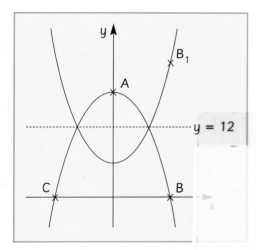

■ **Kevin Evans and Keith Gordon**

■ **Series Editor: Jayne de Courcy**

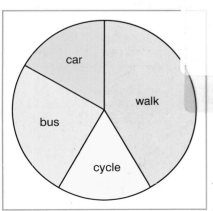

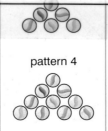

pattern 4

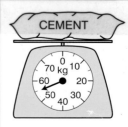

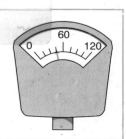

CONTENTS AND REVISION PLANNER

CONTENTS AND REVISION PLANNER

TEST TIPS

On these two pages, you can find the key comments from the most recent QCA Standards report.

Using and applying Mathematics

Solving Problems

You need to take account of all the information given. When you think you have finished a question, you should make sure that all the information given has been used.

(Question 12, page 12)

You need to identify all the necessary steps to solve a problem and your answer should show clearly all the stages in your response to a problem.

Question 4, page 10 and Question 13, page 12)

Communicating

You must be clear and logical when recording your work. This means that examiners can see if you have gained any method marks and also helps you to review and check your work.

(Question 8, page 144)

You must know the signs and symbols of mathematics. There are a lot of special words used in mathematics and lots of special signs such as ± (plus or minus).

(Question 4, page 32

Reasoning

You should apply logical reasoning to solve problems, rather than using inefficient methods such as trial and improvement to solve equations.

(Question 13, page 12)

You need to know when to use a counter-example (an example that shows something is incorrect) and when to use a generalised argument (an example that shows something is always true).

(Question 7, page 180)

Number

Topics tackled well
- Place value
- Negative numbers
- Ratio

Topics tackled less well
- Brackets and hierarchy of operations
- Fractions and calculating with fractions
- Percentages of quantities
- One quantity as a percentage of another
- Division
- Proportional reasoning

You must understand how to calculate with fractions. This means being able to add and subtract fractions with different denominators and to multiply and divide fractions (calculating with fractions).

(Page 109)

You must understand the importance of the hierarchy of operations, especially when using a calculator to evaluate a calculation. This is BODMAS.

(Pages 117, 161)

You need to be able to use formal methods of division and multiplication (column methods) but you also need to be able to use mental methods for simpler calculations.

(Pages 4, 45, 47)

Shape, Space and Measures

Topics tackled well
- Scale factors
- Enlargements

Topics tackled less well
- Time and reading timetables
- Consistent use of units
- Confusion between perimeter and area
- Constructions and the correct use of appropriate equipment

You need to know the difference between morning (a.m.) and afternoon (p.m.) times. You should also understand the 24-hour clock.

(Page 3)

You must use straight edges and compasses to make accurate constructions. Questions tell you to use them, so you will lose marks if you don't.

Page 187)

You need to know the metric and imperial units in everyday use.

(Page 75)

You should know which formula gives the circumference of a circle and which gives the area of a circle, and vice versa.

(Pages 139-140)

You should learn the basic constructions such as perpendicular bisector and angle bisector.

(Pages 133, 187)

Handling Data

Topics tackled well
- Interpreting tables, graphs and charts
- Ways of collecting data

Topics tackled less well
- Understanding the mean of a set of data
- Understanding the median of a set of data
- Understanding the range of a set of data

You should know which totals are required to calculate a mean of a set of grouped data.

(Page 83)

You should understand the significance of the range when asked to compare sets of data. The range measures the spread of the data.

(Pages 37, 84)

Algebra

Topics tackled well
- Simplifying expressions
- Forming equations
- Writing equations for linear graphs

Topics tackled less well
- Understanding mathematical language such as 'coefficient'
- Understanding mathematical symbols such as '±'

You need to understand algebraic terms such as equation, identity and expression. For example, a coefficient is the number in front of a letter in a term such as 2x.

(Page 62)

You need to understand the meaning of letter and operation symbols in algebraic expressions. For example, a^2 means 'a squared' but 2a means 'a times 2'.

(Page 18)

TES

Aı

About this book

We have planned this book to make your revision as active and effective as possible.

How?

- by picking out the key topics by level (levels 4–7)
- by breaking down the content into manageable chunks (Revision sessions)
- by testing your understanding every step of the way (Check Yourself questions)
- by giving you invaluable practice at answering Test questions (Test questions)
- by making it easy for you to plan your revision effectively (Revision website)

Key topics by level

This book is organised by levels so that you can revise easier level 4 topics first and then move on through level 5, 6 and 7 topics. This will provide a secure path through your revision.

Revision sessions

REVISION SESSION 1

- Each topic is covered in one short revision session. You should be able to read through any of these in no more than 20 minutes. That is the maximum amount of time that you should spend on revising without taking a short break.

Check Yourself Questions

- At the end of each revision session there are some Check Yourself questions. By trying these questions, you will immediately find out whether you have understood and remembered what you have read in the revision session. Answers are at the back of the book, along with extra comments and guidance.

- If you manage to answer all the Check Yourself questions for a session correctly, then you can confidently tick off this topic in the box provided in the Contents list at the front of this book. If not, you will need to tick the 'Revise again' box to remind yourself to return to this topic later in your revision programme.

Test questions

There are questions for you to try, linked to the topics that you have revised in each unit. You can try doing these once you have revised all the topics at each level. Or you can save them for last-minute practice just before your Test as a final check on understanding.

Answers and guidance are given at the back of the book. As each question is linked to a topic in the book, if you fail to get the answer right, you can go back and read through the revision session again. You'll then be sure to answer similar questions correctly in your actual Test!

Understanding and Applying Maths Test Questions

There will be some questions in your National Test that test your skills at Understanding and Applying Maths (UAM).
These questions are flagged up in the book with this symbol.

There are three ways that UAM can be tested, the first is problem solving. This will test if you can sort out complex questions and use your maths in unusual situations. The second is communicating. This will test if you can explain your maths and can use appropriate language and symbols. The third is reasoning. This will test if you can write solutions in a logical way and prove your results.

Revision website

The Collins revision website (www.activerevision.com) contains more than a dozen KS3 Maths quick tests. You can get instant feedback on your strengths and weaknesses.

As you complete a test, the results are fed into your own personalised revision planner so that you can manage your revision time effectively.

The website also contains Test Tips compiled by Test markers.

THREE FINAL TIPS

1 Work as consistently as you can during your KS3 Maths course. If you don't understand something, ask your teacher straight away, or look it up in this book. You'll then find revision much easier.

2 Plan your revision carefully and focus on the areas you find hard. The Check Yourself questions in this book will help you to do this.

3 Try to do some Test questions as though you were in the actual exam. Don't cheat by looking at the answers until you've really had a good go at working them out yourself.

The Mathematics National Curriculum explained

First, the technical information! The Mathematics National
Curriculum is divided into four Attainment Targets. These are called:

Ma1 Using and applying mathematics
Ma2 Number and algebra
Ma3 Shape, space and measures
Ma4 Handling data

Each Attainment Target is divided up into level descriptions,
numbered from level 1 to level 8. (There is also a top level called
Exceptional performance.) These describe what you should know
and be able to do at each level.

By the end of Key Stage 3, the majority of students should be
between levels 3 and 7. A typical Key Stage 3 student is expected
to have attained level 5 or 6.

Exceptional performance	•	*Considerably better than*
Level 8	•	*the expected level.*
Level 7	•	*Better than the expected level.*
Level 6	•	*Expected level*
Level 5	•	*for 14-year-olds.*
Level 4	•	
Level 3	•	*Working towards*
Level 2	•	*the expected level.*
Level 1	•	
Age	**14 years**	

Typical 14-year-olds get a level 5 or 6 in the Mathematics National Test.
This book will show you where you are and help you move up the levels.

What's in the Mathematics National Test?

The National Test papers for Maths that you will sit in May of Year 9 have
questions that cover all four Attainment Targets.

The Test papers are available at four different tiers. The first tier covers
National Curriculum levels 3-5, the second tier covers levels 4-6, the third tier
levels 5–7 and the final tier levels 6–8. Everybody has to take their tests in one
of these tiers. Your teacher will decide which tier of papers is best for you to
show what you know and understand about maths.

You have to take two Test papers and a mental Test. Both test papers include
questions in all four Attainment Targets. The Test papers start with the easier
questions and get harder as you work through. You are only allowed to use a
calculator in Paper 2.

REVISION SESSION 1 — The four operations on number

- You should be able to use the four operations of addition, subtraction, multiplication and division in a range of mental and written problems.
- You should know your multiplication tables up to 10 × 10.

What you should already know

- *How to add and subtract numbers up to 20*
- *The 2, 5 and 10 times tables and how to use them in multiplication and division problems*

FOUR RULES

- These are **addition, subtraction, multiplication** and **division**.
- You need to be able to add and subtract numbers with up to three digits and know all of your **tables** up to the 10 times table.
- If you do not know your tables and you find basic addition and subtraction difficult, you might not be able to do some of the problems.
- You need to know the **standard multiplication table** and use it to help you do multiplication and division problems.

×	1	2	3	4	5	6	7	8	9	10
1	1	2	3	4	5	6	7	8	9	10
2	2	4	6	8	10	12	14	16	18	20
3	3	6	9	12	15	18	21	24	27	30
4	4	8	12	16	20	24	28	32	36	40
5	5	10	15	20	25	30	35	40	45	50
6	6	12	18	24	30	36	42	48	54	60
7	7	14	21	28	35	42	49	56	63	70
8	8	16	24	32	40	48	56	64	72	80
9	9	18	27	36	45	54	63	72	81	90
10	10	20	30	40	50	60	70	80	90	100

Worked example

Mary is trying to work out how far the trip is from her home in Leeds to Plymouth, if she goes via Birmingham. She knows that:

Leeds to Birmingham	158 miles
Birmingham to Plymouth	256 miles

Mary works out that the distance is over 500 miles.

a How can you tell that Mary's answer is wrong without working out the correct total?

b Work out the correct answer.

a Leeds to Birmingham is about 150 miles. Birmingham to Plymouth is about 250 miles. Together that is about 400 miles.
As both values were just over their estimates the distance is over 400 miles but not over 500 miles.

b 414 miles
You do not need to show carry digits or other evidence. You will not be allowed to use a calculator on the paper that will ask this sort of question.

Worked example

First-class stamps used to cost 25p. Now they cost 28p.

a Work out the total cost of 9 stamps that cost 28p each.
b How much more is this than the cost of 9 stamps at 25p each?

Think about this problem. There is a very easy way to do it.

a This is a short multiplication.
There are lots of other ways. You can add 28 nine
times or multiply 28 by 10 and take 28 away from
the answer.

$$\begin{array}{r} 28 \\ \times\ 9 \\ \hline 252 \end{array}$$

b $9 \times 25 = £2.25$
$£2.52 - £2.25 = £0.27$
Or, each stamp costs 3p more, so 9 stamps cost 27p more! You may
be able to do this sum in your head. You do not need to show any
working, just write the answer down.

Worked example

Julie is organising a concert for Year 9. There are 232 pupils in Year 9.
The caretaker tells Julie that there are only 178 chairs in the hall.
Julie works out that they need another 146 chairs.

a Explain what she did wrong.
b Work out how many extra chairs are needed.

a Julie just took the smaller number from the bigger
each time and not the bottom number from the
top number.

$$\begin{array}{r} 232 \\ -\ 178 \\ \hline 146 \end{array}$$

b
$$\begin{array}{r} 232 \\ -\ 178 \\ \hline 54 \end{array}$$ So 54 extra chairs are needed.

Hint:

Your explanation
does not need to
be long – just a
sentence.

Worked example

Six pupils can sit at each table in the canteen. The canteen has 40
tables. After the inter-school cross-country race 162 pupils are
expected for tea.

a Without doing an exact calculation, explain why you know there
will be enough tables.
b If the smallest number of tables is to be used, how many will be
needed?

a $6 \times 40 = 240$. This is bigger than 162.

b This is short division.
27 tables are needed.

$$6\overline{)16^42}\ \ \begin{array}{c} 2\ 7 \end{array}$$

CHECK YOURSELF QUESTIONS

Q1 Complete these multiplication squares.

×	7	6	3
2			
5			
10			

×	2	5	9
9			
4			
8			

×	3	7	6
4			
8			
6			

×	5	2	7
7			
9			
3			

Q2 There are 9 pots of yoghurt in a carton.
How many pots of yoghurt are there in seven cartons?

Q3 A piece of string is 147 centimetres long. It is cut into seven equal pieces.
How long is each piece?

Q4 This timetable shows the buses from Wath to Doncaster.

Leave Wath	07.45	08.10	08.45	08.59	09.10
Arrive Doncaster	08.12	08.42	09.15	09.30	09.37

a John needs to arrive in Doncaster by 09.05. Which buses could he catch?
b Lauren has a five-minute walk to the bus stop. What time should she leave home to catch the bus that gets into Doncaster at 09.30?
c Kim is 5 minutes late for the 08.45. How long does she have to wait for the next bus?

Q5 Do these subtractions.
a 235 − 78
b 176 − 97
c 506 − 358

Q6 The train from Edinburgh to London leaves Edinburgh with 418 passengers. At Newcastle 129 get off and 58 get on.
a The guard estimates that there are now fewer than 300 people on the train. Without doing any calculations, explain how you can tell he is wrong.
b How many passengers are there on the train when it leaves Newcastle?

Q7 Time yourself doing these 15 multiplication problems.
a 3 × 3 =   **b** 3 × 4 =
c 3 × 6 =   **d** 3 × 7 =
e 3 × 8 =   **f** 4 × 4 =
g 4 × 6 =   **h** 4 × 7 =
i 4 × 8 =   **j** 6 × 6 =
k 6 × 7 =   **l** 6 × 8 =
m 7 × 7 =   **n** 7 × 8 =
o 8 × 8 =

Answers are on page 221.

Multiplying and dividing by 10 and 100

> - You need to understand the place value of numbers.
> - You should be able to multiply and divide whole numbers by 10 and 100.

What you should already know

- *Which digits in a number represent the units, tens and hundreds*
- *The ten times table*

PLACE VALUE
- In a number such as 453 (four hundred and fifty three)
  - the 4 represents 4 hundreds, or 400
  - the 5 represents 5 tens, or 50
  - the 3 represents 3 units, or 3
  So 453 = 400 + 50 + 3

MULTIPLYING BY 10 AND 100
- When you **multiply** a **whole number** by **10**, you move each digit one place to the **left** and put a zero at the end.
  32 × 10 = 320
- When you **multiply** a **whole number** by **100**, you move each digit two places to the **left** and put two zeros at the end.
  58 × 100 = 5800

H T U
    3 2   × 10
3 2 0

Th H T U
        5 8   × 100
5 8 0 0

DIVIDING BY 10 AND 100
- When you **divide** a **number** by **10**, you move each digit one place to the **right**. If the number ends in zero, it is dropped off the end.
  460 ÷ 10 = 46
- When you **divide** a **number** by **100**, you move each digit two places to the **right**. If the number ends in two zeros, they are dropped off the end.
  7300 ÷ 100 = 73

H T U
4 6 0   ÷ 10
   4 6

Th H T U
7 3 0 0   ÷100
      7 3

Worked example
Jon picks three numbers from these cards.   1   2   3   4   5

a He picks three cards that make the biggest even number. Which three does he pick?

b He picks three cards that make the smallest odd number. Which three does he pick?

a An even number must end in 0, 2, 4, 6 or 8. Jon must choose the biggest number he can for the hundreds value. He must choose the next biggest to be the tens value, then use the biggest even number that is left.

5   4   2

b An odd number must end in 1, 3, 5, 7 or 9. Jon must choose the smallest number he can for the hundreds value. He must choose the next smallest to be the tens value, then use the smallest odd number that is left.

1   2   3

Worked example

You have these cards.

| 3400 | 38 | 65 | 6500 | 380 | 340 | 308 | 650 |

a Pick two cards so that the number on one of them is 10 times the number on the other.

b Pick two cards so that the number on one of them is 100 times the number on the other.

a Any pair from 340 and 3400, 650 and 6500, 38 and 380, 65 and 650. The digits on the second card must be the same as those on the first, with an extra zero at the end.

b 65 and 6500. The digits on the second card must be the same as those on the first, with an extra two zeros at the end.

? CHECK YOURSELF QUESTIONS

Q1 Write down the answers to these.

    a 37×10 **b** 603×10 **c** 78×10 **d** 52×100

    e 307×100 **f** 21×100 **g** $490 \div 10$ **h** $630 \div 10$

    i $90 \div 10$ **j** $4300 \div 100$ **k** $600 \div 100$ **l** $4000 \div 100$

Q2 A pair of socks costs £4. How much would you pay for:

    a 10 pairs   **b** 100 pairs?

Q3 Say if the following statements are true or false.

    a 600 is 6 tens   **b** 600 is 6 hundreds   **c** 600 is 60 tens   **d** 600 is 60 units

Q4 Match these cards in two sets of three that give the same number.

| 40 tens | 40 hundreds | 4000 |

| 4 thousands | 400 | 400 units |

Q5 A box of 10 candles costs £4.50. How much does 1 candle cost?

Q6 22 000 people saw a recent Barnsley match.

    a At half-time, one person in 10 had a cup of tea. How many cups of tea were sold?

    b At half-time, one person in 100 had a snack. How many snacks were sold?

Q7 A rope 20 metres long is divided into 100 equal pieces. How long is each piece?

Q8 Harry has these cards.

| 0 | 1 | 2 | 3 | 4 | 5 |

He picks three cards and makes the number 452.

    a Use the three cards that Harry picked to make a number smaller than 452.

    b Use the three cards that Harry picked to make a number larger than 452.

    c Pick another card so that Harry can make a number 10 times as big as 452. What number does Harry make?

Answers are on page 221.

Addition and subtraction of decimals

- You should be able to add and subtract decimals with up to 2 decimal places.

- When using a calculator to solve problems, you should check that your answers are about the right size.

CALCULATING DECIMAL SUMS AND ESTIMATING ANSWERS

Worked example

Martin goes shopping and buys a shirt that costs £18, a tie that costs £4.65 and a pair of socks priced at £3.99. How much does he spend altogether?

£26.64

When adding decimals it is important to line up the decimal point. Remember that you must write £18 as £18.00. Your working should look like this.

$$
\begin{array}{r}
£18.00 \\
£4.65 \\
+ \ £3.99 \\
\hline
£26.64
\end{array}
$$

Worked example

Owen buys a piece of wood that is 3 metres long and cuts it into two pieces. One of these is 1.65 metres long. How long is the other piece?

1.35 metres

When subtracting decimals it is important to line up the decimal point. Write 3 metres as 3.00 metres.

$$
\begin{array}{r}
3.00 \\
- \ 1.65 \\
\hline
1.35 \quad \text{metres}
\end{array}
$$

Worked example

When working out 378 ÷ 5 on his calculator, Sanjay gets the answer 147.6.

a Explain clearly why he is incorrect.
b What should the answer be, roughly?

a 5 times 100 is 500, so 5 × 146 must be well over 500. This is much bigger than the original number, 378. So, Sanjay must be wrong.
b About 80.
   Make the working easy by taking 378 as about 400.

? CHECK YOURSELF QUESTIONS

Q1 Work these out.
  a 1.63 + 5.24   b 2.05 + 1.87   c 4.56 − 3.81   d 3.08 − 2.16

Q2 Put these decimal numbers in order, smallest first.

1.23	1.20	1.3	1.02	1.00

Q3 Put these decimal numbers in order, largest first.

3.462	3.48	3.5	3.089	3.09

Q4 This is a picture of a child's toy train.
  a How long is the train?
  b How high is the chimney?

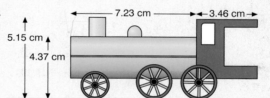

Q5 Robin measures the sides of a triangle as 3.2 cm, 5.8 cm and 10.4 cm.
  a Explain how you know he has made an error in his measuring.
  b The correct measurements are 3.2 cm, 8.5 cm and 10.4 cm. Add up these measurements to find the perimeter.

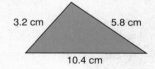

Q6 Ann buys some shoes for £35.50, a skirt for £23.45 and a belt for £5.
  a How much does she spend altogether?
  b If she pays with four £20 notes, how much change will she get?

Q7 What lengths are shown on these rulers?

  a 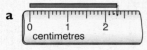   b   c

  d Add your answers to parts (**a**), (**b**) and (**c**) together.

Q8 Two of these are correct and one is wrong.
  a 567 ÷ 9 = 63   b 963 ÷ 9 = 107   c 234 ÷ 9 = 62
  Without using a calculator, explain which is wrong.

Q9 There are 1840 pupils at Wath Comprehensive School. To celebrate her retirement, the head takes them to Alton Towers for the day. The cost is £11 per pupil. Will the £21 000 the head has put aside for the trip be enough? Do not use a calculator and explain your answer fully.

Answers are on page 221.

Simple fractions, decimals and percentages

What you should already know

- *What a fraction is and what a decimal is*
- *Simple percentages and their equivalent decimals and fractions, such as:*
  50% = $\frac{1}{2}$ = 0.5

  25% = $\frac{1}{4}$ = 0.25

- **You should be able to recognise proportions of a whole number and use simple fractions and percentages.**

FRACTIONS, PERCENTAGES AND DECIMALS

- A **fraction** is a part of a whole.
- A **decimal** is a fraction written in a different way. It is also part of a whole.
- A **percentage** is a part of a whole, expressed in hundredths.
- Fractions, decimals and percentages are all different ways of expressing parts of a whole.
- Any fraction can be expressed as a decimal and as a percentage, for example:

  20% = $\frac{1}{5}$ = 0.2   75% = $\frac{3}{4}$ = 0.75   33.3% = $\frac{1}{3}$ = 0.33

ESTIMATING FRACTIONS, DECIMALS AND PERCENTAGES

Worked example

Approximately what percentage of each shape is shaded?

 a   b   c

a 30%   **b** 70%   **c** 95%

An answer that is within 5% of the answer is fine. So, part (a) could be any percentage between 25% and 35%.

Worked example

Approximately what fraction of each shape is shaded?

 a   b   c

a $\frac{2}{3}$ or $\frac{3}{4}$ **b** $\frac{3}{10}$ or $\frac{2}{5}$ **c** $\frac{4}{5}$ or $\frac{9}{10}$

RECOGNISING FRACTIONS AND DECIMALS

- Fractions may be difficult to recognise, but the shapes can usually be measured and they divide up easily.
- All the fractions you are expected to find will be simple, with a **denominator** (the bottom number) such as 2, 3, 4, 5 or 10.
- Decimals may also be difficult to recognise, but again the shapes can usually be measured and they divide up easily.
- All the decimals you are expected to find will have only one decimal place, or will be 0.25 or 0.75.

Worked example

If each of these squares represents one whole, approximately what decimal is shaded?

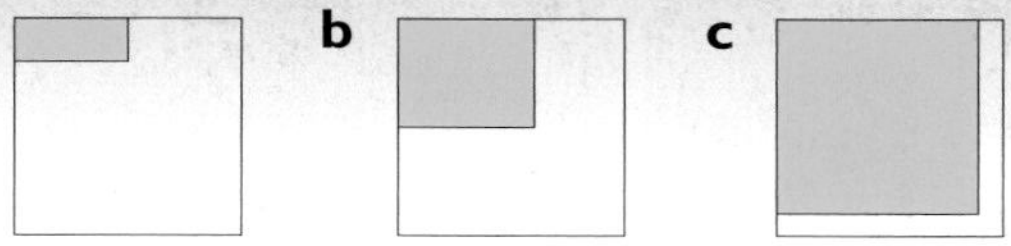

a
b
c

a 0.1 **b** 0.3 **c** 0.8

CHECK YOURSELF QUESTIONS

Q1 Martin is painting a wall. These pictures show how much he has done at different times.

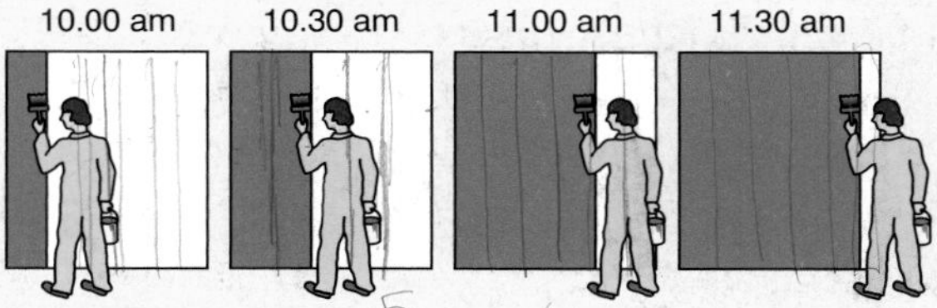

10.00 am
10.30 am
11.00 am
11.30 am

Approximately what percentage has he painted at each time?

Q2 Approximately what fraction of each flag is shaded?

a 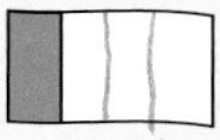 **b** 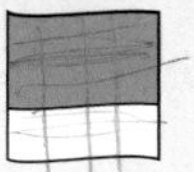 **c** 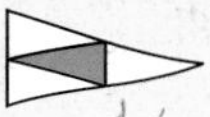 **d** 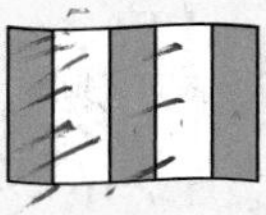

Q3 Copy this shape twice and shade in:

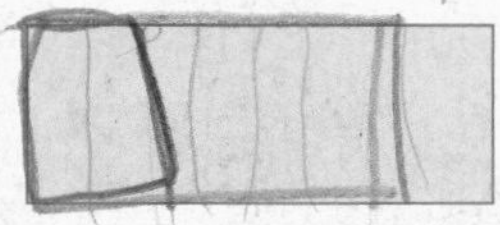

a $\frac{1}{5}$ **b** $\frac{3}{4}$.

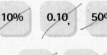

Q4 The picture shows how far up the scale of a 'Test your Strength' machine the marker has moved when different people have hit the pad.

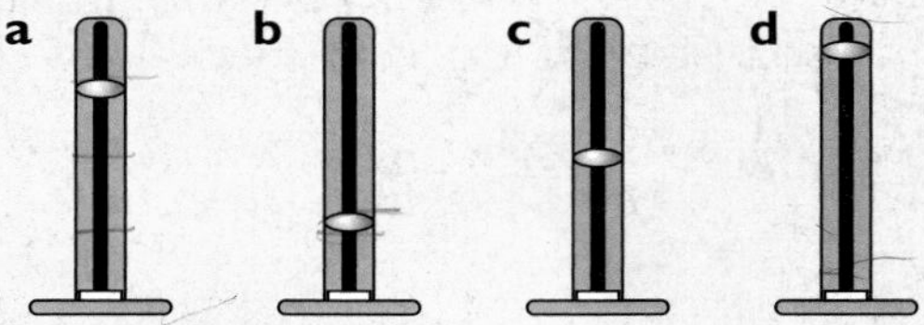

a
b
c
d

Approximately what fraction of the total distance is each marker from the bottom?

Q5 Match these cards into six sets that show the same number.

10% | 0.10 | 50% | 0.80 | $\frac{4}{5}$ | $\frac{1}{3}$ | 33% | 0.05 | $\frac{1}{20}$

$\frac{1}{2}$ | 80% | 0.50 | $\frac{1}{10}$ | 25% | 0.33 | 5% | 0.25 | $\frac{1}{4}$

Q6 Find 10% of each amount.

a £100 **b** £300 **c** £50 **d** £10

Q7 Find one-third of each amount.

a £3 **b** £300 **c** £150 **d** £30

Q8 Pupils in a class are trying to save £30 for a Christmas party. This is the chart they keep over the term.

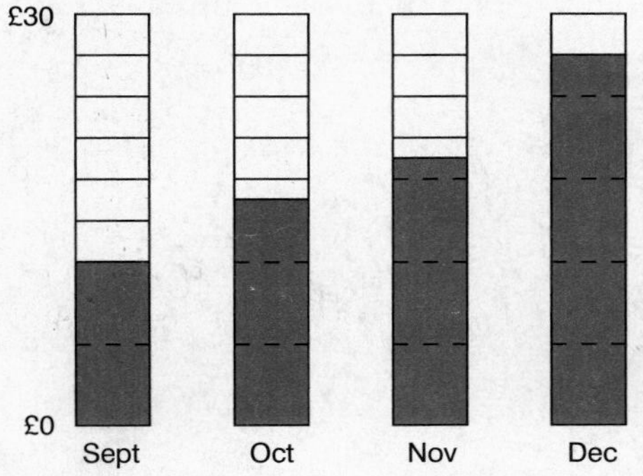

£30
£0
Sept
Oct
Nov
Dec

a What percentage of their target do they reach each month?

b How much money do they have each month?

c What percentage of their target are they down by in December?

Q9 Find three-quarters of each number.

a 4 **b** 40 **c** 120 **d** 400

Answers are on page 222.

1 Write **one** number at the end of each equation to make it correct.

Example: 26 + 34 = 16 + ...44

a 38 + 17 = 28 + ...   **b** 38 − 17 = 28 − ......

c 40 × 10 = 4 × ......   **d** 7000 ÷ 100 = 700 ÷ ......   *4 marks*

2 Look at these three signs.

<	=	>
is **less** than	is **equal** to	is **greater** than

Examples:

5 < 6	4 − 3 = 2 − 1	6 − 2 > 9 − 6
5 is **less** than 6	4 − 3 is **equal** to 2 − 1	6 − 2 is **greater** than 9 − 6

Put the correct sign, <, = or >, into each number sentence.

a ⁻7 .... ⁻2   **b** 3 − 2 ...... ⁻5   **c** 5 − 5 ...... 4 − 6   *3 marks*

3 Mark and James have the same birthday.
They were born on 15 March but in different years.

a Mark was **12** years old on 15 March **2001**.
How old will he be on 15 March 2010?   *1 mark*

b In what year was Mark born?   *1 mark*

c James was **half** as old as Mark on 15 March 2001.
In what year was James born?   *1 mark*

4 The table shows how much it costs to go to a cinema.

Mrs Jones (aged 35), her daughter (aged 12), her son (aged 10) and a friend (aged 65) want to go to the cinema.

They are not sure if they want to go before 6 pm or after 6 pm.

	Before 6 pm	After 6 pm
Adult	£3.20	£4.90
Child (14 or under)	£2.50	£3.50
Senior Citizen (60 or over)	£2.95	£4.90

How much will they save if they go **before** 6 pm?
Show you working.   *3 marks*

5 **a** Fill in the missing numbers.

50% of ...... = 27   *1 mark*

a quarter of ...... = 27   *1 mark*

b Write numbers in each space to make the calculation correct.

...... ÷ ...... = 27   *1 mark*

6 The arrow by this thermometer shows a temperature of 20°C.

    a In New York the temperature was ⁻2°C.
       In Atlanta the temperature was **7 degrees higher**.

       What was the temperature in Atlanta?   5   *1 mark*

    b In Amsterdam the temperature was **3°C**.
       In Helsinki the temperature was ⁻**8°C**.

       How many degrees warmer was it in
       Amsterdam than in Helsinki?   *1 mark*

20°C ➞

7 How much does it cost to park
for **40 minutes**?

Show your working.

> **P** **Car Park**
> Car Park Charges
> **15p** for **8 minutes**

     2 marks

8 Use **+**, **−**, × or ÷ to make each calculation correct.

     Examples: 2 ..**+**... 4 = 7 ..**−**.. 1   5 ..×... 3 = 3 ..×.. 5

    a 5 ...... 2 = 10 3   **b** 12 ...... 3 = 3 3

    c 2 ...... 1 = 9 3   **d** 6 ...... 6 = 7 7   *4 marks*

9 **a** Peter's height is **0.9 m**. Lucy is **0.3 m taller** than Peter.

       What is Lucy's height?   *1 mark*

    b Lee's height is **1.45 m**. Misha is **0.3 m shorter** than Lee.

       What is Misha's height?   *1 mark*

    c Zita's height is **1.7 m**.

       What is Zita's height in **centimetres**?   *1 mark*

10 Here are some number cards.   **1** **7** **3** **5**

     You can use each card once to make the number 1735 like this.   **1** **7** **3** **5**

     Use all four number cards to make numbers that are **as close
as possible** to the numbers written below.

     Example   **8000** ➞ **7** **5** **3** **1**

     You must **not** use the same card more than once in each answer.

    a 4000 ➞ ☐☐☐☐   **b** 1500 ➞ ☐☐☐☐

    c 1600 ➞ ☐☐☐☐   *3 marks*

11 **a** A club wants to take **3000 people** on a journey to London. The club secretary says:

> We can go in coaches.
> Each coach can carry **52** people.

How many coaches do they need for the journey?

Show your working.

2 marks

b Each coach costs **£420**.

What is the **total cost** of the coaches? *1 mark*

c How much is each person's share of the cost? *1 mark*

12 There are two small tins and
one big tin on these scales.

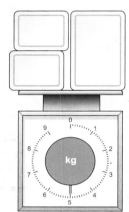

The two small tins have the same mass.

The mass of the big tin is **2.6 kg**.

What is the mass of one small tin?
Show your working.

2 marks

13 Alice and Ben each buy a bicycle, but they pay in different ways.

Alice pays
£179.99

Ben pays **£8.62**
every week for
24 weeks

Ben pays more than Alice.

How much more?
Show your working.

2 marks

Answers are on page 243.

> • You should be able to explore and describe number patterns.

What you should already know

• *How to work out the difference between two numbers*

NUMBER PATTERNS

• A **number pattern** is a list or series of numbers that are connected by a **rule**.
• You need to be able to recognise a simple number pattern and describe how it builds up. Each of these is a number pattern.
  a 2, 4, 6, 8, 10, 12, ... This goes up in twos: it's the two times table.
  b 3, 7, 11, 15, 19, 23, ... This goes up in fours, but it isn't the four times table because it starts at 3.
  c 6, 9, 12, 15, 18, ... This goes up in threes and is part of the three times table, but it doesn't start at 3. Instead it starts at 6, the second number in the three times table.
  d 2, 5, 9, 14, 20, 27, ... This one is different from the others because it does not go up by the same amount each time. It is still a pattern though, as from 2 to 5 is a jump of 3, from 5 to 9 is a jump of 4, from 9 to 14 is a jump of 5, and so on. It's a good idea to write down the 'jumps' under the pattern like this.

This makes it much easier to work out the next terms.

NEXT TERMS

• There are lots of ways to write down how a pattern builds up. At this level you will only have to find the next two or three terms.

Worked example
Find the next three terms in the number patterns shown in **a** to **d** above. Explain how you worked out your answers.

a goes up in 2s, so you add 2s to get 14, 16 and 18.
b goes up in 4s, so you add 4s to get 27, 31 and 35.
c goes up in 3s, so you add 3s to get 21, 24 and 27.
d goes up in jumps. Looking at the diagram above, you need to add 8 to 27 to get 35. Then you add 9 to 35 and get 44. Finally, you add 10 to 44 and get 54. So, the next three terms are 35, 44, 54. You can see this by extending the diagram.

```
       27           35           44           54
....      +8           +9          +10
```

- You will often need to explore number patterns shown in diagrams. You usually have to count matches or squares to try to spot the pattern.

Worked example

John is making matchstick patterns. Here are his first three patterns.

pattern 1

pattern 2

pattern 3

a Draw the next pattern.

b How many matches are needed for the 6th pattern?

a One more layer of squares is added each time. So, the next pattern looks like this.

b If you list the number of matches used in each pattern, you get 10, 15 and 20. This makes it really clear that the pattern goes up in 5s. The next three numbers are 25, 30 and 35. So, you can work out that 35 matches are needed to make the 6th pattern, without drawing all the diagrams.

Worked example

A company hires out bikes. The cost is £10, plus £3 per hour.
This table shows how much it costs to hire a bike for different times.
Fill in the missing numbers.

Number of hours bike is hired	1	2	3	4	5	6	7	8
Cost (£)	13	16	19	22				

Number of hours bike is hired	1	2	3	4	5	6	7	8
Cost (£)	13	16	19	22	25	28	31	34

You can see that the cost is going up by £3 for every extra hour. It is also possible to work out the time for which the bike was hired, if you know only the total cost.

CHECK YOURSELF QUESTIONS

Q1 Describe how each of these number patterns is building up.

   a 3, 6, 9, 12, 15, …   **b** 1, 3, 5, 7, 9, …

   c 2, 5, 8, 11, 14, 17, …   **d** 2, 4, 7, 11, 16, 22, …

   e 1, 4, 9, 16, 25, …

Q2 For each of the number patterns in question 1, write down the next three terms.

Q3 For each series of pictures on the right:

   a draw the next picture

   b write down (without drawing) how many matches you would need to make the 5th pattern.

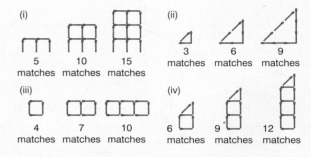

Q4 A block of flats with five floors has the flats numbered like this.

   a Describe the number pattern for each floor.

   b What do all the patterns have in common?

   c The next block of flats has four floors and three flats on each floor. On which floor is flat number 7?

Q5 Denise is making square patterns with marbles. These are her first four patterns.

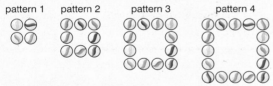

   a Draw her next square.

   b This list shows the numbers of marbles used for each pattern.

      4, 8, 12, 16, … .

      Describe how the pattern is building up.

   c How many marbles will Denise need for her 6th pattern?

Q6 Jason is making triangle patterns with marbles. Here are his first few patterns.

   a Draw his next triangle.

   b Describe how the pattern is building up.

   c How many marbles will Jason need for his 6th triangle pattern?

Q7 Mia is making square patterns with marbles. These are her first four patterns.

   a Draw her next square.

   b This list shows the numbers of marbles she uses.

      1, 4, 9, 16, …

      Describe how the pattern is building up.

   c How many marbles will Mia need for her 6th square?

Answers are on page 223.

Multiples, factors, primes and squares

- **You should be able to use multiples, factors, primes and squares.**

MULTIPLES

- A **multiple** is any number in the times table.
- The multiples of 4 are 4, 8, 12, 16, 20, 24, ... You should recognise this as the 4 times table.

> **Worked example**
> Write out the first five multiples of: **a** 5 **b** 7 **c** 12.
>
> **a** 5, 10, 15, 20, 25, ...   **b** 7, 14, 21, 28, 35, ...   **c** 12, 24, 36, 48, 60, ...

- In each case, the answers are just the first five numbers of the times tables. For example, the last one is 1×12, 2×12, 3×12, 4×12 and 5×12.

FACTORS

- A **factor** is a number that goes into another number exactly.
- The factors of 20 are $\{1, 2, 4, 5, 10, 20\}$. All these numbers divide into 20 exactly.
- Here are some tips to help you find factors of a number.
  - 1 is a factor of every number.
  - The number itself is always a factor.
  - Most other factors come in pairs. For example, $1 \times 20 = 20$, $2 \times 10 = 20$, $4 \times 5 = 20$. If you find one factor, you can find another by finding its 'pair'.

> **Worked example**
> Find all the factors of: **a** 24 **b** 15 **c** 18 **d** 16.
>
> **a** $\{1, 2, 3, 4, 6, 8, 12, 24\}$ The 'pairs' are 1×24, 2×12, 3×8 and 4×6.
> **b** $\{1, 3, 5, 15\}$ The pairs are 1×15 and 3×5.
> **c** $\{1, 2, 3, 6, 9, 18\}$ The pairs are 1×18, 2×9 and 3×6.
> **d** $\{1, 2, 4, 8, 16\}$ The pairs are 1×16, 2×8 and 4 is its own pair because $4 \times 4 = 16$.

PRIMES

- A **prime number** is a number with only two factors, itself and 1. For example, factors of 3 are $\{1, 3\}$. Factors of 17 are $\{1, 17\}$. 3, 17 and 53 are all examples of prime numbers.
- Here are two important facts about prime numbers.
  - There is only one even prime number – this is 2.
  - 1 is not a prime number (it only has 1 factor).
- The prime numbers up to 50 are:
  2, 3, 5, 7, 11, 13, 17, 19, 23, 29, 31, 37, 41, 43, 47
- There is no pattern to prime numbers. You just have to learn them or learn how to work them out.

> **Worked example**
> Give a reason why 9 is not a prime number.
>
> It is in the 3 times table, so it has 3 as a factor.

Worked example

You have cards with the numbers 1, 2, 3 and 10 on them. Fit the numbers into the four spaces on the grid so that each number is correct for its column and row.

	Multiples of 2	Factors of 12
Prime numbers		
Factors of 10		

	Multiples of 2	Factors of 12
Prime numbers	2	3
Factors of 10	10	1

1   2   3   10

SQUARES

- A **square number** is the result of multiplying a number by itself.
  16 is a square number because $4 \times 4 = 16$.

Worked example

a Continue this pattern for another three lines.

$$1 = 1$$
$$1 + 3 = 4$$
$$1 + 3 + 5 = 9$$

b What sort of numbers are on the left-hand side?

c What do you call the numbers on the right-hand side?

a
$$1 + 3 + 5 + 7 = 16$$
$$1 + 3 + 5 + 7 + 9 = 25$$
$$1 + 3 + 5 + 7 + 9 + 11 = 36$$

b These are odd numbers

c These are square numbers,
$1 \times 1 = 1, 2 \times 2 = 4,$
$3 \times 3 = 9, 4 \times 4 = 16, \ldots$

CHECK YOURSELF QUESTIONS

Q1 Write down the first five multiples of each number.
  a 4   **b** 6   **c** 9   **d** 11   **e** 20

Q2 Work out the factors of each number.
  a 6   **b** 10   **c** 30   **d** 18   **e** 32

Q3 Write down:
  a an even prime number
  b all the prime numbers between 30 and 40
  c all the prime numbers that are less than 20.

Q4   3   5   20   17   18

From these cards, find a number that is:
  a a prime number bigger than 10
  b a multiple of 6
  c a factor of 10
  d a multiple of 4 and a multiple of 5 (one card)
  e a multiple of 3 and a prime number.

Q5 You have cards with the numbers 1, 2, 5 and 15 written on them. Fit them into the four spaces on the grid so that each number is correct for its column and its row.

15   1
5   2

	Factors of 15	Prime numbers
Multiples of 5	15	5
Factors of 20	1	2

Q6 The factors of 16 are {1, 2, 4, 8, 16}.
  a How many factors does 16 have?
  b Is your answer to (a) an odd number or an even number?
  c What happens when you try to match the factors of 16 up in pairs?

Q7 What number are these people describing?

It's a multiple of 3

It's also a multiple of 4

It's also between 10 and 20

Answers are on page 223.

What you should already know

- *How to use a simple number machine*

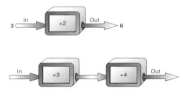

- You should be able to use simple formulae expressed in words.

WHAT IS A FORMULA?

- A **formula** is just a rule that changes a number into another number. At the simplest level this could be 'multiply by 2'.
- A formula can be shown as a **number machine**. For the rule 'multiply by 2', if 3 goes in, 6 comes out.
- The numbers that go in and the numbers that come out can be shown as a table. Check that you agree with each of these.
- For more complicated formulae the number machine may have more than one part. For example, this one is for 'multiply by 3 and add 4'.
- The formulae you will use include only the four basic rules of **addition**, **subtraction**, **multiplication** and **division**.
- Formulae may be sometimes be expressed in words.

In	Out
2	4
4	8
5	10
8	16

TO COOK:

Allow 20 minutes cooking time for each pound plus an additional 30 minutes. This bird weighs **5 pounds**.

Worked example

Look at the label on a chicken from my local supermarket. How long would it take to cook a 5-pound chicken?

The time is $5 \times 20 + 30 = 100 + 30 = 130$ minutes.

This could be written as 2 hours and 10 minutes.

? CHECK YOURSELF QUESTIONS

Q1 Work out the outputs from these number machines.

 a $7 \rightarrow \boxed{-3} \rightarrow ?$ b $18 \rightarrow \boxed{\div 3} \rightarrow ?$

Q2 Work out the outputs from these number machines.

 a $8 \rightarrow \boxed{+2} \rightarrow \boxed{-2} \rightarrow ?$ b $6 \rightarrow \boxed{\times 4} \rightarrow \boxed{+1} \rightarrow ?$

Q3 The following label was stuck inside an American cookery book.
  a What temperature is 45°C equal to in °F?
  b Water boils at 100°C. What is this temperature in °F? Show how you worked out your answer.

> **To change from °C to °F:**
> Step 1 – Divide by 5.
> Step 2 – Multiply by 9.
> Step 3 – Add 32

Q4 In the local garden centre, the price of a plant is £4.00 plus £2 for every leaf. What is the cost of the plants shown?

 a   b   c

Answers are on page 224.

COORDINATES

- **Coordinates** are used to describe the position of a point on a grid.
- The coordinates you will use at this level are all in the **first quadrant**.

FINDING A POINT ON A GRID

- There are two important rules to help you find coordinates.
  - Always start at the **origin**.
  - Move **across first**, then move **up second**.
- The origin is the point at the bottom left-hand corner of the grid. It is usually marked with an O. Its coordinates are (0, 0).
- Point A on the grid is 3 across and 2 up from the point marked O which is the origin. Write this as (3, 2).
- The pair of numbers (3, 2) is called an **ordered pair**, as the order is important.
- The ordered pair (3, 2) gives the coordinates of A.
- The first number is the x-coordinate, or the 'across' number.
- The second number is the y-coordinate, or the 'up' number.
- On the same grid, point B is at (6, 2). Point C is at (1, 5), point D is at (4, 0) and point E is at (0, 2).

What you should already know

- *How to use grids to draw shapes*
- *In games such as 'Battleships', how to identify a position*

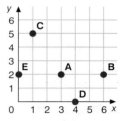

Worked example

Andrea draws a rectangle with corners at A(0, 2), B(6, 2), C(6, 4) and D(0, 4).

a What is the area of Andrea's rectangle?

b John multiplies all of Andrea's coordinates by 2. For example, his point A is at (0, 2) × 2 = (0, 4).
What other coordinates does John get? Draw his points on a grid.

c What is the area of John's rectangle?

d Fred also multiplies Andrea's coordinates by a number. Two points of Fred's rectangle are drawn on the grid. What are the other two coordinates?

e What is the area of Fred's rectangle?

a 12 squares
b (12, 4), (12, 8) and (0, 8).
See the grid on right.
c 48 squares
d (3, 2) and (0, 2)
e 3 squares

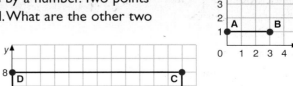

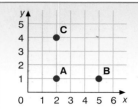

Worked example

a What are the coordinates of the points A, B and C?

b Another point D is placed on the grid so that ABCD is a square. What are the coordinates of D?

a A is (2, 1), B is (5, 1), C is (2, 4).

b The point D must be at (5, 4).

CHECK YOURSELF QUESTIONS

Q1 Give the coordinates of the points A, B, C, D, E and F from the grid.

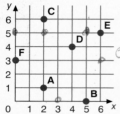

Q2 Copy the grid in question 1 and mark on the points G(6, 3), H(3, 0), J(2, 5), K(0, 5) and L(5, 5).

Q3 From the grid, give the coordinates of the points A, B and C.

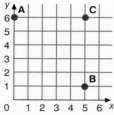

Q4 a From the grid, give the coordinates of the points P, Q and R.

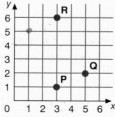

b Another point S is placed on the grid to make a rectangle PQRS. What are the coordinates of S?

Q5 The grid shows some black, white and grey counters. Four counters must be in a line. They do not have to be next to each other.

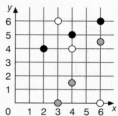

a Where should the next black counter be placed to give a line of four black counters?

b Where should the next white counter be placed to give a line of four white counters?

c Where should the next grey counter be placed to give a line of four grey counters?

Q6 a From this grid, write down the coordinates of the points A, B, C, D and E.

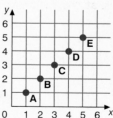

b What do you notice about the numbers in the coordinates?

c Could the point (8, 9) be on the same line as A, B, C, D and E?

Answers are on page 224.

I Daniel has some parallelogram tiles.
He puts them on a grid, in a continuing pattern.
He numbers each tile.

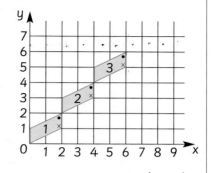

The diagram shows part of the pattern of tiles on the grid.

Daniel marks the **top right corner** of each tile with a •.
The coordinates of the corner with a • on **tile number 3**
are (6, 6).

a What are the coordinates of the corner with a • on
tile number 4?

I mark

b What are the coordinates of the corner with a • on **tile number 20**?
Explain how you worked out your answer.

I mark

c Daniel says:

> One tile in the pattern has a • in the corner at **(25, 25)**.

Explain why Daniel is **wrong**.

I mark

d Daniel marks the **bottom right corner** of each tile with a **x**.
Fill in the table to show the coordinates of each corner with a **x**.

Tile number	Coordinates of the corner with a x
I	(...2..., ...1.)
2	(......, ...)
3	(......, ...)
4	(......, ...)

I mark

Fill in the missing numbers below.

e Tile number **7** has a **x** in the corner at (......, ...).

I mark

f Tile number ...... has a **x** in the corner at **(20, 19)**.

I mark

2 Look at the diagram.

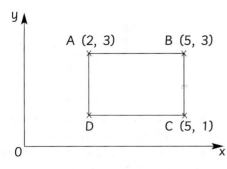

a The point K is halfway between points B
and C. What are the coordinates of point K?

I mark

b Shape ABCD is a rectangle.
What are the coordinates of point D?

I mark

3 **a** I can think of three different rules to change 6 to 18.

6 ➡ 18

Complete these sentences to show what the rules could be.

First rule: add …   *1 mark*

Second rule: multiply by …   *1 mark*

Third rule: multiply by 2 then …   *1 mark*

b Now I think of a new rule.
The new rule changes 10 to 5 **and** it changes 8 to 4.

10 ➡ 5   8 ➡ 4

Write down what the new rule could be.   *1 mark*

4 A book shows two ways to change °C to °F.

Exact rule	**Approximate rule**
Multiply the °C temperature by 1.8 then add 32.	Double the °C temperature then add 30.

a Fill in the gaps.

Using the **exact** rule, **25°C** is …… °F.   *1 mark*

Using the **approximate** rule, **25°C** is …… °F.   *1 mark*

b Fill in the gaps.

Using the **exact** rule, **0°C** is …… °F.   *1 mark*

Using the **approximate** rule, **0°C** is …… °F.   *1 mark*

c Show that at **10°C**, the exact rule and the approximate rule give the same answers.

2 marks

5 A cookery book shows how long, in minutes, it takes to cook a joint of meat.

Microwave oven
Time = (12 × weight in pounds) + 15

Electric oven
Time = (30 × weight in pounds) + 35

a How long will it take to cook a **3 pound** joint of meat in a **microwave oven**?   *1 mark*

b How long will it take to cook a **7 pound** joint of meat in an **electric oven**?   *1 mark*

c How much quicker is it to cook a **2 pound** joint of meat in a microwave oven than in an electric oven? Show your working.   *1 mark*

6 There are **four** different ways to put six pupils into equal size groups.

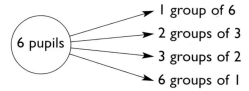

6 pupils
→ I group of 6
→ 2 groups of 3
→ 3 groups of 2
→ 6 groups of I

a Show the **five** different ways to put 16 pupils into equal size groups.

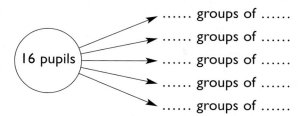

16 pupils
→ ...... groups of ......
→ ...... groups of ......
→ ...... groups of ......
→ ...... groups of ......
→ ...... groups of ......

2 marks

c Circle the numbers below that are **factors of twelve**.

    I   2   3   4   5   6

    7   8   9   10   II   12

2 marks

7 Here is some information about a school.

There are **3 classes** in Year 8. Each class has **27 pupils**.
There are **4 classes** in Year 9. Each class has **25 pupils**.

a Use the information to match each question with the correct calculation. The first one has been done for you.

Question	Calculation
How many **classes** are there altogether in Years 8 and 9?	$3 + 4$
	$3 - 4$
	$4 - 3$
There are more **classes** in Year 9 than in Year 8. How many more?	$(3 \times 27) + (4 \times 25)$
	$(3 + 27) + (4 + 25)$
How many **pupils** are there altogether in Years 8 and 9?	$(3 \times 27) - (4 \times 25)$
	$(4 + 25) - (3 + 27)$
There are more **pupils** in Year 9 than in Year 8. How many more?	$(4 \times 25) - (3 \times 27)$

I mark

b Use the information about the school to write what the missing question could be.

Question   Calculation

4×25

I mark

Answers are on page 243.

2-D and 3-D shapes

What you should already know

- *How to recognise and name shapes such as the square, rectangle, cube, cuboid and pyramid*

- You should be able to recognise a 3-D shape from a 2-D drawing and identify linking edges and corners.

- You should be able to draw common 3-D shapes on a 2-D grid.

NETS AND SOLIDS

- To make a 3-D shape you need to start by drawing a **net** for the shape.
- Drawing the net on a grid helps to make it more accurate.
- Add **tabs** to join the edges and make the actual shape.
- The nets of most solids allow you to count the numbers of **edges**, **corners** and **faces** on the 3-D shape.
- Try to learn the numbers of edges, corners and faces for simple 3-D shapes.

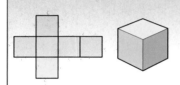

Worked example

This net can be folded to make a cube. How many edges, corners and faces does the cube have?

The cube has 12 edges, 8 corners and 6 faces.

Worked example

Use a grid to draw a net for a pyramid.

PLANS AND ELEVATIONS

- The **plan** of a shape is the view from above, looking down.
- The **elevations** of a shape are the views from the back, sides or front.

Worked example

Draw the plan and the front and side elevations for this T-shape.

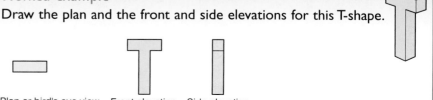

Plan or bird's eye view   Front elevation   Side elevation

CHECK YOURSELF QUESTIONS

Q1 Which of these nets could you use to make a cube?

a   b   c 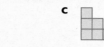 d

Q2 Use a grid to draw an accurate net for this open box.

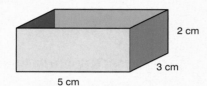

2 cm

3 cm

5 cm

Q3 Draw front, side and top elevations for this L-shape.

Q4 Find the number of edges, corners and faces for this 4-sided dice.

Q5 Use a dotted grid to draw a net for this chocolate box.

Answers are on page 224.

What you should already know

- *How to recognise symmetry*

- *That 2-D shapes may have:*
  – line symmetry, sometimes called reflective symmetry
  – rotational symmetry

- **You should recognise rotational symmetry and line symmetry.**
- **You should be able to reflect shapes in a mirror line.**

LINE SYMMETRY

- A shape has **line symmetry** if you can draw a line on the shape to divide it into two equal, matching parts.
- You can use tracing paper or a mirror to test for a line of symmetry on a shape.
- A line of symmetry is sometimes called a **mirror line**.
- The line of symmetry divides the shape so that one half is a 'mirror image' of the other.
- Shapes can have more than one line of symmetry.

Worked example

How many lines of symmetry does this road sign have?

It has just one line of symmetry.

Lines of symmetry are usually dotted. Check by tracing the shape and folding the tracing paper on the line of symmetry or by placing a mirror on the line of symmetry.

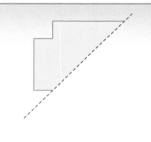

Worked example

Use the dotted diagonal line as a mirror line to reflect this shape.

You may find it easier to turn the page so that the mirror line is horizontal.

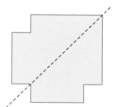

ROTATIONAL SYMMETRY

- A shape has **rotational symmetry** if you can draw round it, pick it up and turn it around so that it fits exactly over its outline.
- The **order** of rotational symmetry is the number of times a rotated shape can be turned to fit exactly over its own outline, before it returns to its original position.
- You can use tracing paper to help you find the order of rotational symmetry.
- Shapes that do not have rotational symmetry are of order 1.

Worked example

Find the order of rotational symmetry for each
of these shapes.

a   b   c   d   e

a order 2
b order 4
c order 2
d order 3
e order 6

CONGRUENT SHAPES

- **Congruent** shapes are exactly the same size and shape but they
  may be in different positions.
- To check if two shapes are congruent, trace one of them and see
  if it fits exactly on top of the other. Remember that you may
  have to turn your tracing paper over.

Worked example

How many of these letters are congruent?

All the letters are congruent.

❓ CHECK YOURSELF QUESTIONS

Q1 Draw in all the lines of symmetry for these shapes.

Q2 Find the order of rotational symmetry for these shapes.

a   b   c   d

Q3 Find pairs of congruent shapes.

a   b   c   d   e   f

Answers are on page 224.

What you should already know

- *The metric units: metres, grams and litres*

- You should be able to choose appropriate measuring instruments and units and measure accurately from a variety of scales.

MEASURING
- Generally, you need to use a ruler for measuring length, a set of scales or a balance for weighing, a thermometer for taking temperatures and so on.
- The **scale** on measuring instruments is usually graduated in small divisions.
- Take care to work out how many units there are for each division.

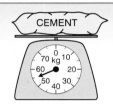

Worked example

What is the mass of the bag of cement?

Each division is 5 kg. The bag of cement weighs 55 kg.

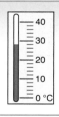

Worked example

What is the temperature shown on the thermometer?

Between 0 and 10 there are 5 divisions. So each division is 2°.
The temperature shown is 20 + (4 × 2) = 28°C.

CHECK YOURSELF QUESTIONS

Q1 Measure the lengths of these lines.

a ———————————————————

b ——————————

c ————

Q2 How much liquid is in the measuring jug?

Q3 How much time is left on the parking meter?

Answers are on page 225.

> • You should be able to find perimeters of simple shapes, find areas by counting squares and volumes by counting cubes.

What you should already know

• *The basic ideas of length, area and volume*

PERIMETER

• To find the **perimeter** of a shape, you find the total distance all the way around the outside.
• Remember the units are **millimetres** (mm), **centimetres** (cm) and **metres** (m).

Worked example
Find the perimeter of the hexagon.

The perimeter of the shape is 6 cm.
Remember not to count the lines inside the shape.

Worked example
Find the perimeter of the H-shape.

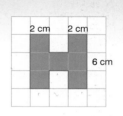

Start at the top left corner of the shape and add up the lengths around the outside.
Perimeter = 2 + 2 + 2 + 2 + 2 + 6 + 2 + 2 + 2 + 2 + 2 + 6
= 32 cm

AREA

• To find the **area** of a 2-D shape, place it over a square grid and count the number of whole squares covered by the shape.
• The units of area are **square centimetres** (cm^2) or **square metres** (m^2).

Worked example
Find the area of this rectangle.

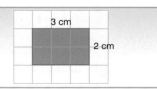

There are 6 squares inside the rectangle, so the area is 6 cm^2.

Worked example
Find the area of each of these shapes.

For examples like these, it is a good idea to mark the half squares with a cross first.

a
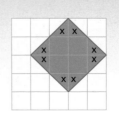

b
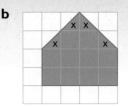

a Inside this shape, there are 4 whole squares and 8 half squares. So, the total area is 4 + 4 = 8 cm^2.
b Inside this shape, there are 10 whole squares and 4 half squares. So, the total area is 10 + 2 = 12 cm^2.

VOLUME

- To find the **volume** of a 3-D shape. count the number of cubes inside the shape.
- The units of volume are **cubic centimetres** (cm³) or **cubic metres** (m³).

Worked example

Find the volume of this T-shape.

Count the cubes.
The volume of the shape is **9 cm³**.

 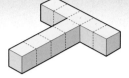

1 cm³

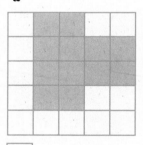

Worked example

Find the volume of this cuboid.

On the top layer there are 12 cubes, so in 2 layers there are 24 cubes. Each cube is 1 cm³, so the volume of the cuboid is 24 cm³.

CHECK YOURSELF QUESTIONS

Q1 Find the perimeter and area of each of these shapes.

a

b

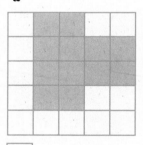 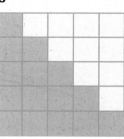

□ = 1 cm²

Q2 The area of this square is 16 cm². Can you draw a rectangle which has the same area?

Q3 This diamond tile has a perimeter of 4 cm. Find the perimeter of a larger diamond shape that is made by putting 9 of these tiles together.

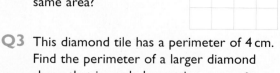

Q4 Find the area of this carpet.

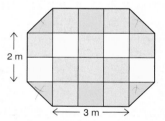

2 m

3 m

Q5 What is the volume of this shape?

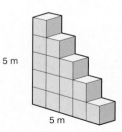

5 m

5 m

Answers are on page 225.

1   A pupil recorded how much rain fell on five different days.

	Amount in cm
Monday	0.2
Tuesday	0.8
Wednesday	0.5
Thursday	0.25
Friday	0.05

   a   Fill in the gaps with the correct days.

     The **most** rain fell on ....   The **least** rain fell on ....   *2 marks*

   b   How much **more** rain fell on Wednesday than on Thursday?   *1 mark*

   c   How much rain fell altogether on **Monday**, **Tuesday** and **Wednesday**?   *1 mark*

     Now write your answer in millimetres.   *1 mark*

2   Look at the shaded shape.

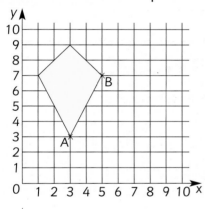

   a   **Two** statements below are correct.
Tick the correct statements.

     The shape is a **quadrilateral**.   ☐

     The shape is a **trapezium**.   ☐

     The shape is a **pentagon**.   ☐

     The shape is a **kite**.   ☐

     The shape is a **parallelogram**.   ☐   *1 mark*

   b   What are the coordinates of point **B**?   *1 mark*

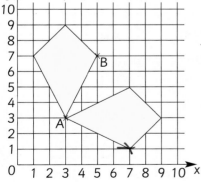

   c   The shape is **reflected** in a mirror line.

     Point A stays in the same place.

     Where is point **B** reflected to?

     Put a cross on the grid to show the correct place.   *1 mark*

   d   Now the shape is **rotated**.

     Point A stays in the same place.

     Where is point **B** rotated to?

     Put a cross on the grid to show the correct place.

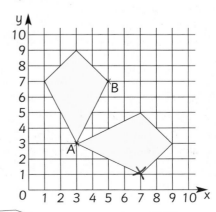

     1 mark

3 Two pupils drew angles on square grids.

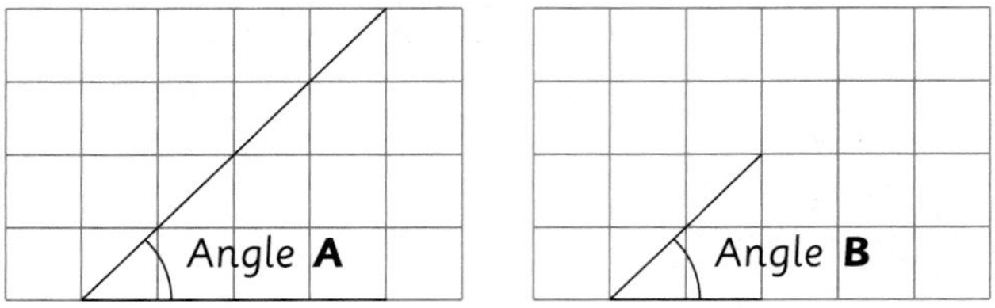

Angle **A**

Angle **B**

a Which word below describes angle **A**? Tick (✓) the correct box.

acute ☐   obtuse ☐   right angle ☐   reflex ☐   *I mark*

b Is angle **A bigger** than angle **B**?

Tick (✓) yes or no.

Yes ☐   No ☐

Explain your answer.   *I mark*

4 Look at the hexagon and the triangle.

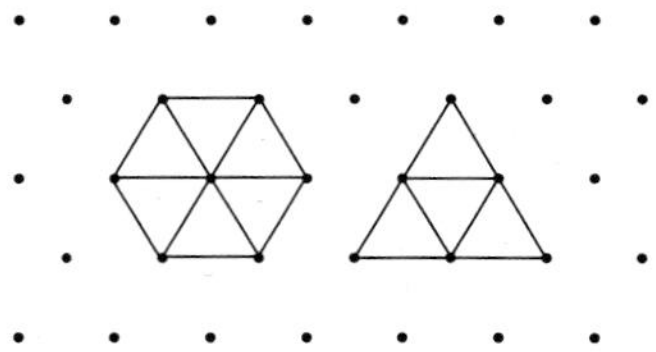

a Do the hexagon and triangle have the **same area**?

Tick (✓) yes or no.

Yes ☐   No ☐

Explain your answer.   *I mark*

b Do the hexagon and triangle have the **same perimeter**?

Tick (✓) yes or no.

Yes ☐   No ☐

Explain your answer.   *I mark*

5

a The time on this clock is **3 o'clock**.
What is the **size** of the **angle** between the hands?

I mark

b What is the size of the **angle** between the hands
at **I o'clock**?

I mark

c What is the size of the **angle** between the hands
at **5 o'clock**?

I mark

d How long does it take for the tip of the **minute**
hand to move through **360°**?

I mark

6 The shaded rectangle has an **area** of **4 cm²** and a **perimeter** of **10 cm**.

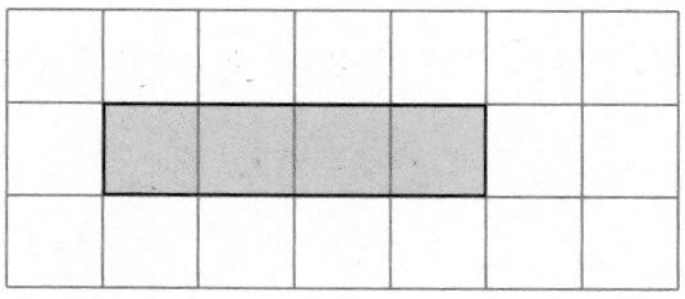

a Look at the cross-shape.

Fill in the gaps below.

The cross-shape has an **area** of ...... **cm²** and a **perimeter** of ...... **cm**.

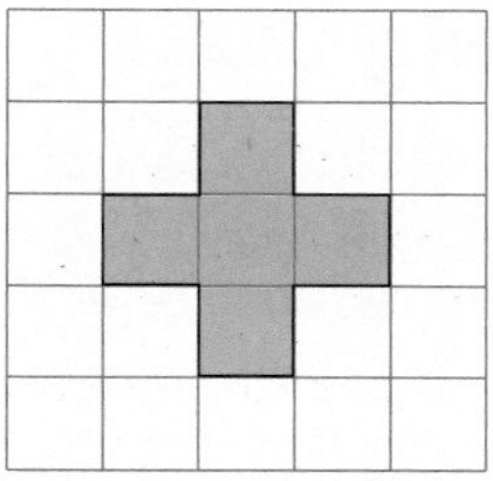

2 marks

b Draw a shape with an **area** of **6 cm²**.   1 mark

c What is the **perimeter** of your shape?   1 mark

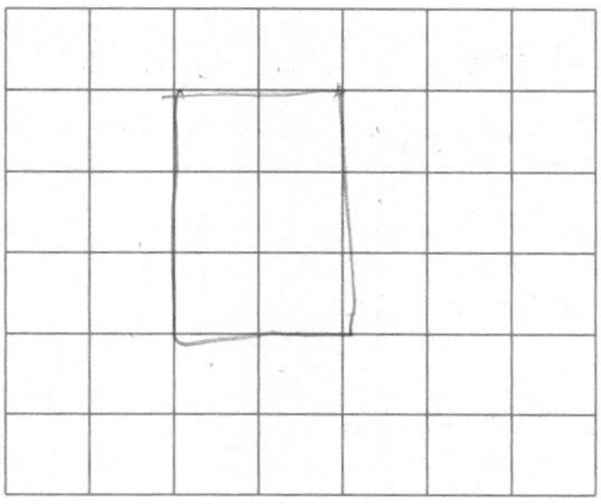

d Look at the octagon.

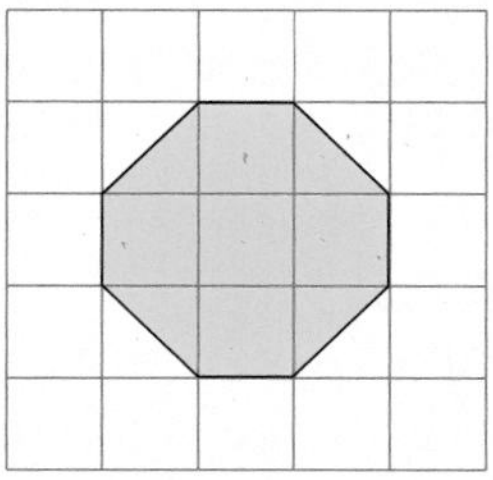

What is the area of the octagon?   1 mark

e Explain how you know that the perimeter of the octagon is **more than 8 cm**.

1 mark

7 a I have a square piece of card.

I cut along the dashed line to make two pieces of card.

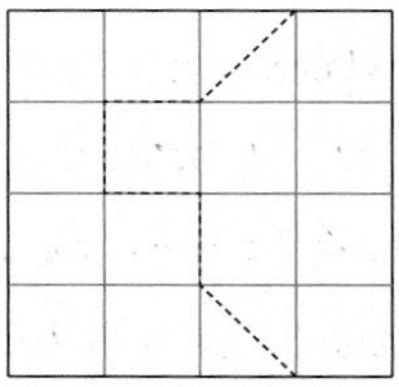

Do the two pieces of card have the same area?

Tick (✓) yes or no.

Yes ☐   No ☐

Explain your answer.   1 mark

b The card is shaded grey on the front and black on the back. I turn piece A over to see its black side.

Which of the shapes below shows the black side of piece A?

Put a tick (✓) under the correct answer.

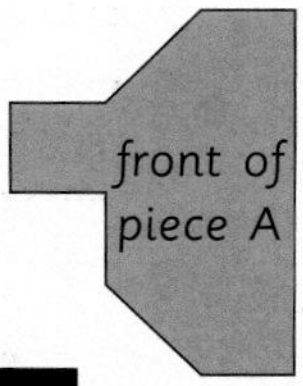

front of piece A

☐   ☑   ☐   ☐   ☐

1 mark

Answers are on page 244.

What you should already know

- *How to read information from tables*
- *How to draw a simple bar chart*

- You should be able to collect discrete data and record it in a table.
- You should be able to group data and represent this in a frequency diagram.
- You should be able to interpret such diagrams.

COLLECTING DATA

- You may need to collect data from a wide variety of sources.
- When collecting data, you usually start by designing a survey sheet or writing a questionnaire.
- You can use a tally to enter data onto a **frequency table**.
- When you have completed the frequency table, you can draw suitable diagrams to make the data easier to understand.
- **Frequency diagrams** are usually drawn as **bar charts**.
- Computer **databases** are a quick and convenient way for collecting a lot of data. Your school is likely to have a database of its pupils.

DISCRETE DATA COLLECTION

- Data that involves counting in whole numbers, such as the numbers of children in families, is called **discrete data**.
- If you collect data from a small group (or sample), you can use a **tally** to construct a frequency table.

Worked example

```
8  7  5  10  4  8
7  6  7  7  10  5  ←— These are their marks out of 10.
8  9  8  9  8  8
5  8  8  7  8  9
```

The 24 pupils in Class 9Q were given 10 mental arithmetic questions. These are their marks out of 10.

a Use a tally to draw up a frequency table for the data.
b Draw a bar chart to illustrate the data.
c What mark did most pupils obtain?

a

Mark	Tally	Frequency
4	I	1
5	III	3
6	I	1
7	ɪɪɪɪ	5
8	ɪɪɪɪ IIII	9
9	III	3
10	II	2
	TOTAL	24

b

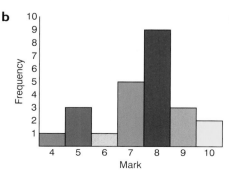

c Most pupils obtained a mark of 8.

Remember to label the axes. Notice that the marks are placed under the middle of each bar.

Notice that for every 5 counted you use a 'gate' ɪɪɪɪ .

Worked example

James in Form 9P designed a survey sheet to find the favourite colour of his class. His completed survey sheet looked like this.

How could James improve his survey sheet?

James could use a tally to make counting easier. He could also use the frequency column to find the total for each colour. He could then add the frequencies to check that he had included everyone.

Colour	Frequency
Red	✓✓✓✓✓✓
Blue	✓✓✓
Green	✓✓✓✓✓
Yellow	✓✓
Black	✓
Purple	✓✓
Brown	✓✓✓
Others	✓✓✓✓✓

COLLECTION OF GROUPED DATA

- If you have to collect a lot of data and it is spread out over a wide range of numbers, it is more convenient to put the data into a **grouped frequency table**.
- There should be fewer than 10 groups all of equal width.
- The groups are called **class intervals**.

Worked example

Mrs Whitehead recorded her pupils' Science SATS marks.

45 57 35 34 37 38 40 29 42 56 28 19 34 56 35 28
20 39 35 40 45 24 17 36 37 42 27 46 55 38 50 22

She wanted to show how well the class had done, so she decided to draw a bar chart. She started by constructing a grouped frequency table, putting the marks into class intervals of 10 marks width.
a Draw up a grouped frequency table to show how she did this.
b Draw a bar chart to illustrate the data.
c A Level 5 was awarded to anyone who scored over 40.
How many pupils obtained a Level 5?

a

Class interval	Tally	Frequency
1–10		0
11–20	|||	3
21–30	⧪⧪⧪⧪⧪		6
31–40	⧪⧪⧪⧪⧪ ⧪⧪⧪⧪⧪ |||	13
41–50	⧪⧪⧪⧪⧪		6
51–60	||||	4
	TOTAL	32

b

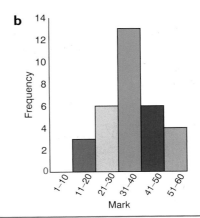

c 10 pupils obtained a Level 5 (6 + 4).

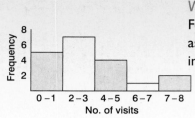

Worked example

For a school project, Jonathan was doing a survey on the cinema. He asked a sample of friends how many times they had visited the cinema in the past month. His bar chart is shown on the left.

a How many friends took part in the sample?
b How many visited the cinema more than five times?
c How many visited the cinema exactly once?

a Add together the heights of all the bars.
$5 + 7 + 4 + 1 + 2 = 19$
b Add together the heights of the last two bars.
$1 + 2 = 3$
c You cannot tell this from the bar chart. The first bar shows the number of Jonathan's friends who didn't go to the cinema at all, added to the number who visited the cinema once.

CHECK YOURSELF QUESTIONS

Q1 Mr Rhodes accessed the school database to find the number of absences last week for the pupils in class 9R. His data is given in the frequency table.

Day	Mon	Tue	Wed	Thur	Fri
Absences	2	4	10	1	3

a Draw a bar chart for his data.
b How many pupils are there in class 9R?
c Can you think of a reason why so many pupils were absent on Wednesday?

Q2 The vertical line diagram (bar chart with bars replaced by lines) shows the number of drinks served in a school's canteen on Tuesday.
a Which drink sold the most?
b How many drinks were sold altogether?
c What was the weather like on Tuesday?

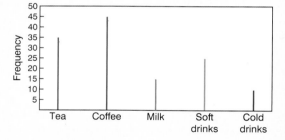

Q3 Jenny wanted to find out how much pupils at her school spent on sweets. She asked 30 pupils how much they had spent on sweets the previous day. This is her data.

23p, 56p, £1.20, 50p, 0p, 48p, 90p, £1.45, 60p, 32p, £2.30, 38p, 0p, £2.10, 75p, 18p, 65p, £1.60, 40p, 18p, 28p, £1.50, £1.52, 65p, 0p, 22p, 50p, £2.35, £1.82, 85p.

a Draw up a grouped frequency table for her data, using class intervals 0p–49p, 50p–99p, £1.00–£1.49… and so on.
b Draw a bar chart to illustrate her data.

Q4 This extract is taken from Shakespeare's *A Midsummer Night's Dream*.

Count the letters in each word and draw up a frequency table. How many words are there in the extract?

> Thou speak'st aright;
> I am that merry wanderer of the night.
> I jest to Oberon and make him smile
> When I a fat and bean-fed horse beguile,
> Neighing in likeness of a filly foal:
> And sometimes lurk I in a gossip's bowl,
> In very likeness of a roasted crab.

Answers are on page 225.

14 Mode and median

- You should understand and be able to used the mode and median of a set of data.
- You should know what the range of a set of data is.

What you should already know

- *The term frequency*
- *How to list numbers in numerical order*

AVERAGES AND RANGE

- An **average** value is the best representative value for a set of data.
- There are three common averages: the **mode**, the **median** and the **mean**.
- The **range** of a set of data is the difference between the biggest number and the smallest number.

THE MODE

- In any set of data, the mode is the value that has the highest frequency. It is the value that occurs most often in the data.
- The mode is a useful average because it gives the most common value. For example, Number 1 in the charts is the most common single sold in the UK in a particular week.

Worked example

City United scored the following numbers of goals in their first 10 matches of the season.

0, 1, 3, 0, 2, 1, 0, 1, 3, 1

a Find their modal score.

b Find the range of the data.

a The score of 1 occurs the greatest number of times (4 times), so this is the score with the highest frequency. Therefore, the modal score is 1.

b The highest value is 3 and the lowest is 0, so the range is 3 − 0 = 3.

Worked example

Denise kept a record of how many minutes the school bus was late over a four-week period. This is her data.

2, 10, 5, 15, 3, 0, 0, 2, 8, 4, 5, 0, 0, 8, 20, 0, 5, 0, 10, 3

a Find the modal average for these times.

b Do you think this average value will help Denise to explain why she is often late for school?

a 0 occurs 6 times and this is the time with the highest frequency. The modal time is 0 minutes.

b No. It is obvious from her data that the bus is late quite often but the modal average makes it seem as if the bus is always on time.

THE MEDIAN

- The median is the middle value in a set of data, once the values have been put into numerical order.
- The median is a useful average because it does not take into account the very high or very low values which can sometimes distort the data.

Worked example

A newspaper article discussing average wages quotes the annual salaries of a group of people in a table like this.

Civil servant	Bank clerk	Fireman	Shop manager	Teacher	Footballer	Lorry driver	Lawyer	Nurse
£24 000	£14 000	£16 500	£19 500	£21 000	£80 000	£13 500	£32 000	£14 500

a Find the median salary.

b Why is the median a good average to use?

a List the salaries in order:

£13 500, £14 000, £14 500, £16 500, £19 500, £21 000, £24 000, £32 000, £80 000

There are nine values and the middle one is the fifth value. The median salary is therefore £19 500.

b It does not take into account the high salary of the footballer which is not consistent with the rest of the data.

CHECK YOURSELF QUESTIONS

Q1 Find the mode and median for each of these sets of numbers.
   a 2, 7, 5, 2, 1, 3, 2
   b 9, 18, 32, 16, 9, 7, 29, 10, 14
   c 4, 5, 4, 4, 7, 8, 9, 5
   d 42, 50, 46, 54, 38, 44, 52, 48, 40, 56

Q2 Find the range of each of the sets of data in question 1.

Q3 Sam wanted to find the average height of all the boys in his football team. After measuring all their heights to the nearest centimetre, he recorded the following data.

159, 155, 153, 158, 162, 160, 172, 161, 163, 165, 168

Find the median height of the team.

Q4 'LikeAglove' shoe shop kept a frequency table of the sizes of 'Sporty' shoes they sold on a particular day.
   a Find the modal shoe size.
   b Find the median shoe size.

Size	No. sold
3	1
4	3
5	3
6	4
7	8
8	5
9	1

Answers are on page 226.

REVISION SESSION 15 Line graphs

> • You should be able to construct simple line graphs.

What you should already know

- *How to read information from graphs*

- *How to read and understand decimal notation*

USING LINE GRAPHS

- **Line graphs** are statistical diagrams which show how data changes between consecutive values, for example, how temperature changes at various times of the day.
- They can be used to show **trends** or patterns over a time period, for example, the global warming of the Earth.
- In line graphs, data points are connected by straight lines.

Worked example

Mark recorded the outside temperature every two hours and drew a line graph to show his data.

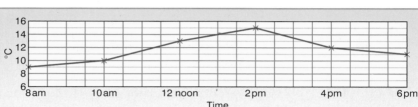

a What was the temperature at 2 pm?

b Find the increase in temperature between 10 am and 1 pm.

c Which two-hour period had the greatest increase in temperature? How can you tell this from the graph?

a 15°C

b At 10 am it was 10°C and at 1 pm it was 14°C. The increase is 4°C.

c The greatest increase in temperature was between 10 am and midday. The line on the graph between these two times has the steepest upward slope.

Worked example

Lizzie is in hospital with a fever. Her medical chart shows her temperature on a line graph over a three-day period.

a What was Lizzie's temperature at 6 pm on Tuesday?

b What was her highest temperature?

c Normal body temperature is 37°C. When did Lizzie have a normal body temperature?

d Why does the temperature axis not start at 0°C?

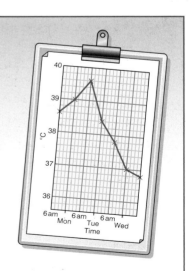

a 38.4°C. On the temperature axis there are five divisions for every one whole degree, so each division on the axis is 0.2 of a degree.

b 39.6°C.

c 6 pm on Wednesday. Readings were taken every 12 hours.

d A lot of space would be wasted and the line graph would be difficult to read because the scale would be much smaller.

CHECK YOURSELF QUESTIONS

Q1 A holiday brochure for Greece has a line graph to show the average daily high and low temperatures for different months.

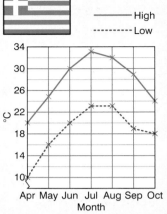

a What are the average daily high and low temperatures in May?

b What is the difference between the high and low temperatures in September?

c In which month is the difference between the two temperatures the least?

Q2 The table shows the sales figures of the book, *A Mathematician's Diary*, by Dr Easisome, for the 25 years after it was first published.

Year	1970	1975	1980	1985	1990	1995
Sales	2100	2400	2800	3000	2900	2700

a Draw a line graph to show the sales of the book.

b Could we use the graph to estimate how many books were sold in the year 2000?

Answers are on page 226.

REVISION SESSION 16 Probability

> • You should understand and use simple words associated with probability, such as 'fair', 'certain 'and 'likely'.

What you should already know

• *Simple ideas about chance*

WHAT IS PROBABILITY?

• The idea of **chance** comes up every day: *What will the weather be like tomorrow? What's the chance the SATs will be easy?*
• **Probability** is about measuring the chance of something happening. When you talk about probability, you use words such as: *possible, likely, 50–50, fair, impossible.*
• You need to know how these words are used in probability questions: *impossible, very unlikely, unlikely, equally likely, likely, very likely* and *certain.*
• In probability, you consider **events** that have one or more possible **outcomes**.
• This probability line shows where each of the words come on a scale from *least chance* to *greatest chance.*

Impossible	Very unlikely	Unlikely	Evens	Likely	Very likely	Certain

---

Worked example

When you roll an ordinary dice, what is the chance of getting a 6?

There are six different numbers on a dice and you could score any one of them. Therefore, the chance is not very good. Scoring a 6 is unlikely.

? CHECK YOURSELF QUESTION

Q1 Choose one of the following to describe each of (a) to (g):
impossible, very unlikely, unlikely, equally likely, likely, very likely, certain.
   a picking a heart from a well-shuffled pack of cards
   b rolling a dice and getting an even score
   c winning the jackpot in the National Lottery
   d running a 1500 m race in 3 minutes
   e the next car you see having been made in Europe
   f doing some revision for your SATs
   g picking a consonant from a bag of 'Scrabble' letters

Answers are on page 226.

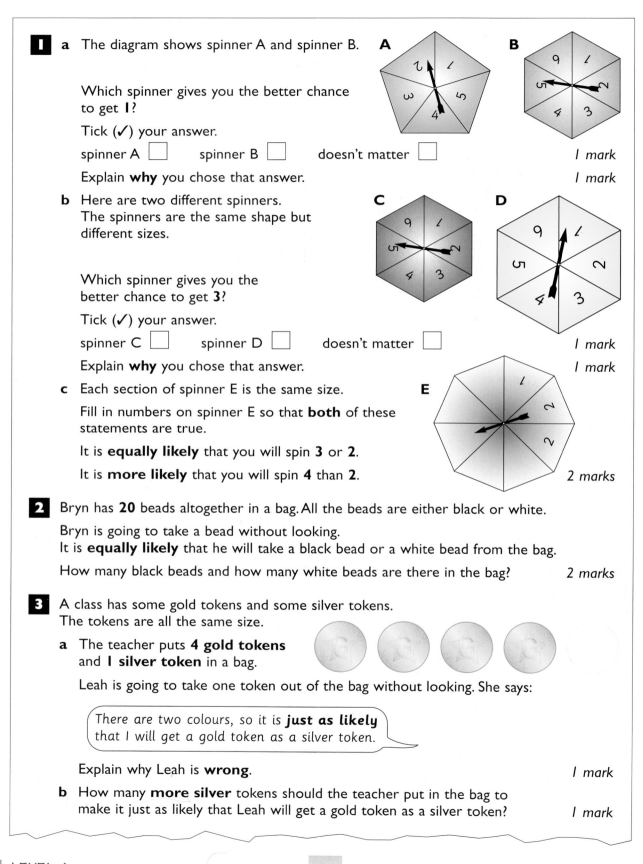

1 a The diagram shows spinner A and spinner B.

Which spinner gives you the better chance to get **1**?

Tick (✓) your answer.

spinner A ☐   spinner B ☐   doesn't matter ☐   *1 mark*

Explain **why** you chose that answer.   *1 mark*

b Here are two different spinners.
The spinners are the same shape but different sizes.

Which spinner gives you the better chance to get **3**?

Tick (✓) your answer.

spinner C ☐   spinner D ☐   doesn't matter ☐   *1 mark*

Explain **why** you chose that answer.   *1 mark*

c Each section of spinner E is the same size.

Fill in numbers on spinner E so that **both** of these statements are true.

It is **equally likely** that you will spin **3** or **2**.

It is **more likely** that you will spin **4** than **2**.   *2 marks*

2 Bryn has **20** beads altogether in a bag. All the beads are either black or white.

Bryn is going to take a bead without looking.
It is **equally likely** that he will take a black bead or a white bead from the bag.

How many black beads and how many white beads are there in the bag?   *2 marks*

3 A class has some gold tokens and some silver tokens.
The tokens are all the same size.

a The teacher puts **4 gold tokens** and **1 silver token** in a bag.

Leah is going to take one token out of the bag without looking. She says:

> *There are two colours, so it is **just as likely** that I will get a gold token as a silver token.*

Explain why Leah is **wrong**.   *1 mark*

b How many **more silver** tokens should the teacher put in the bag to make it just as likely that Leah will get a gold token as a silver token?   *1 mark*

c Jack has a different bag with **8** tokens in it.
It is **more likely** that Jack will take a gold token than a silver token from his bag.

How many **gold** tokens might there be in Jack's bag? *1 mark*

4 The diagram shows what pupils in years 7, 8 and 9 choose to do at dinner time.

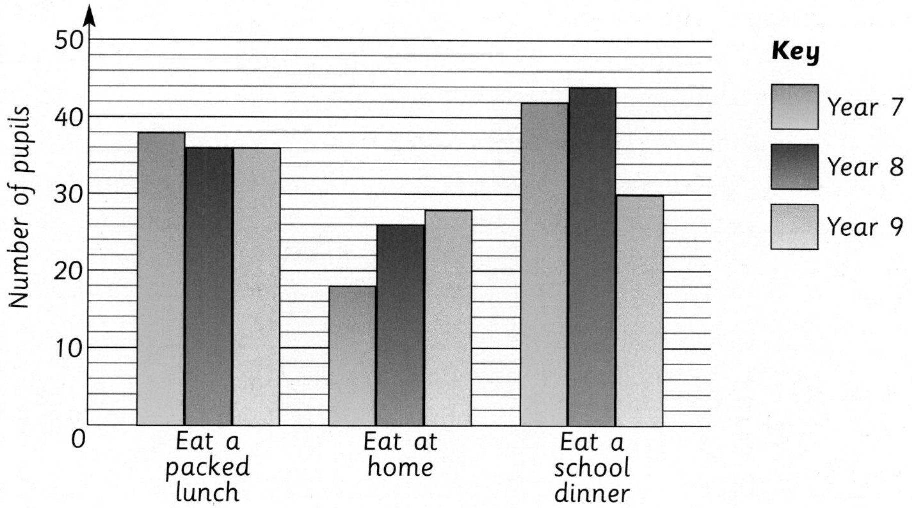

a A pupil from each year is chosen at random.

Are they **more likely** to eat a packed lunch, eat at home or eat a school dinner?

Tick (✓) the correct boxes.

	Eat a packed lunch	Eat at home	Eat a school dinner
Pupil from Year 7	☐	☐	☐
Pupil from Year 8	☐	☐	☐
Pupil from Year 9	☐	☐	☐

2 marks

b How many **more** pupils are there in Year **8** than in Year **9**?
Show your working. *2 marks*

5 A teacher has five number cards.
She says:

'I am going to take a card at random.
Each card shows a **different** positive whole number.
It is **certain** that the card will show a number less than 10.
It is **impossible** that the card will show an even number.'

What numbers are on the cards?

2 marks

Answers are on page 245.

REVISION SESSION |

Long multiplication and long division

What you should already know

- *How to do 'short division' and 'short multiplication', where a two- or three-digit number is multiplied or divided by a single-digit number*

- You should be able to multiply a three-digit number by a two-digit number without using a calculator. This is called 'long multiplication'.

- You should be able to divide a three-digit number by a two-digit number without using a calculator. This is called 'long division'.

LONG MULTIPLICATION

- Questions on this topic come up on Paper 1 of the National Tests, a non-calculator paper.
- There are several ways to do long multiplication. Three of them are shown in the examples below. Some others are mentioned in the tutorial for the *Check yourself* section. You need to be sure of at least one of the methods described.

Worked example
Small tins of beans weigh 146 grams. How much do 23 tins weigh?

The question is 23 × 146. Do this by the **standard column method**. This is the method that your parents probably remember.

Step 1	Step 2	Step 3	Step 4	Step 5
1 4 6	1 4 6	1 4 6	1 4 6	1 4 6
× 2 3	× 2 3	× 2 0	× 2	× 2 3
	4 3 8			4 3 8
		0	2 9 2 0	2 9 2 0
				3 3 5 8

Step 1: Write down the multiplication, remembering to line up the units on the right-hand side.

Step 2: Ignore the tens digit in the bottom number and multiply 146 by the units digit 3. (This is short multiplication.)

Step 3: Ignore the units digits and multiply by the 10s digit which is really 20. Do this by putting the zero in the second line of the answer.

Step 4: Multiply 146 by the 2 (short multiplication again).

Step 5: Add both answers to get the final total.
The answer is 3358.

Worked example

Seventeen buses are booked to take pupils on a school trip. Each bus holds 46 people. How many pupils will the 17 buses carry in total?

The multiplication is 17 × 46. Do this one by the **box method**.

Step 1

46 = 40 + 6

×	40	6
10		
7		

17 = 10 + 7

Step 2

×	40	6
10	400	60
7	280	42

Step 3

```
    4 0 0
      6 0
    2 8 0
+     4 2
  ───────
    7 8 2
```

Step 1: Draw a box 2 squares by 2 squares (because it is a two-digit by two-digit multiplication). Split the numbers into their tens and units along the top and down the side.

Step 2: Multiply the numbers at the top and the numbers at the side and put each answer in each box.

Step 3: Take the numbers from the boxes and write them down, lining up the units on the right. Then, add them together.

The answer is 782.

Worked example

Thirty-five students each pay £157.00 for a weeks' trip to France. How much do they pay altogether?

The multiplication is 35 × 157. Do this by the **Chinese multiplication** or **Napier's bones method**.

Step 1: Draw a box 3 squares by 2 squares (this is three-digit by 2-digit multiplication). Draw diagonals across each section. Write the digits of each number across the top and down the right-hand side.

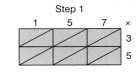

Step 2: Multiply each pair of digits together and write the answer in the two spaces created by the diagonal. Note that the tens digit (even if it is zero) goes in the top left space while the units go into the bottom right space.

Step 3: Add up the numbers along each diagonal 'path', starting at the bottom right. Note the 'carry' digit of 1. Reading the numbers from left to right gives the final answer.

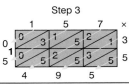

The answer is 5495.

LONG DIVISION

- There are two ways to do this without a calculator. The first method is similar to short division. You need to use carried figures. You can also use a method which involves subtraction.

Worked example

Divide 612 by 18.

Step 1

$$18\overline{)6\ \ 1\ \ 2}$$

Step 2

$$\overset{3}{18\overline{)6\ \ {}^6 1\ \ 2}}$$

Step 3

$$\overset{3\ \ 4}{18\overline{)6\ \ {}^6 1\ \ {}^7 2}}$$

Step 1: 18 into 6 does not go, so carry the 6 to the 1 to make 61.

Step 2: 18 into 61 goes 3 times, with remainder 7. Write the 3 over the 1 and carry the 7 to the 2 to make 72. (You do not need to know your 18 times table. Just work out how the table builds up: 18, 18 + 18 = 36, 36 + 18 = 54, and so on.)

Step 3: 18 into 72 goes 4 times exactly.
Write the 4 over the 2. 54 + 18 = 72.

The answer is 34.

```
        3  4
18 ) 6  1  2
     5  4
     7  2
     7  2
     0  0
```

Worked example

962 football fans need to travel to an away game in 37-seater coaches. How many coaches will they need?

Use a method based on subtraction.
37 × 10 is 370 which is not as big as 962, so take it away. Take away 370 again. Take away 185 which is 5 × 37 (half of 370). There is 37 left so take away 1 lot of 37. We have taken away 10 lots twice, 5 lots and 1 lot. This is a total of 26 lots of 37.
The answer is 26.

```
  1  0  ×  3  7  =     9  6  2
                       3  7  0  –
                       5  9  2
  1  0  ×  3  7  =     3  7  0  –
                       2  2  2
     5  ×  3  7  =     1  8  5  –
                       2  2  2
     1  ×  3  7  =        3  7  –
  +                      3  7
     2  6                 0  0
```

CHECK YOURSELF QUESTIONS

Q1 Work out these long multiplications. Use any method you are happy with.

a   48
    × 24

b   256
    × 52

c   362
    × 36

d   178
    × 48

Q2 A milkman has to put 432 milk bottles into crates that hold 24 bottles. How many crates does he need?

Q3 Work out these long divisions.

a $16\overline{)928}$ **b** $28\overline{)924}$

c $23\overline{)782}$ **d** $31\overline{)961}$

Use any method you are happy with.

Q4 Stamps cost 19p each.
a How many can you buy for £5.00?
b How much change will you get?

Answers are on page 226.

REVISION SESSION **2** Decimals

> - You should be able to multiply and divide whole numbers and decimals by 10, 100 and 1000.
> - You should be able to add, subtract, multiply and divide using decimal numbers expressed to 2 decimal places.

What you should already know

- *How to multiply and divide whole numbers by 10 and 100*
- *How to put decimals in order of size*
- *How to add and subtract whole numbers*

MULTIPLYING AND DIVIDING DECIMALS BY 10 AND 100

- When you multiplied or divided by 10 and 100 at level 4 (see page 4), you put on or took off one or two zeros at the end of the number. This does not always work, particularly with whole numbers and decimals. For example, this is what happens when you multiply decimals.

34.7 × 10 = 347   59.61 × 100 = 5961
56.23 × 10 = 562.3   1.205 × 10 = 12.05

When you **multiply** any number by 10 or 100 the digits move one or two places to the **left**.

34.7 × 10

        U
   3 4 . 7 × 10
  3 4 7 .

59.61 × 100

            U
      5 9 . 6 1 × 100
   5 9 6 1 .

- When you **divide** decimals by 10 or 100 the same thing happens but in reverse: the digits move one or two places to the **right**.

 34.7 ÷ 10 = 3.47   59.6 ÷ 100 = 0.596
562 ÷ 100 = 5.62   607 ÷ 10 = 60.7

   U
3 4 . 7 ÷ 10
   3 . 4 7

      U
5 6 2 . 6 ÷ 100
      5 . 6 2

FOUR RULES WITH DECIMALS

- Adding and subtracting decimals is similar to adding and subtracting whole numbers.
- For whole numbers, you line up the units. You still have to do this, but the unit digit is not always the last digit on the right. The units are the numbers in front of the decimal point.
- At level 5, you will be expected to do multiplication and division where one of the numbers involved is a single-digit number.
- In all four types of calculation, you must line up the decimal points.

NUMBER . . . . **47** . . . . LEVEL 5

Fill any 'gaps' with zeros. Complete the calculation in the usual way, making sure that the decimal points are lined up.

Worked example

Work out 39.73 + 4.2.

Write this as:
```
   39.73
+   4.20
   43.93
```

Worked example

Work out 5.7 − 3.49.

Write this as:
```
   5.70
−  3.49
   2.21
```

Hint:

Treat it as a short multiplication and then put the decimal point directly below where it started.

Worked example

Work out 34.56 × 7.

Write this as:
```
   34.56
×      7
  241.92
```

Hint:

Do the short division and put the point directly above where it started.

Worked example

Work out 34.51 ÷ 7.

Write it as:
```
      4.93
7 )34.51
```

Worked example

Jason has these cards.   2   3   4   5   6   .   0

He makes the number 463 with three of the cards.   4   6   3

a What other card should he choose to make a number ten times bigger than 463?
b What other card should he choose to make a number ten times smaller than 463?

a He should choose zero to make: 4   6   3   0

b He should choose the decimal point to make: 4   6   .   3

Worked example

Jenny wrote her homework in her book. After her teacher marked them as correct Jenny spilt ink on the page. Can you find the missing number or sign in each answer?

1.	● × 10 = 23 ✓
2.	2.3 ●100 = 230 ✓
3.	23 ÷ ● = 2.3 ✓
4.	23 ●100 = 0.23 ✓

In (1) the missing number must be 2.3.
In (2) the missing sign must be ×.
In (3) the missing number must be 10.
In (4) the missing sign must be ÷.

Worked example

A lottery syndicate of 9 people won a prize of £147.33. If they share it equally, how much does each person win?

They each win £16.37.

Hint:

$$9\overline{)147{\cdot}33} = 16{\cdot}37$$

CHECK YOURSELF QUESTIONS

Q1 Complete these decimal calculations.
  a 2.6 + 5.7   **b** 5.3 − 2.8   **c** 7 × 3.4   **d** 4.8 ÷ 3

Q2 Complete these decimal calculations.
  a 3.47 + 6.85 **b** 6.53 − 3.86 **c** 8 × 2.36   **d** 20.16 ÷ 8

Q3 Ahmed has these cards.

  | 4 | 5 | 6 | 7 | 8 | . | 0 |

  He makes the number 758 with three of them.

  | 7 | 5 | 8 |

  a Choose a card to make a number 10 times bigger than 758.
  b Change a card to make a number 10 less than 758.
  c Choose another card to make a number that is 10 times smaller than 758.

Q4 Paul buys a shirt for £18.45, a tie for £5.60 and a pair of cufflinks for £15.32. How much does he pay altogether?

Q5 A sack of potatoes weighs 5.63 kilograms (kg). The chef takes out 2.75 kg of potatoes. What is the weight of the potatoes left in the sack?

Q6 Unleaded petrol costs 81.2p per litre. How much do 9 litres cost?

Q7 Water rates for a small house are £123.21. This is paid by 9 equal monthly payments. How much is each payment?

Q8 Fill in the missing numbers or signs.
  a 4.6 × ☐ = 46
  b 4.6 × 100 = ☐
  c 4.6 ☐ 10 = 0.46
  d 4.6 ÷ ☐ = 0.046

Answers are on page 227.

- You should be able to arrange in order, add and subtract negative numbers.

NUMBERS ON THE NUMBER LINE
- This is a number line.

$$-11\ -10\ -9\ -8\ -7\ -6\ -5\ -4\ -3\ -2\ -1\ 0\ 1\ 2\ 3\ 4\ 5\ 6\ 7\ 8\ 9\ 10\ 11\ 12$$

- As the numbers go to the right they get bigger. As the numbers go to the left they get smaller. In the number line, 8 is bigger than 3, ⁻2 is bigger than ⁻6, ⁻6 is smaller than 3.
- You can use the signs > (bigger than) and < (smaller than) to compare numbers.

Worked example

Put these numbers: ⁻4, 8, ⁻6, 2, ⁻1 in order, with the smallest first.

Put the numbers on a number line.

$$-8\ -7\ -6\ -5\ -4\ -3\ -2\ -1\ 0\ 1\ 2\ 3\ 4\ 5\ 6\ 7\ 8\ 9$$

In order, with the smallest first, the numbers are ⁻6, ⁻4, ⁻1, 2 and 8.

Worked example

Put the signs > (bigger than) and < (smaller than) between the numbers in these pairs to make true statements.

a ⁻4 2   **b** ⁻8 ⁻10   **c** 2 ⁻8

First, draw a number line.

$$-11\ -10\ -9\ -8\ -7\ -6\ -5\ -4\ -3\ -2\ -1\ 0\ 1\ 2\ 3$$

a ⁻4 < 2   **b** ⁻8 > ⁻10   **c** 2 > ⁻8

ADDING AND SUBTRACTING NEGATIVE NUMBERS
- When you add and subtract negative numbers there are two rules.
  - Always start counting at zero.
  - Positive (+) numbers count to the right and negative (–) numbers count to the left.

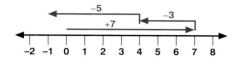
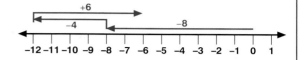
CHECK YOURSELF QUESTIONS

Q1 Arrange the numbers in each set in order of size, smallest first.
  a $^-3, 5, ^-6$ **b** $^-3, ^-6, ^-1, ^-2$
  c $^-4, 7, 3, ^-1$

Q2 Put the sign < or > between the numbers in each pair to make a true statement.
  a $^-5 \quad ^-6$ **b** $^-12 \quad 6$
  c $7 \quad ^-8$

Q3 Work these out.
  a $^-5 + 8$ **b** $6 - 4$
  c $^+3 - 5 + 8$ **d** $^-5 + 8 - 6 + 2$
  e $^-3 - 3 - 3$ **f** $^-7 + 6 - 4$
  g $^-5 - 1 + 7 - 6$ **h** $^-3 + 4 - 5 + 6 - 7$
  i $^-3 + 7 + 3$ **j** $^-4 + 4 - 8$
  k $^-1 - 6 + 1$ **l** $^+7 - 8 - 7$

Q4 Complete this number pattern.

$^+3 + ^-2 = ^+1$

$^+2 + ^-2 = 0$

$^+1 + ^-2 = ^-1$

$0 + ^-2 = ^-2$

$\square + ^-2 = ^-3$

$\square + ^-2 = \square$

$\square + ^-2 = \square$

Q5 You may use a calculator for this question. The diagram shows a mountain and cave system.

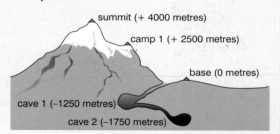

  a How high above cave 1 is the summit?
  b How far below the summit is camp 1?
  c How far is cave 1 above cave 2?
  d How far below camp 1 is cave 2?

Q6 Read the numbers from these scales.

  a

  b

  c

Q7 You may use a calculator for this question. Just before Christmas I had £56.22 in my bank account. I wrote cheques for presents totalling £75.89. My Aunt Jane then gave me a cheque for £20 which I paid in to the bank. How much did I have in my account after Christmas?

Answers are on page 227.

What you should already know

- *How to recognise proportions of a whole number*
- *How to use simple fractions and percentages*
- *That 10% is one-tenth*
- *How to express 25% and 50% as fractions*

- **You should be able to calculate fractional or percentage parts of quantities and measurements, using a calculator where appropriate.**

FRACTIONS AND PERCENTAGES OF VARIOUS QUANTITIES

- At this level you will use only the simpler values and your answers will always be a simple number or decimal.
- 10% is the same as one-tenth.
- 10% is the easiest percentage to work out, particularly if you are using pounds (£).
- Finding one tenth is the same as dividing by 10, which moves the digits one place to the right.

> **Worked example**
> Find 10% of £23.50.
>
> £23.50 ÷ 10 = £2.35.
>
> You could also your calculator to find 10% × £23.50. If your calculator has a % button, try it to see if it gives the correct answer. If it doesn't then you can work out 10 × 23.50 ÷ 100 or 10 ÷ 100 × £23.50.

- Most of the other percentages that you will be asked to find can be worked out by first finding 10%. One special percentage that you should know is that $\frac{1}{3} = 33\frac{1}{3}\%$.

> **Worked example**
> Increase 300 by 20%.
>
> 10% of 300 is 30. 20% is 2 lots of 10%.
> 20% of 300 is 2 × 30 = 60.
> 300 increased by 20% is 300 + 60 = 360.

> **Worked example**
> Find 45% of 340.
>
> 45% of 340 can be calculated as
> 45 × 340 ÷ 100 = 153

> **Worked example**
> Find $\frac{4}{5}$ of 120.
>
> Fractions of quantities can be found in two ways. Firstly, find $\frac{1}{5}$ of 120, which you can do by dividing 120 by 5. 120 ÷ 5 = 24.
>
> $\frac{4}{5}$ is 4 × $\frac{1}{5}$, and 4 × 24 is 96. So, $\frac{4}{5}$ of 120 is 96.
>
> The second way to do this problem is to multiply by 4 and then divide by 5.
>
> 4 × 120 = 480, 480 ÷ 5 = 96

CHECK YOURSELF QUESTIONS

Q1 Find 10% of:
   a £320   b £410   c £60   d £32
   e £7   f £32.50   g £12.70   h 70p
   i 150 elephants   j 25 packets of sweets.

Q2 Find 20% of:
   a £320   b £410   c £60   d £32
   e £9   f £41.50   g £16.40   h 60p
   i 250 elephants   j 45 packets of sweets.

Q3 Find:
   a 30% of £400   b 40% of £40   c 50% of £80
   d 25% of £360   e 1% of £100   f 5% of £300
   g 75% of £370   h 24% of £56   i 65% of £7
   You will need a calculator for (g) (h) and (i).

Q4 Find $\frac{2}{3}$ of:
   a 300   b 180   c 45   d 60.

Q5 Find $\frac{3}{4}$ of:
   a 100   b 32   c 40   d 20.

Q6 Find:
   a $\frac{2}{3}$ of 21   b $\frac{2}{3}$ of 30   c $\frac{4}{5}$ of 35   d $\frac{3}{8}$ of 40.

Q7 A kitchen wall is to have a window put into it.
   The area of the wall is 70 square feet. Because it is an outside wall,
   the window cannot cover more than $\frac{2}{7}$ of the area of the wall.
   What is the biggest area that the window could have?

Q8 A bottle of shampoo contains 25% extra.
   a   A regular bottle contains 400 ml. How much does the new bottle
       contain?
   b   Mark uses a regular bottle to wash his hair 32 times.
       How many washes will he get out of the new bottle?

Answers are on page 227.

• You should be able to reduce a fraction to its simplest form or lowest terms.

• You should be able to solve simple problems involving ratio and direct proportion.

Worked example

Cancel these fractions.

a $\frac{14}{20}$ **b** $\frac{16}{24}$

a The HCF of 14 and 20 is 2.
$$\frac{14^{\,7}}{20_{\,10}} = \frac{7}{10}$$

b The HCF of 16 and 24 is 8.
$$\frac{16^{\,2}}{24_{\,3}} = \frac{2}{3}$$

CANCELLING FRACTIONS

• The fraction $\frac{15}{25}$ is not in its simplest form. It is **equivalent** to $\frac{3}{5}$.

• To cancel a fraction, look for the **highest common factor** (HCF) of the denominator and numerator, and divide both numbers by it.

• The highest common factor of two numbers is is the highest times table that includes both numbers.

• As 15 and 25 are both in the 5 times table, their HCF is 5. Divide both numerator and denominator of $\frac{15}{25}$ by to get $\frac{3}{5}$. $\frac{15^{\,3}}{25_{\,5}} = \frac{3}{5}$

• When the numerator and denominator have no more common factors, the fraction is in its **lowest terms**.

RATIO AND DIRECT PROPORTION

• Use ratio and direct proportion to compare quantities and prices.

• Usually you need to find out what one thing measures or costs and use that information to work out what you need to know.

Worked example

A box of six pens costs £1.80. How much will 8 pens cost?

One pen costs £1.80 ÷ 6 = £0.30. Eight pens cost 8 × £0.30 = £2.40

Worked example

A fruit drink recommends 'Mix 1 part of juice with 7 parts of water'.

a How much water should Emily add to 7 centilitres of juice?
b What quantity of juice should John add to half a litre of water?

a There needs to be 7 times as much water as juice.
So add 7 × 7 = 49 centilitres of water.
b Change half a litre to millilitres (500 ml). There should be one-seventh as much juice as water. So add 500 ÷ 7 = 71 millilitres of juice.

❓ CHECK YOURSELF QUESTIONS

Q1 Cancel these fractions to their lowest terms.
   a $\frac{12}{18}$ **b** $\frac{9}{21}$ **c** $\frac{15}{45}$

Q2 A fraction in its simplest form is $\frac{3}{4}$.
Write down two equivalent fractions that mean the same.

Q3 A 6-pack of cans of cola costs £1.32. How much would 7 tins cost?

Q4 To make filler, Fred mixes 1 kg of powder with 20 centilitres of water.
   a How much water should he mix with a $2\frac{1}{2}$ kg bag of powder?
   b How much powder should Fred add to $2\frac{1}{2}$ litres of water?

Q5 It costs £1.25 to travel 5 miles on a bus. How much will an 8-mile journey cost?

Answers are on page 228.

1 Here is a list of numbers.

⁻7 ⁻5 ⁻3 ⁻1 0 2 4 6

You can choose some of the numbers from the list and add them to find their **total**.

For example: ..6.. + ..⁻1.. = 5

a Choose **two** of the numbers from the list which have a **total** of **3**.

...... + ... = 3   *I mark*

b Choose **two** of the numbers from the list which have a **total** of ⁻1.

...... + ... = ⁻1   *I mark*

Choose **two** other numbers from the list which have a **total** of ⁻1.

...... + ... = ⁻1   *I mark*

c What is the **total** of **all eight** of the numbers on the list?
Write the three numbers and their total.
You must not use the same number more than once.   *I mark*

d Choose the **three** numbers from the list which have the **lowest possible total**.

...... + ... + ... = ...   *2 marks*

2 The table shows some percentages of amounts of money. **You can use this table to help you work out the missing numbers.**

	£10	£30	£45
5%	50p	£1.50	£2.25
10%	£1	£3	£4.50

a 15% of £30 = £......   c £3.50 = ... % of £10

b £6.75 = 15% of £......   d 25p = 5% of £......   *4 marks*

3 a A football club is planning a trip.
The club hires **234** coaches. Each coach holds **52** passengers.
How many passengers is that altogether?
Show your working.   *I mark*

b The club wants to put one first aid kit into each of the 234 coaches.
These first aid kits are sold in **boxes of 18**.
How many boxes does the club need?   *I mark*

4 a Look at these fractions. $\frac{1}{2}$ $\frac{1}{3}$ $\frac{5}{6}$

Mark each fraction on the number line.
The first one is done for you.

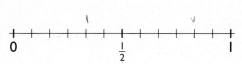

0                     $\frac{1}{2}$ 1

b Fill in the missing numbers in the boxes.

$\frac{2}{12} = \frac{\square}{6}$ $\frac{1}{2} = \frac{12}{\square}$ $\frac{1}{\square} = \frac{6}{24}$ *I mark*

5 **a** What **fraction** of shape A is shaded?

Write your fraction as simply as possible.

b What **percentage** of shape B is shaded?

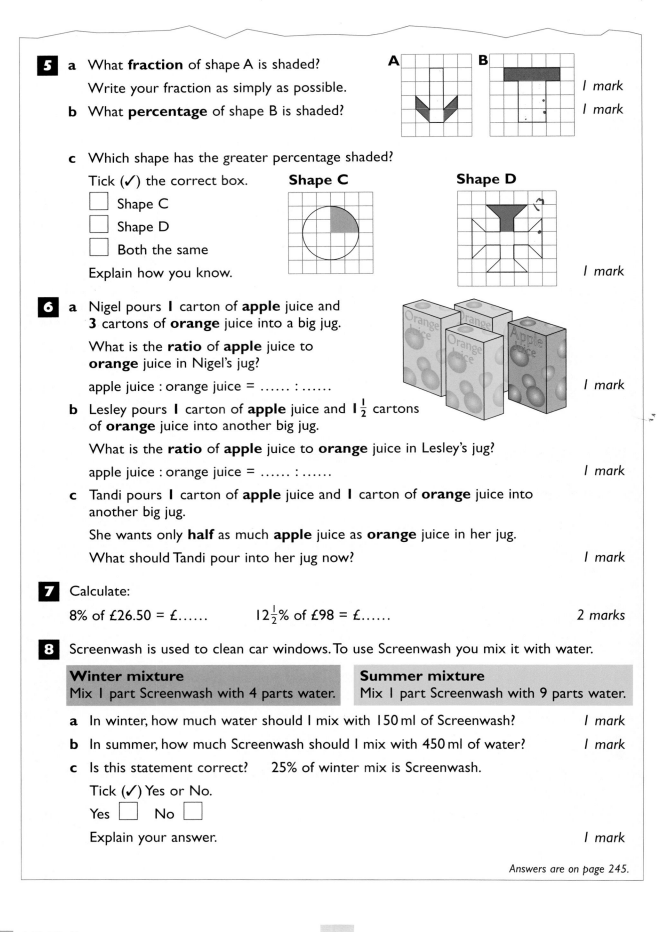

1 mark

1 mark

c Which shape has the greater percentage shaded?

Tick (✓) the correct box.

☐ Shape C

☐ Shape D

☐ Both the same

Explain how you know.

Shape C

Shape D

1 mark

6 **a** Nigel pours **1** carton of **apple** juice and **3** cartons of **orange** juice into a big jug.

What is the **ratio** of **apple** juice to **orange** juice in Nigel's jug?

apple juice : orange juice = ... : ......

1 mark

b Lesley pours **1** carton of **apple** juice and $1\frac{1}{2}$ cartons of **orange** juice into another big jug.

What is the **ratio** of **apple** juice to **orange** juice in Lesley's jug?

apple juice : orange juice = ... : ......

1 mark

c Tandi pours **1** carton of **apple** juice and **1** carton of **orange** juice into another big jug.

She wants only **half** as much **apple** juice as **orange** juice in her jug.

What should Tandi pour into her jug now?

1 mark

7 Calculate:

8% of £26.50 = £...... $12\frac{1}{2}$% of £98 = £......   *2 marks*

8 Screenwash is used to clean car windows. To use Screenwash you mix it with water.

Winter mixture	**Summer mixture**
Mix 1 part Screenwash with 4 parts water.	Mix 1 part Screenwash with 9 parts water.

a In winter, how much water should I mix with 150 ml of Screenwash?   *1 mark*

b In summer, how much Screenwash should I mix with 450 ml of water?   *1 mark*

c Is this statement correct?   25% of winter mix is Screenwash.

Tick (✓) Yes or No.

Yes ☐   No ☐

Explain your answer.   *1 mark*

Answers are on page 245.

Number patterns, square numbers and opposite operations

> - You should be able to check your answers by working backwards.

INVERSE OPERATIONS

- In maths, working backwards means 'undoing' mathematical operations.
- To undo a maths operation, do the opposite of the operation that you did first.
- The mathematical name for opposite is **inverse**.
- At this level, you need to know these facts.
  - The inverse operation for multiplication (times) is division.
  - The inverse operation for division is multiplication.
  - The inverse operation for addition is subtraction.
  - The inverse operation for subtraction is addition.

SQUARE NUMBERS

- A special set of numbers that you need to know is the **square numbers**.
- This is the pattern made by the first four square numbers.

| 1 | 4 | 9 | 16 |

The next pattern will contain 25 dots.
- A square number is made by multiplying another number by itself.

| $1 \times 1 = 1$ | $3 \times 3 = 9$ | $5 \times 5 = 25$ |
| $2 \times 2 = 4$ | $4 \times 4 = 16$ | $6 \times 6 = 36$ |

- You need to know the square numbers up to $15 \times 15 = 225$.
- Because square numbers are so special, there is a special mathematical sign. 4×4 is written as 4^2 and you say 'four squared'.
- Most calculators have a special button that works out the square of a number. To find the square of 3, key in:

 3 **x^2** **=** to get the answer 9.

> **Worked example**
>
> **a** Describe how this pattern is building up.
>
> 1, 4, 9, 16, 25, ...
>
> **b** Find the next two terms in the number pattern.
>
> **a** The terms start at 1 and go up by 3, then by 5, then by 7 and so on.
> **b** The next terms are 36 and 49.
>
> You can find these by adding 11 to 25 and then by adding 13 to 36.

> **Worked example**
>
> Write down the next two lines of this number pattern.
>
> | | | | | | |
> |---|---|---|---|---|---|
> | 1 | | = 1 | = | $1 \times 1 = 1^2$ |
> | 1 + 3 | | = 4 | = | $2 \times 2 = 2^2$ |
> | 1 + 3 + 5 | | = 9 | = | $3 \times 3 = 3^2$ |
> | 1 + 3 + 5 + 7 | | = 16 | = | $4 \times 4 = 4^2$ |
> | 1 + 3 + 5 + 7 + 9 | | = 25 | = | $5 \times 5 = 5^2$ |
>
> Each line starts by adding up odd numbers. This gives the square numbers which can be written either as a number multiplied by itself, or as the number followed by the special sign for 'squared'.

SQUARE ROOTS $\sqrt{\ }$

- To 'undo' squaring a number, you need to take the square root.
  The square root of 9 is 3. $\sqrt{9} = 3$
  The square root of 81 is 9. $\sqrt{81} = 9$
- The square root also has its own button on most calculators. You will need to find out how your calculator works out a square root.

  On most scientific calculators you type in: **1** **2** **1** **√**

  On DAL calculators you type in: **√** **1** **2** **1** **=**

  In both types of calculator, the display gives the answer 11.

> **Worked example**
>
> Find the square root of each of these numbers.
>
> **a** 81   **b** 169   **c** 75
>
> You won't need a calculator for the first two if you know your tables, but it will be useful for the last one.
>
> **a** 9   **b** 13   **c** 8.66
>
> The last answer is not exact. It is rounded to three significant figures, or two decimal places (see page 60).

NUMBER MACHINES AND INVERSES

- If you are told the number that comes out of a number machine, you can find out the number that went into that machine by using the **inverse operation**.

Worked example

Find the numbers that went into each of these machines.

a The number 4 went in because $5 \times 4 = 20$. You can find this out by reversing the number machine and calculating $20 \div 5 = 4$.

b The number 30 went in. If you reverse this machine you get:

Worked example

Use the rule: 'Start with a number and multiply by 2 and then add 1' to find which numbers are missing from this table.

The 5 in the first column goes to 11 in the second column.
The 21 goes back to 10, the 12 goes to 25 and the 15 goes back to 7.

Start	End
1	3
5	☐
☐	21
12	☐
☐	15

CHECK YOURSELF QUESTIONS

Q1 Find the opposite operation for each of these.

    a + 7   **b** − 6   **c** × 5   **d** ÷ 9

Q2 Find the numbers that went into these machines.

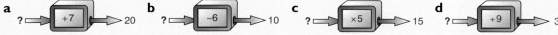

Q3 What numbers went into these machines?

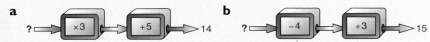

Q4 Answer this question without using a calculator.

    a Find the square of each number.
      (i) 3 (ii) 9 (iii) 10
    b Find the square root of each number.
      (i) 36 (ii) 64 (iii) 1

Answers are on page 228.

What you should already know

- *How to multiply and divide by 10*

- **You should be able to check your solutions by approximating.**

WHY ROUND OR APPROXIMATE NUMBERS?

- Rounding off is useful as it gives a rough idea of what an answer should be before you work it out.

ROUNDING

- At this level you need to be able to round to the nearest whole number, or to the nearest 10, 100 or 1000.

HALFWAY NUMBERS

- When rounding to the nearest whole number, if the decimal part is 0.5 or more, then you go up to the next whole number. If it is below 0.5, go down to the whole number.
- In general, if a number is 'halfway', the rule is to go upwards.

Worked example
Round each of these calculator displays to the nearest whole number.

a `3.89` b `6.23`
c `15.4` d `0.763`

a 4 b 6 c 15 d 1

Worked example
Round these numbers to the nearest 10.
a 17   b 34   c 123   d 85   e 22.9

a 20   b 30   c 120   d 90   e 20
The number in (d) goes upwards as it is halfway.

Worked example
Round these numbers to the nearest 100.
a 172   b 345   c 123   d 85   e 250

a 200   b 300   c 100   d 100   e 300
The number in (e) goes upwards as it is halfway.

Worked example
Round these numbers to the nearest 1000.
a 1340   b 3405   c 2780   d 8500   e 250

a 1000   b 3000   c 3000   d 9000   e 0
The number in (d) goes upwards as it is halfway. In part (e), 250 is nearer to zero than 1000.

MULTIPLYING MULTIPLES OF TEN AND A HUNDRED

- Multiples make up the times tables.
- Multiples of 10 are 20, 30, and so on, and multiples of 100 are 200, 300, and so on.
- If you want to work out 40×30 you find $4 \times 3 = 12$ and then, as there are two zeros in the numbers being multiplied, put two zeros on the end of your answer.

$$3\ 0 \times 4\ 0 = 1\ 2\ 0\ 0$$
$$3 \times 4$$

Worked example
Write down the answers to:
a 20×30
b 40×500
c 70×3000

a 600   b 20 000
c 210 000
In (b), $4 \times 5 = 20$. You still have to put the three zeros on the end.

DIVIDING MULTIPLES OF 10 AND 100

- Most divisions you will be asked to do will be straightforward.
- If you want to find 1200 ÷ 60, work out 12 ÷ 6 = 2. Then, because there were two zeros in the first number and one zero in the second number, and 2 zeros minus 1 zero equals 1 zero, you write down one zero at the end. You can also cancel or 'cross off' the zeros.

$$1\ 2\ 0\ \cancel{0} \div 6\ \cancel{0} = 2\ 0$$
$$1\ 2\quad\div\quad 6$$

ESTIMATING ANSWERS

- To estimate an answer, round the numbers and then do the calculation in your head.

Worked example
Find an approximate answer for each of these.

a 19.6×5.3 **b** $\dfrac{99.6 - 42.1}{12.1}$ **c** $\dfrac{11.8 \times 56.3}{5.8}$

a The answer is about 100, because $19.6 \approx 20$, $5.3 \approx 5$ and $20 \times 5 = 100$.

b $\dfrac{99.6 - 42.1}{12.1} \approx 6$ because $99.6 \approx 100$, $42.1 \approx 40$ and $12.1 \approx 10$.
100 take away 40 is 60 and 60 divided by 10 is 6.

c $\dfrac{11.8 \times 56.3}{5.8} \approx 100$ because $11.8 \approx 10$, $56.3 \approx 60$ and $5.8 \approx 6$.
10 multiplied by 60 is 600, and 600 divided by 6 is 100.

Hint:

If you use a calculator you will not get any marks.

Hint:

≈ means 'is approximately'

❓ CHECK YOURSELF QUESTIONS

Q1 Round each of these calculator displays to the nearest whole number.
   a 2.134   **b** 16.78   **c** 10.06

Q2 Round these numbers to the nearest 10.
   a 44   **b** 52   **c** 69
   d 75   **e** 109   **f** 99
   g 51   **h** 501

Q3 Round these numbers to the nearest 100.
   a 170   **b** 620   **c** 308
   d 450

Q4 Round these numbers to the nearest 1000.
   a 2700   **b** 2034   **c** 1450
   d 4500

Q5 Write down the answers to these.
   a 40×60 **b** 10×700
   c 50×700 **d** 300×600

Q6 Write down the answers to these.
   a $400 \div 20$ **b** $700 \div 70$
   c $500 \div 100$ **d** $1800 \div 60$

Q7 Estimate answers to these.
   a 47×62 **b** 11.4×69
   c 5.1×73 **d** 285×613

Q8 Estimate the answer to this.

$$\frac{55.7 + 41.6}{27.3 - 19.1}$$

Answers are on page 228.

What you should already know

- *How to use simple formulae expressed in words*

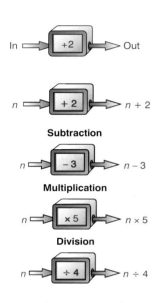

Subtraction

Multiplication

Division

- You should be able to use mathematical symbols to write down a formula or rule.

WRITING FORMULAE OR RULES WITH MATHEMATICAL SYMBOLS
- In algebra you can use letters for numbers.
- A **formula** is just a rule that changes one number into another.
- You can use number machines to show formulae, for example, for the simple rule 'add 2':
  if 3 goes in, then 3 + 2 = 5 comes out,
  if 7 goes in, then 7 + 2 = 9 comes out.
- You can say that if a number goes in, then the number plus 2 comes out, or, more mathematically, 'If n goes in, then $n + 2$ comes out'.
- You can use the letter n to stand for any number.
- You can use number machines for the other three basic mathematical rules: subtraction, multiplication and division.
- The multiplication $5 \times n$ can also be written as $5n$ and the division $n \div 4$ can be written as $\frac{n}{4}$.
- You assume there is a multiplication sign between numbers and letters, even though the sign is not written in.
- A line, like the one in a fraction, means divide.
- Formulae can be more complicated and the number machine may

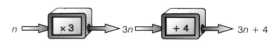

  need more than one part, for example: 'multiply by 3 and add 4'.
- The formulae at this level use only the four basic rules of addition, subtraction, multiplication and division. You might also use the operation of squaring, written as n^2.

Worked example
Write down the algebraic formula that comes out of each of these number machines.

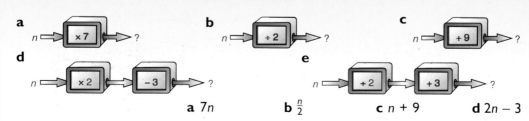

a $7n$ **b** $\frac{n}{2}$ **c** $n + 9$ **d** $2n - 3$ **e** $\frac{n}{2} + 3$

There are other ways to write some of these.
a could be $7 \times n$, or $n \times 7$. You should not write it as $n7$.
b could be $n \div 2$.
d could be $2 \times n - 3$, or $n \times 2 - 3$.
e could be $n \div 2 + 3$.

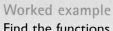

Worked example

Find the functions that are missing from these machines.

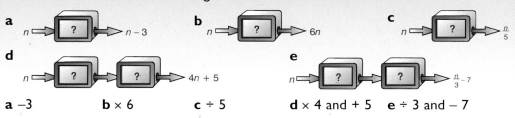

a −3   b × 6   c ÷ 5   d × 4 and + 5   e ÷ 3 and − 7

LETTERS FOR NUMBERS

- You can use algebra to describe everyday situations, for example,
  my brother is two years younger than I am. If I am x years old,
  how old is my brother? Whatever my age, my brother's age is 2
  years less. So, if I am x years old, my brother is $x - 2$ years old.
  If I am 14, he is 14 − 2, which is 12.

Worked example

Pupils in a class are baking biscuits. Ann bakes B biscuits. Barry bakes
three more biscuits than Ann. Carol bakes twice as many biscuits as Ann.
Derek bakes four fewer biscuits than Carol.

Write down in the table how many biscuits each person bakes. Then
write down the total number of biscuits baked.

Person	Biscuits
Ann	B
Barry	$B + 3$
Carol	
Derek	
Total	

Carol bakes $2B$ biscuits. Derek bakes $2B - 4$ biscuits. Altogether they
bake: $B + B + 3 + 2B + 2B - 4 = 6B - 1$ biscuits.

? CHECK YOURSELF QUESTIONS

Q1 Write down the formula from each of these number machines.

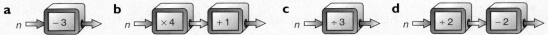

Q2 Find the rule that is missing from each of these machines.

Q3 Mrs Jones has written the following terms on the board and
    asked the class to add them up.

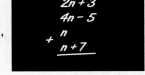

   a These are the answers for three pupils. Alf: $13n$, Bert: $8n - 15$,
      Charles: $8n + 5$ Who is correct?

   b Add these terms together. $3n - 6 + 7 - n + 2n + 4$.

Q4 This square has a side of n centimetres.

   a Explain why the perimeter of the square is $4n$ cm.

   b Two identical squares are put together in a line.
      Rod thinks that the perimeter of this shape is $8n$. Explain why he is wrong.

   c What is the perimeter of the shape made by the two squares?

Answers are on page 229.

Using formulae and rules: coordinates in all four quadrants

- You should be able to use simple rules or formulae involving one or two operations.

USING RULES WITH ALGEBRA TO SOLVE PROBLEMS

- The axes on a graph divide the grid into four **quadrants**.
- The coordinates of any point can be found by using positive and negative numbers.

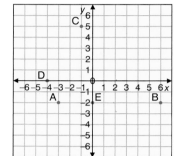

- Follow the two rules when using coordinates.
  - 'Start at the origin (0, 0).'
  - 'Move across first and up second.'
- For a negative number, move to the left or downwards. Point A on the grid is 3 to the left and 2 down from the origin (0,0). Write this as A($^-$3, $^-$2). Point B is at (6, $^-$2), point C is at ($^-$1, 5), point D is at ($^-$4, 0) and point E is at (0, $^-$2).

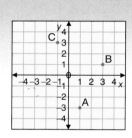

Worked example

a What are the coordinates of the points A, B and C in the grid on the right?

b Another point, D, is placed on the grid so that ABCD is a square. What are the coordinates of D?

a A is (1, $^-$3), B is (3, 1), C is ($^-$1, 3).
b The point D must be at ($^-$3, $^-$1).

MULTIPLYING AND DIVIDING NEGATIVE NUMBERS

- To multiply and divide negative numbers, ignore the negative signs, complete the calculation and then put a minus sign in front if necessary.
- To multiply, for example, $3 \times {}^-2$, start with 3×2, which is 6, then put in the minus sign to give $^-6$.
- To divide, for example, $^-16 \div 2$, start with $16 \div 2$, which is 8, then put the minus in front to give $^-8$.
- From the table, multiplying two negative numbers together gives a positive (plus) number.
- Again, dividing one negative number by another negative number gives a positive number.

$$3 \times {}^-2 = {}^-6$$
$$2 \times {}^-2 = {}^-4$$
$$1 \times {}^-2 = {}^-2$$
$$0 \times {}^-2 = 0$$
$${}^-1 \times {}^-2 = 2$$
$${}^-2 \times {}^-2 = 4$$
$${}^-3 \times {}^-2 = 6$$

Worked example
a Use this number machine to complete the table.

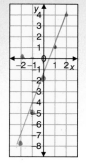

In	Out
2	4
1	
0	
⁻1	⁻5
⁻2	

b The coordinates (2, 4) and (⁻1, ⁻5) are plotted
on the grid. Use the other three sets of coordinates
in the table to plot three more points on the grid.
What do you notice about the five points?

a The pairs of numbers are (2, 4), (1, 1), (0, ⁻2), (⁻1, ⁻5), (⁻2, ⁻8).
b If you join the points together, you get a straight line.

MAPPINGS

- A **mapping** is a rule that changes one number to a different number.
- Mappings are sometimes shown as diagrams. For example, these are mapping diagrams for $y = 2x$, $y = x - 2$ and $y = 2x - 2$.

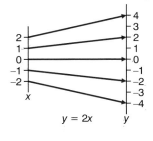

$y = 2x$

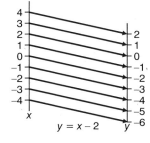

$y = x - 2$

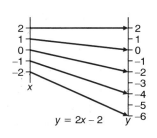

$y = 2x - 2$

Worked example

Draw mapping diagrams for these number machines. They only use whole numbers.

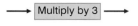 → Multiply by 3 →

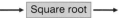 → Square root →

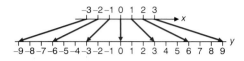

CHECK YOURSELF QUESTIONS

Q1 Give the coordinates of points A, B, C, D, E and F on the grid.

Q2 Copy the grid in question 1. Mark on it the points G(⁻5, 3), H(⁻4, 0), J(2, ⁻3), K(0, ⁻2), L(⁻3, ⁻4).

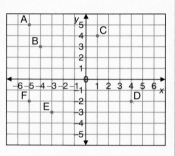

Q3 a From the grid on the right, give the coordinates of points A, B and C.

    b Another point, D, is placed on the grid to make a parallelogram ABCD. What are the coordinates of D?

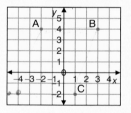

Q4 The mapping diagram below shows $y = x + 3$. The lines for $x = 2$ and $x = 1$ are drawn.

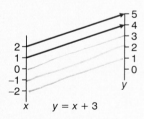

$y = x + 3$

    a Complete the mapping diagram for $x = 0, ⁻1$ and $⁻2$.

    b The two lines drawn give coordinates (2, 5) and (1, 4). These have been plotted on the grid. Plot the points given by the other three lines. What do you notice about the points?

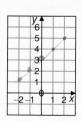

Answers are on page 229.

1 Write each expression in its simplest form.

7 + 2t + 3t   *1 mark*

b + 7 + 2b + 10   *1 mark*

2 Maria and Kay ran a 1500 metres race.
The distance–time graph shows the race.

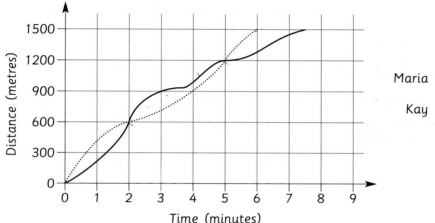

Use the graph to help you fill in the gaps in this report of the race.

Just after the start of the race, Maria was in the lead.

At 600 metres, Maria and Kay were level.

Then Kay was in the lead for …… minutes.

At …… metres, Maria and Kay were level again.

…… won the race.   *2 marks*

Her total time was …… minutes.

…… finished …… minutes later.   *2 marks*

3 Look at this table.

	Age (in years)
Ann	a
Ben	b
Cindy	c

Write in words the meaning of each equation below.

b = 30   Ben is 30 years old.

a + b = 69   ...   *1 mark*

b = 2c   ...   *1 mark*

$\dfrac{a + b + c}{3} = 28$ ...   *1 mark*

4 Jeff makes a sequence of patterns with black and grey triangular tiles.

pattern 1   pattern 2   pattern 3

The rule for finding the number of tiles in pattern number *N* in Jeff's sequence is:

number of tiles = **1 + 3N**

a The **1** in this rule represents the **black tile**.
What does the **3N** represent?   *1 mark*

b Jeff makes **pattern number 12** in his sequence.
How many **black** tiles and how many **grey** tiles does he use?

...... black and ...... grey   *1 mark*

c Jeff uses **61 tiles** altogether to make a pattern in his sequence.
What is the number of the pattern he uses?   *1 mark*

d Barbara makes a sequence of patterns with **hexagonal** tiles.

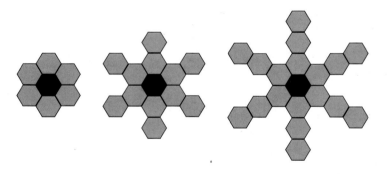

pattern 1   pattern 2   pattern 3

Each pattern in Barbara's sequence has **1 black** tile in the middle. Each new pattern
has **6 more grey** tiles than the pattern before.
Write the rule for finding the number of tiles in pattern number *N* in Barbara's
sequence.

number of tiles = ...1... + ..6.n.   *1 mark*

e Gwenno uses some tiles to make a **different** sequence of patterns. The rule for
finding the the number of tiles in pattern number *N* in Gwenno's sequence is:

number of tiles = **1 + 4N**

Draw what you think the first 3 patterns in Gwenno's sequence could be.

2 marks

5 A teacher has **5 full packets** of mints and **6 single** mints.
The number of mints inside each packet is the same.

The teacher tells the class:

'**Write an expression** to show **how many mints**
there are **altogether**. Call the number of mints
inside each packet y.'

Here are some of the expressions the pupils write.

$5 + 6 + y$ $5y6$ $5y + 6$

$6 + 5y$ $5 + 6y$ $(5 + 6) \times y$

a Write down **two** expressions that are correct.

.... and ....   *2 marks*

b A pupil says:
'I think the teacher has a total of **56 mints**.'

Could the pupil be right? Tick (✓) Yes or No.

Yes ☐   No ☐

Explain how you know.   *1 mark*

6 You pay £2.40 each time you go swimming.
Complete the table.

Number of swims	0	10	20	30
Total cost (£)	0	24		

1 mark

b Now show this information on a graph.
Join the points with a straight line.   *2 marks*

c A different way of paying is to pay a yearly fee of **£22**.
Then you pay **£1.40** each time you go swimming.
Complete this table.

Number of swims	0	10	20	30
Total cost (£)	22	36		

1 mark

d Now show this information on the same graph.
Join these points with a straight line. *2 marks*

e For **how many swims** does the graph show that the cost is the **same** for
both ways of paying?   *1 mark*

Answers are on page 246.

LEVEL 5   SHAPE, SPACE AND MEASURES

What you should already know	• You should be able to measure angles to the nearest degree and know the language associated with angle.

• *That an angle is a measure of turn and is measured in degrees*

• *A complete turn is 360°, a half-turn is 180° and a right angle is 90°*

DESCRIBING ANGLES
• There are different types of angle.

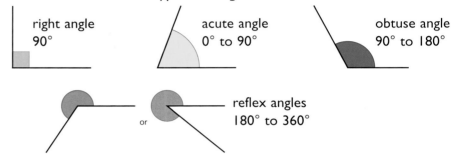

right angle
90°

acute angle
0° to 90°

obtuse angle
90° to 180°

or

reflex angles
180° to 360°

MEASURING AND DRAWING ANGLES
• You can use a **protractor** to measure or draw angles.
• A protractor has an inside scale and outside scale so that you can measure an angle from both sides.
• You should be able to measure or draw angles accurately to within 1°.
• Always use a sharp pencil for drawing and marking.

Worked example
Measure these angles.

a

b

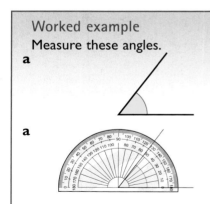

a

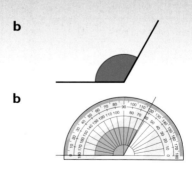

b

The angle is acute so it must be less than 90°. Line up your protractor as shown in the diagram. You need to line up the base line on the protractor, the line that starts from 0°, with the horizontal line that makes the angle. Use the inside scale.

Count round anticlockwise in steps of 10 degrees until you meet the other line of the angle. Now count the units. The angle is 53°.

The angle is obtuse, so it must be greater than 90°. Line up your protractor as shown. The base line on the protractor must start from 0°, so use the outside scale. Count round clockwise in steps of 10 degrees until you meet the other line of the angle. Now count the units. The angle is 118°.

CALCULATING ANGLES

- You can calculate the size of an angle on a diagram without having to measure it if you know these facts.

$a + b = 90°$
a and b are
complementary angles.

$a + b = 180°$
a and b are
supplementary angles.

$a + b = 360°$
a and b are
conjugate angles.

- The angle sum of a triangle is 180°.
  $a + b + c = 180°$

60°

90° ⌐   30°

Worked example

Calculate the missing angle in each of these triangles.

a

67°
a 48°

b

80°
b

a $a + 67° + 48° = 180°$
$a + 115° = 180°$
$a = 65°$

b For an isosceles triangle
$2b + 80° = 180°$
$2b = 100°$
$b = 50°$

Worked example

Calculate the size of the angle marked x on each diagram.

a

x
40°

b

x
62°

c

123°
x

a The two angles add up to 90°, so $x = 90° - 40° = 50°$
b The two angles add up to 180°, so $x = 180° - 62° = 118°$
c The two angles add up to 360°, so $x = 360° - 123° = 237°$

? CHECK YOURSELF QUESTIONS

Q1 Measure these angles to the nearest degree.

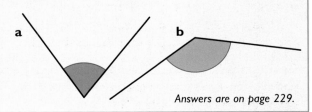

a   **b**

Q2 Use a protractor to draw these angles.
    a 39°   **b** 172°

Answers are on page 229.

Symmetry of 2-D shapes

- You should be able to recognise all the symmetries of 2-D shapes.

POLYGONS

- A **polygon** is a 2-D shape with any number of straight sides.
- A **regular polygon** has equal sides and equal angles.
- Learn the special names of polygons listed in this table.

Number of sides	3	4	5	6	7	8	9	10
Name	triangle	quadrilateral	pentagon	hexagon	heptagon	octagon	nonagon	decagon

LINE SYMMETRY FOR 2-D SHAPES

- Some 2-D shapes have line symmetry – you can use straight lines to cut them exactly in half.
- If there is only one line that will cut the shape exactly in half, the shape has one line of symmetry.
- If there are two different lines that can each cut the shape exactly in half, the shape has two lines of symmetry, and so on.
- You can use tracing paper or a mirror to check whether shapes show line symmetry, for example:

isosceles triangle
1 line of symmetry

equilateral triangle
3 lines of symmetry

rectangle
2 lines of symmetry

square
4 lines of symmetry

regular hexagon
6 lines of symmetry

Worked example

Draw the lines of symmetry on each of these 2-D shapes.

a

a kite

b

a diamond (or rhombus)

c

an egg shape (or ellipse)

a

1 line of symmetry

b

2 lines of symmetry

c
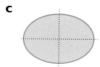
2 lines of symmetry

ROTATIONAL SYMMETRY FOR 2-D SHAPES

- A shape that has rotational symmetry can be turned, or rotated and will look the same from different angles.
- You can use tracing paper to check whether a shape has rotational symmetry, for example:

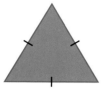

equilateral triangle
order 3

rectangle
order 2

square
order 4

parallelogram
order 2

regular hexagon
order 6

Worked example

Find the order of rotational symmetry for these hexagons.

a

b

c

a Order 2

b Order 3

c Order 1 (no rotational symmetry).

? CHECK YOURSELF QUESTIONS

Q1 Without looking at any diagrams, write down the number of lines of symmetry for:
  a a rectangle   **b** an isosceles triangle   **c** a diamond.

Q2 Without looking at any diagrams, write down the order of rotational symmetry for:
  a a parallelogram   **b** a regular hexagon   **c** a square.

Q3 Draw a regular octagon accurately. How many lines of symmetry does it have? What is its order of rotational symmetry?

Answers are on page 229.

What you should already know

- *The standard units of the metric system – the metre (m), the gram (g) and the litre (l)*

- *How to multiply and divide by powers of 10*

- *The imperial units still in common use*

> • You should know the rough metric equivalents of imperial units in common use and be able to convert between one metric unit and another.

METRIC UNITS
- Learn these measures.

Length	Mass	Capacity (volume)
10 mm = 1 cm	1000 mg = 1 g	1000 ml = 1 l
100 cm = 1 m	1000 g = 1 kg	100 cl = 1 l
1000 m = 1 km	1000 kg = 1 tonne	1000 cm³ = 1 l

- Remember these important rules.

  – 'To change from a larger unit to a smaller unit – multiply'.

  LARGE ⟶ small ⟶ ×

  – 'To change from a smaller unit to a larger unit – divide'.

  small ⟶ LARGE ⟶ ÷

Worked example

Mr Hardy's passport states his height as 1.83 m.

What is his height in centimetres?

Larger to smaller unit, so multiply.
1.83 × 100 = 183 cm

Worked example

Express each quantity in terms of the unit given in brackets.

a 3.2 m (cm) **b** 2500 g (kg) **c** $1\frac{1}{2}$ l (cl)
d 78 mm (cm) **e** 3.2 tonnes (kg) **f** 850 ml (l)

a 3.2 × 100 = 320 cm **b** 2500 ÷ 1000 = 2.5 kg
c 1.5 × 100 = 150 cl **d** 78 ÷ 10 = 7.8 cm
e 3.2 × 1000 = 3200 kg **f** 850 ÷ 1000 = 0.85 l

Worked example

Mrs Hall is making a Christmas cake.

Her recipe requires these ingredients: $\frac{1}{4}$ kg plain flour, $\frac{1}{4}$ kg butter, 400 g sultanas, 350 g raisins, 300 g currants, 250 g brown sugar and 60 g candied peel.

Find the total mass of ingredients required, in kilograms.

First change all masses to grams (changing them all to kilograms would give you difficult fractions to work with). Then add them together. ($\frac{1}{4}$ kg = 250 g)
250 + 250 + 400 + 350 + 300 + 250 + 60 = 1860 g
Smaller to larger unit – divide. 1860 ÷ 1000 = 1.86 kg

IMPERIAL UNITS
- You need to know these conversion tables.

Length
12 inches (ins) = 1 foot (ft)
3 feet = 1 yard (yd)
1760 yards = 1 mile (m)

Mass
16 ounces (oz) = 1 pound (lb)
14 pounds = 1 stone (st)
2240 pounds = 1 ton

Capacity (volume)
8 pints (pt) = 1 gallon (g)

IMPERIAL UNITS AND THEIR METRIC EQUIVALENTS
- You need to know these approximate metric equivalents for the imperial units still in use.

Length
1 in is about 2.5 cm
1 ft is about 30 cm
1 yd is about 90 cm
1 mile is about 1.6 km

Mass
1 oz is about 30 g
1 lb is about 450 g
1 st is about 6.5 kg
1 ton is about 1 tonne

Capacity (volume)
1 pint is about 0.5 l
1 gallon is about 4.5 l

Remember: to change imperial to metric units, multiply.

> **Worked example**
> The world's heaviest man was alleged to be Jon Minnoch who weighed in at about 980 lb. How many stones did he weigh?
>
> Smaller to larger unit, so divide.
> 980 ÷ 14
> = 70 stones

A useful conversion is 5 miles ≈ 8 km

> **Worked example**
> Monsieur Braun sees a road sign on the M1 stating it is 120 miles to Birmingham. Approximately, how many kilometres is this?
>
> 120 × 1.6 = 192. So the distance is approximately 192 km.

> **Worked example**
> Mr Hargreaves buys a firkin of beer for his firm's Christmas Party. The beer is to be served in $\frac{1}{2}$-litre glasses. How many glasses of beer can be served? (A firkin is a barrel of beer containing 9 gallons.)
>
> Change 9 gallons into litres. This is 9 × 4.5 = 40.5 l. The number of glasses is 40.5 ÷ $\frac{1}{2}$ = 40.5 ÷ 0.5 = 81
>
> So, approximately 81 glasses of beer can be served.

? CHECK YOURSELF QUESTIONS

Remember: you can use your calculator.

Q1 Express each quantity in the unit in brackets.

a 8.32 km (m)   b 152 cm (m)
c 4385 g (kg)   d 800 mg (g)
e 4.7 l (cl)   f 420 cm³ (l)

Q2 A lorry carrying 85 sacks of potatoes to a local supermarket comes to a bridge displaying this sign.

> **MAXIMUM WEIGHT 10 TONNES**

The driver knows that the mass of the lorry is $4\frac{1}{2}$ tonnes and that the mass of each sack is 50 kg. Can the lorry cross the bridge safely?

Q3 Using the conversions tables given above, find the approximate metric equivalents for these measures. The units required are in brackets.

a
6 feet
(metres)

b
500 gallons crude oil
(litres)

c

2 lb flour
(grams)

d
To the Beach 1/2 mile
(metres)

Answers are on page 229.

What you should already know

- *The metric system of units for length, mass and capacity*

- *Some everyday items that measure about 1 metre, 1 kilogram and 1 litre*

- You should be able to make a sensible estimate of a range of measures in relation to everyday situations.

Worked example

Which units would you use to estimate these measures?

a the length of a school playing field
b the mass of a train
c the distance from London to Moscow
d the volume of water in Lake Windermere
e the thickness of an exercise book
f the mass of a sheet of paper

a metres	**b** tonnes	**c** kilometres
d litres	**e** millimetres	**f** grams

Worked example

The coach is 10 m long. Make sensible estimates for the length of the lorry, motor bike and taxi.

Lorry: about 20 m; motor bike: about 2 m; taxi: 3–4 m

CHECK YOURSELF QUESTIONS

Q1 Make sensible estimates for these measures.
  a the thickness of a glass (in mm)
  b the mass of a packet of crisps (in g)
  c the capacity of a full bath of water (in *l*)
  d the height of your front door (in cm)
  e the mass of a large dictionary (in kg)

Q2 A ream of photocopying paper (500 sheets) has a mass of about 2.5 kg. Use this information to estimate the mass of a single sheet of paper.

Answers are on page 230.

• You should understand and be able to use the formula for the area of a rectangle.

What you should already know

• *How to find area by counting squares*

THE AREA OF A RECTANGLE

• Rectangles have two **dimensions**. These are usually called the **length** and the **width** or **breadth**.
• To work out the area of a rectangle, use the formula:
area of a rectangle = length × width.

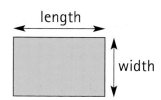

Hint:

Write this as
$A = l \times w = lw$

Worked example
Find the area of each of these rectangles.

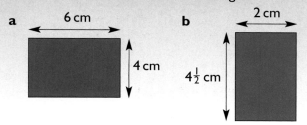

a 6 cm
4 cm

b 2 cm
$4\frac{1}{2}$ cm

a The length is 6 cm and the width is 4 cm.
The area is $4 \times 6 = 24\,cm^2$.
Don't forget to include the units in your answer.
b The area is length × width = $4\frac{1}{2} \times 2 = 9\,cm^2$.

Worked example
Find the area of a square of side 6 cm.

A square is a special rectangle where the length and width are the same.
Area = $6 \times 6 = 36\,cm^2$

Worked example
A rectangle with an area of $12\,cm^2$ has been drawn on the grid.
Draw two other rectangles with different dimensions that also have areas of $12\,cm^2$.

Any other rectangles with areas of $12\,cm^2$ will do.
Three are shown.

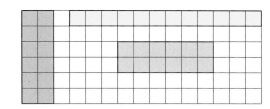

CHECK YOURSELF QUESTIONS

Q1 Work out the area of a rectangle with length 7 cm and width 5 cm.

Q2 A rectangle has a length of 10 cm. Its area is 40 cm.
What is its width?

Q3 Which of the rectangles below have the same area?

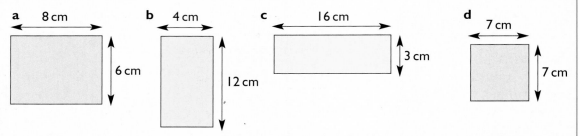

Q4 A square has an area of 16 cm². A rectangle has the same area.
Give two possible different sizes for the rectangle.

Q5 Rectangle A has a length of 8 cm and a width of 6 cm.
Rectangle B has a length of 4 cm and a width of 3 cm.
Mary thinks that rectangle B will have an area half that of
rectangle A. Show that Mary is wrong.

Answers are on page 230.

1 An equilateral triangle has **3 lines of symmetry**.

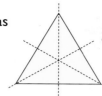

It has **rotational symmetry** of **order 3**.

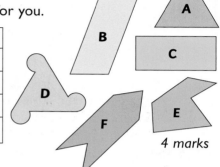

Write the letter of each shape in the correct space in the table below.
You may use a mirror or tracing paper to help you.
The letters for the first two shapes have been written for you.

		Number of lines of symmetry			
		0	1	2	3
Order of rotational symmetry	1				
	2	B			
	3				A

4 marks

2 Helen has **these eight rods**.

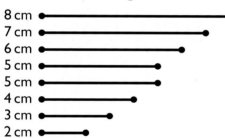

8 cm
7 cm
6 cm
5 cm
5 cm
4 cm
3 cm
2 cm

She can use **5** of her rods to make a **rectangle**.

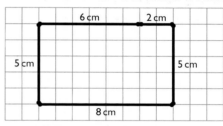

a Show how to make a **different rectangle** with a **different shape** with **5** of Helen's rods.

b Show how to make a rectangle with **6** of Helen's rods.

c Show how to make a **square** with all **8** of Helen's rods.

3 marks

3 The diagram shows a box.

Complete the **net** for the box.

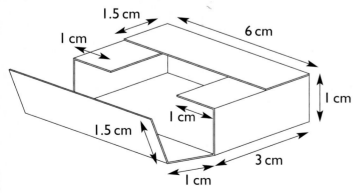

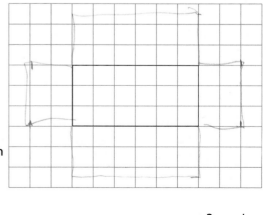

3 marks

4 **Four** squares join together to make a bigger square.

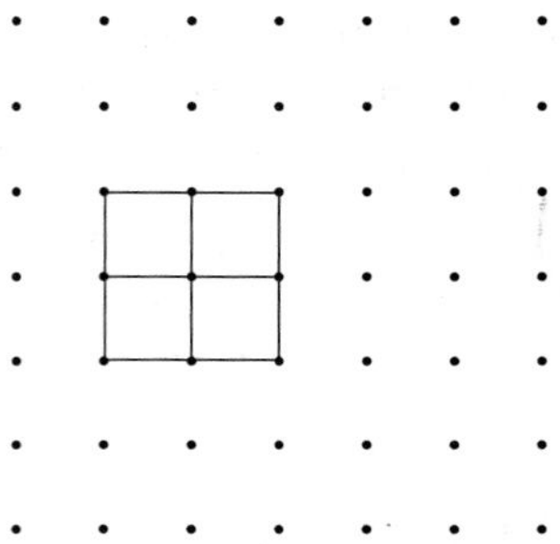

a **Four** congruent triangles join together to make a bigger triangle. Draw **two more** triangles to complete the drawing of the bigger triangle.

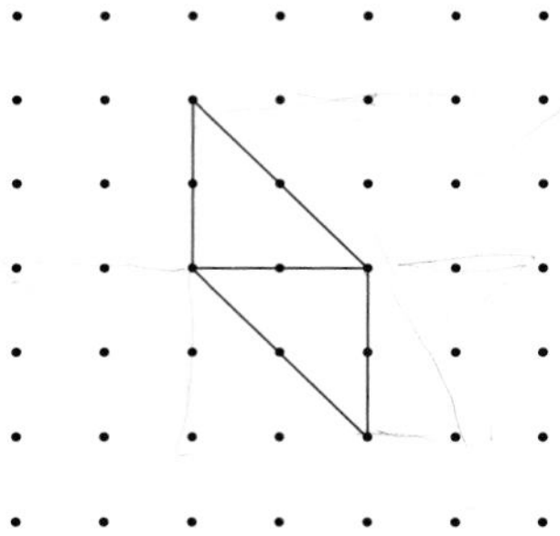

1 mark

b Four congruent trapeziums join to make a bigger trapezium. Draw **two more** trapeziums to complete the drawing of the bigger trapezium.

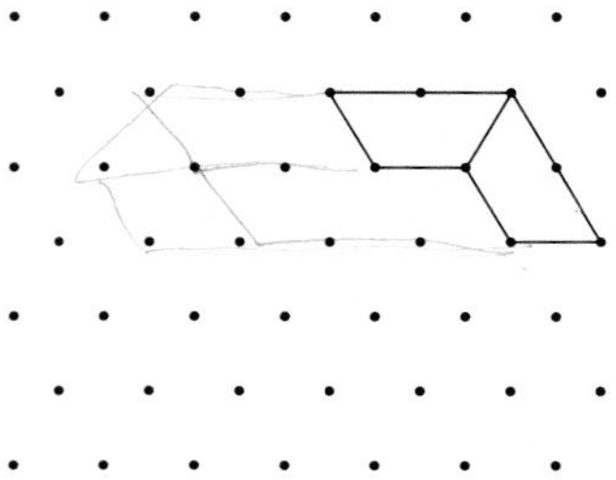

1 mark

c

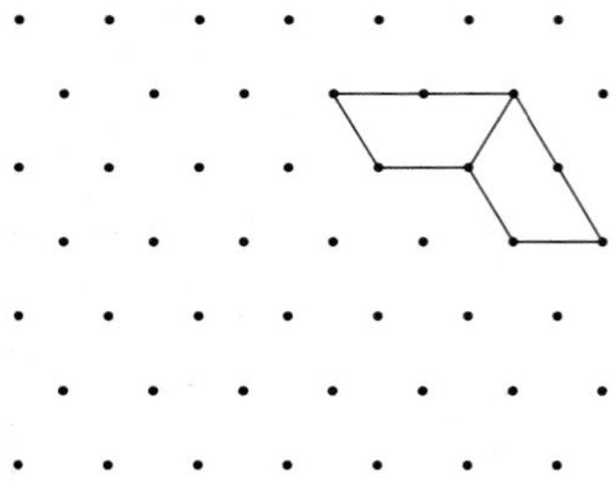

Four congruent trapeziums join together to make a parallelogram.
Draw **two more** trapeziums to complete the drawing of the parallelogram.

1 mark

5 This cuboid is made from **4** small cubes.

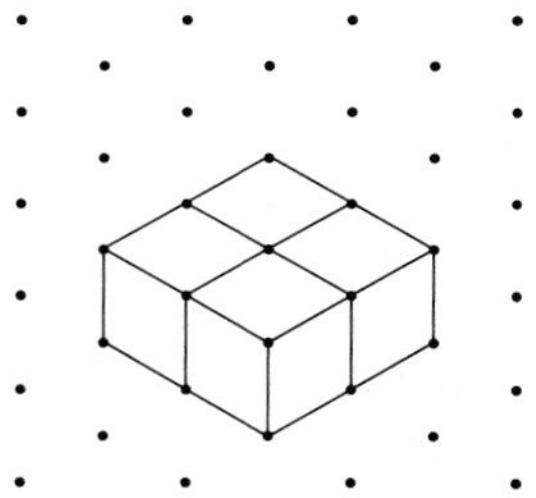

a Draw a cuboid which is **twice** as **high**, **twice** as **long** and **twice** as **wide**.

2 marks

b Graham made this cuboid from **3** small cubes.

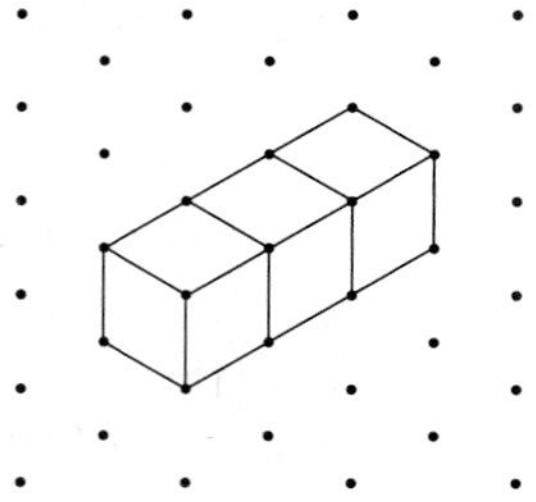

Mohinder wants to make a cuboid which is **twice** as **high**, **twice** as **long** and **twice** as **wide** as Graham's cuboid.
How many small cubes will Mohinder need altogether?

1 mark

6 a You can **rotate** triangle **A** onto triangle **B**.
Put a cross on the **centre of rotation**.
You may use tracing paper to help you.

b You can **rotate** triangle **A** onto triangle **B**.
The rotation is **anti-clockwise**.
What is the **angle** of rotation?

Angle: ......°

1 mark

c **Reflect** triangle **A** in the mirror line.
You may use a mirror or tracing paper
to help you.

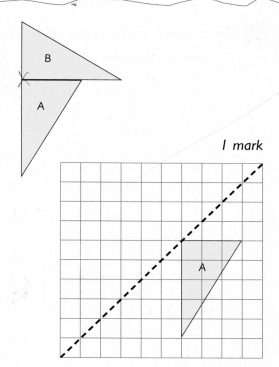

1 mark

7 a Tick (✓) any rectangles below that have an area of **12 cm²**.

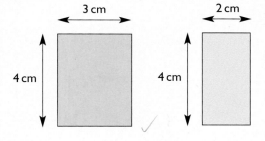

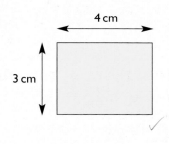

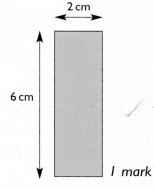

1 mark

b A **square** has an area of **100 cm²**. What is its **perimeter**?
Show your working.

2 marks

8 How may kilometres are there in **5 miles**?
Complete the missing part of the sign.

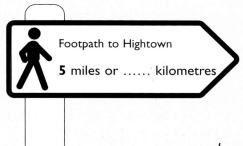

Footpath to Hightown

5 miles or ...... **kilometres**

1 mark

9 Here is a plan of a ferry crossing.
(Not drawn accurately)

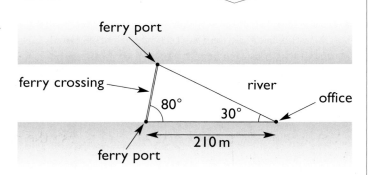

ferry port

ferry crossing

river

office

80°   30°

210 m

ferry port

a Complete the accurate scale
drawing of the ferry crossing
below.

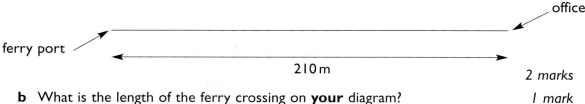

office

ferry port

210 m

2 marks

b What is the length of the ferry crossing on **your** diagram?   *1 mark*

c The scale is **1 cm** to **20 m**. Work out the length of the real ferry crossing.
Show your working and **write the units with your answer**.   *1 mark*

10 A scale measures in **grams** and in **ounces**.

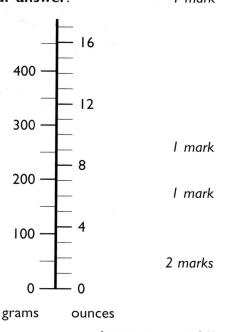

Use the scale to answer these questions.

a About how many ounces is **400 grams**?

1 mark

b About how many grams is **8 ounces**?

1 mark

c About how many ounces is **1 kilogram**?
Explain your answer.

2 marks

16

400

12

300

8

200

4

100

0   0

grams   ounces

Answers are on page 246.

15 Mean and range

> • You should understand and be able to use the mean of a set of discrete data.
>
> • You should be able to use the range and one of the averages to compare two distributions.

THE MEAN

- An average such as:
  - the average contents of a box of drawing pins is 144
  - the average annual rainfall in Borrowdale is 43.9 cm (the wettest place in England!)

  is the **mean** or the **mean average**.
- There are three types of average: mean, mode and median (see pages 37–38).
- The mean is a useful average because it takes all values into account.
- To find the mean of a set of data, add up all the values and divide by the number of values in the list.
- The mean (the symbol is $\bar{x}$) = $\dfrac{\text{all the values added together}}{\text{the total number of values}}$

Worked example

A sponsored cycle race was held to help raise money for a school minibus. 10 pupils gave in the following amounts of money:
£6, £10, £8, £12, £14, £20, £5, £10, £15, £16.

Find the mean amount that the pupils raised.

The total amount raised is £116.
The mean is £116 ÷ 10, which is £11.60.

Number of children	Frequency
1	6
2	7
3	5
4	2

Worked example

After watching the TV news about life in China, Mandy wanted to find out the average number of children per family in her class at school. She asked 20 of her friends how many children there were in their families, including themselves. She then made a frequency table for her data.

From the table she decided that she could calculate the mean average for the number of children in each family. Show how she could do this. Why could Mandy's answer not show an accurate estimate of the average family size for all families in Britain?

The table shows that 6 families had 1 child, 7 families had 2 children, and so on. Add a column to the table to work out the total for all 20 families.

Number of children	Frequency	Total number of children in all 20 families
1	6	1×6
2	7	2×7
3	5	3×5
4	2	4×2

Now add together all the totals.
$6 + 14 + 15 + 8 = 43$
The mean is $43 \div 20 = 2.15$ children per family. Notice that it is usual to leave the answer as a decimal.

It would not be a good estimate because Mandy chose only 20 families: this is too small a sample to represent the whole country. For example, it did not include any families with no children.

THE RANGE

- The **range** of a set of data shows how the values are spread out.
- The range is the difference between the highest and lowest values (highest value – lowest value).
- The range is useful when you need to compare two sets of data.

Worked example

Steve and Joanne kept a record in their school work diaries of all their maths' test marks. The table shows their results at the end of the year.

Steve's marks	42%	53%	68%	59%	64%	48%	70%	40%
Joanne's marks	55%	52%	66%	50%	55%	51%	53%	50%

a Find the mean and range of their marks.
b Comment on these results.

a Steve's mean mark = $444 \div 8 = 55.5\%$.
   The range of Steve's marks is $70 - 40 = 30\%$.
   Joanne's mean mark is $432 \div 8 = 54\%$.
   The range of Joanne's marks is $66 - 50 = 16\%$.
b Steve's average mark was higher, but Joanne had a smaller range.
   This shows that she was more consistent.

Worked example

Mrs Corbett and Mr Baxter both do their shopping at 'SuperShop' once a week. The amounts they spent over a 5-week period are given in the table.

	Mrs Corbett	Mr Baxter
Week 1	£95.70	£86.90
Week 2	£102.30	£84.00
Week 3	£93.00	£87.80
Week 4	£98.10	£79.40
Week 5	£101.60	£80.50

a Find the mean and range of the amounts they spent.
b What can you deduce from these values?

a Mrs Corbett's mean amount spent is £490.70 ÷ 5 = £98.14.
Her range is £102.30 – £93 = £9.30.
Mr Baxter's mean amount spent is £418.60 ÷ 5 = £83.72.
His range is £87.80 – £79.40 = £8.40.
b On average Mrs Corbett spends more. The Corbett family might be larger than the Baxter family. The ranges are very close, showing both of them are very consistent in their shopping habits.

❓ CHECK YOURSELF QUESTIONS

Remember that you can use your calculator.

Q1 Find the mean and range of each set of numbers.
   a 12, 14, 18, 17, 14, 11, 16, 10
   b 135, 143, 150, 149, 158, 162
   c 3.2, 5.4, 2.5, 4.6, 3.8

Q2 These are the average monthly temperatures for Narvic in Norway, over a year.

$^-6°C, ^-5°C, ^-3°C, 2°C, 6°C, 10°C, 14°C, 13°C, 9°C, 4°C, 0°C, ^-2°C$

Find the mean and range of these temperatures.

Q3 The bar graph shows the amounts of time Claire and Sarah spent on homework during the week.

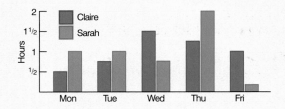

   a Find the average amount of time each one spent on homework during the week.
   b Find the range of times for each of them.
   c Using these values, comment on what you notice.

Answers are on page 230.

REVISION SESSION 16 Pie charts

What you should already know

- *How to interpret frequency tables and diagrams*

- **You should be able to interpret graphs and diagrams, including pie charts, and make sense of them.**

DISPLAYING DATA

- Data can be displayed on **bar charts** and **frequency diagrams** so that it can be readily interpreted.
- If there are not too many categories, it is often useful to display the data on a **pie chart** or circular **diagram**.
- Pie charts are very easy to understand at a glance. This is why they are often used in advertising and in the business world.

Worked example

Mr Hebson was doing surveys with his Year 9 class. Each pupil had to do a survey of their own choice and then draw a pie chart to display their data.

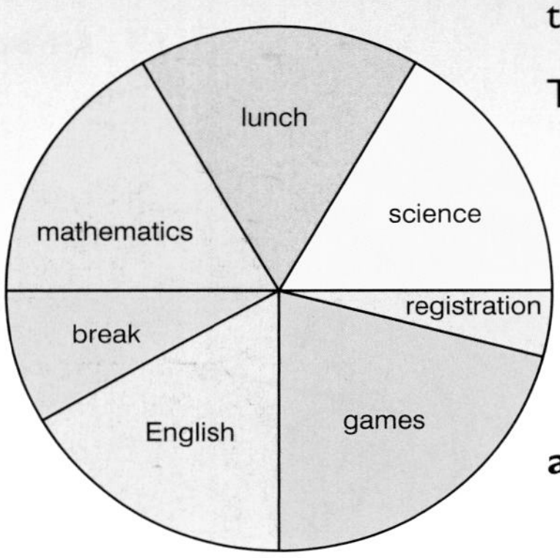

This is Val's pie chart to show how she has spent her day at school.

a Which lesson was the longest? How can you tell?

b Val spent six hours at school.

(i) How long was the maths lesson?

(ii) If maths and English lessons lasted for the same time, how long was break?

a Games

The slice or sector labelled 'games' is the largest.

b (i) 1 hour

The sectors for maths, lunch and science are all the same size and take up half of the diagram. This represents 3 hours so maths is 1 hour.

(ii) $\frac{1}{2}$ hour

The sectors for English and break take up $\frac{1}{4}$ of the diagram which represents $1\frac{1}{2}$ hours.

English is 1 hour, so this leaves $\frac{1}{2}$ hour for break.

Worked example

In the same survey, David decided to find out what method of transport the pupils in the class had used to get to school that morning.

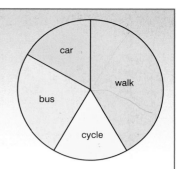

a What does the diagram tell you about those pupils who cycled or came by car?

b If 9 pupils came on the bus, how many pupils were in the class?

c Can you tell how many pupils walked?

a The same number of pupils cycled or came by car, since the sectors are the same size.

b 36. The bus sector is $\frac{1}{4}$ of the chart which represents 9 pupils, so total number of pupils is $4 \times 9 = 36$.

c Not easily, since it is difficult to find the fraction of the diagram for those who walked. It is more than $\frac{1}{4}$ which is 9 pupils, and less than $\frac{1}{2}$ which is 18 pupils. You could estimate that about 15 pupils walked to school.

CHECK YOURSELF QUESTIONS

Q1 The pie chart shows the age distribution of people in Britain.
  a Estimate the size of the fraction for:
     (i) the under-10 age group   (ii) the 21–40 age group.
  b Can you find the population of Britain from the diagram?
  c The population of Britain is nearly 60 million. Estimate the number of people who are over 65.

Q2 The pie chart shows how Mr and Mrs Hadwin spend their money during a typical week of the year.
  a Estimate the percentage amount they spend on food.
  b One week, Mr and Mrs Hadwin have £400 to spend.
     (i) If they spend 15% on fuel, how much money is this?
     (ii) If they spend £48 on transport, what percentage of the total is this?

Q3 Mitchell drew a pie chart to show how he spent the day. He calculated that each hour of the day is represented by 15° on the pie chart.
  a Show how he calculated that 1 hour equals 15°.
  b By measuring the angle for each sector, complete the frequency table.

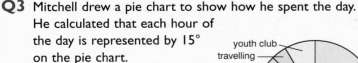

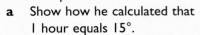

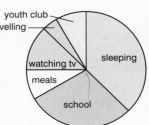

Activity	Angle of sector	No. of hours
Sleeping		
School		
Meals		
Watching TV		
Travelling		
Youth Club		

Answers are on page 230.

<table>
<tr><td>

What you should already know

- *The terms 'unlikely', 'likely', 'fair' and 'certain'*

- *The range of the probability of an outcome*

</td><td>

- You should understand and be able to use the probability scale from 0 to 1.

- You should be able to find and justify probabilities using either experimental evidence or theoretical probabilities.

</td></tr>
</table>

PROBABILITY

- The probability of an outcome of an event can be anywhere between impossible and certain, as this probability scale shows.

- Probability may be calculated by using **theory**, by doing **experiments** or by **collecting data**.
- The probability that the outcome of an event will happen is usually written as a fraction, but it can also be given as a decimal or a percentage.
- An event that is impossible has a probability of 0 and an event that is certain has a probability of 1. All other probabilities lie between 0 and 1.

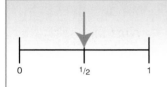

Worked example

Draw an arrow on a scale to show the probability of tossing a head with a normal coin.

The two possibilities are heads or tails. This is a 1 in 2 chance or $\frac{1}{2}$.

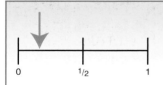

Worked example

Draw an arrow on a scale to show the probability of throwing a 6 on an ordinary dice.

The six possible scores are 1, 2, 3, 4, 5, 6. This is a 1 in 6 chance or $\frac{1}{6}$.

CHECK YOURSELF QUESTION

Q1 Draw arrows on a probability scale to show the probabilities for these events.
  a Picking a club from a well shuffled pack of cards.
  b Choosing a letter at random from the word 'ABSTEMIOUS' that is a vowel.
  c Winning a game of chess, playing against a very skilled player.
  d Your getting maths homework next week.

Answers are on page 231.

- **You should know that different outcomes may result from repeating the same experiment.**

PROBABILITY FROM EXPERIMENTAL OR STATISTICAL DATA
- Probabilities can be calculated by using different methods.

EQUALLY LIKELY OUTCOMES
- An **event** is something that happens.
- Every event has a set of possible **outcomes**: different results.
- You can often find the probability for a specific or favourable outcome.
- On a fair coin or dice, all the outcomes have the same chance of happening. They are **equally likely** outcomes.
- The probability of tossing a coin and scoring a head is a 1 in 2 chance or $\frac{1}{2}$. Write this as P(head) = $\frac{1}{2}$.
- P(outcome) = $\dfrac{\text{number of ways of getting that outcome}}{\text{total number of possible outcomes}}$

- This formula for calculating a probability gives a **probability fraction**. This fraction can also be written as a decimal or a percentage.
- A probability must lie between 0 and 1.
- The total of the probabilities for all possible outcomes of an event is 1.

EXPERIMENTAL DATA
- Sometimes it is necessary to carry out an experiment, to show all the possible outcomes of an event, before estimating probabilities for particular or favourable outcomes.

> ### Worked example
> Alison dropped 50 drawing pins onto a table, to estimate the probability that a drawing pin lands point-up or point-down.
>
>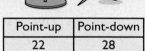
>
> | Point-up | Point-down |
> |----------|------------|
> | 22 | 28 |
>
> Estimate the probability that a drawing pin lands point-up. If Alison repeats the experiment will she get the same results?
>
> There are 22 favourable outcomes out of 50 possible outcomes.
>
> P(drawing pin lands point-up) = $\frac{22}{50} = \frac{11}{25}$
>
> It is unlikely that she will get exactly the same results, but her probability fraction should be about the same.

What you should already know

- *How to use the probability scale from 0 and 1*

Hints:

Tossing a coin has two possible outcomes: heads or tails.

Throwing a dice has six possible outcomes: 1, 2, 3, 4, 5 or 6.

The probability of throwing a 6 on a normal dice is a 1 in 6 chance or $\frac{1}{6}$. Write this as P(6) = $\frac{1}{6}$.

Worked example
Find the probability of choosing a picture card from a well-shuffled pack of cards.

There are 12 favourable outcomes (4 kings + 4 queens + 4 jacks). There are 52 equally likely possible outcomes: the number of cards in a pack.

P(picture card)
= $\frac{12}{52} = \frac{3}{13}$

● Sometimes it is necessary to carry out a survey or look at historical data, before estimating probabilities for particular or favourable outcomes.

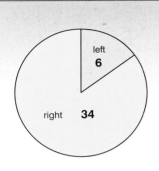

Worked example

Louise wanted to estimate the percentage of the people in England who are left-handed. She carried out a survey on 40 pupils in her year at school and drew a pie chart to show her data.

Use Louise's chart to estimate the percentage of people who are left-handed. How could Louise obtain a more realistic percentage?

$$P(\text{left-handed}) = \frac{6}{40} = \frac{3}{20}$$

So, an estimate for the number of left-handed people is 15%. To obtain a more realistic percentage, she would have to survey a complete age range of people and ask more people.

CHECK YOURSELF QUESTIONS

Q1 A card is chosen from a well-shuffled pack. Find:
  a P(choosing an ace)
  b P(choosing a heart)
  c P(choosing a king or a queen).

Q2 This 8-sided spinner is used in a game. Find:
  a P(a score of 3)
  b P(a score greater than 2)
  c P(an even score).

Q3 The National Lottery uses 49 balls numbered 1 to 49. What is the probability that the first ball that comes out has at least one 3 on it?

Q4 A box contains coloured counters for the game 'Tiddlywinks'. If there are 40 red, 30 blue, 20 green and 10 yellow counters, and one is taken out at random, find the percentage probability of getting:
  a a blue counter
  b a green or red counter
  c a counter that is not green.

Q5 James is ill at home and, to keep himself occupied, decides to do a survey on the types of vehicle that pass his house as he looks through his bedroom window. After one hour he had collected these results.

Vehicle	Car	Van	Lorry	Bus	Motorbike
Frequency	35	7	4	2	12

Estimate the probability that the next vehicle to pass James' house is:
  a a car or van
  b a large vehicle
  c a vehicle with more than 2 wheels.

Answers are on page 231.

HANDLING DATA　　　TEST QUESTIONS

1 This graph shows the **range** in the **temperature** in Miami each month.

For example, in January the temperature ranges from 17°C to 24°C.

a In which month does Miami have the **smallest range** in temperature?　　*1 mark*

b In **July**, the **range** in the temperature in Miami is 5 degrees.
There are **five** other months in which the range in the temperature is 5 degrees.
Which five months are they?　　*2 marks*

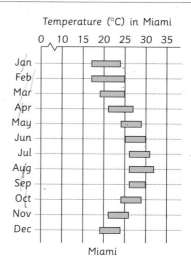

Temperature (°C) in Miami

Miami

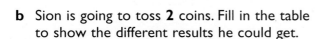

Temperature (°C) in Orlando

Orlando

c This graph shows the range in the temperature in Orlando each month.
In which **three** months is the **maximum** temperature in **Miami greater** than the maximum temperature in Orlando?　　*1 mark*

2 A coin has two sides, heads and tails.

a Chris is going to toss a coin. What is the **probability** that Chris will get **heads**?
Write your answer as a **fraction**.

heads　　　tails

1 mark

b Sion is going to toss **2** coins. Fill in the table to show the different results he could get.

First coin	Second coin
heads	heads

1 mark

c Sion is going to toss **2** coins.
What is the **probability** that he will get **tails** with **both** his coins?
Write your answer as a fraction.　　*1 mark*

d Dianne tossed one coin. She got tails.
Diane is going to toss another coin.
What is the **probability** that she will get **tails again** with her next coin?
Write your answer as a **fraction**.　　*1 mark*

3 Look at these angles.

angle P angle Q angle R angle S angle T

a One of the angles measures 120°.
Write its letter.

1 mark

b Complete the drawing below to show an angle of **157°**.
Label the angle 157°.

_____

2 marks

c 15 pupils measured two angles. Here are their results.

Angle A	
Angle measured as	Number of pupils
36°	1
37°	2
38°	10
39°	2

Angle B	
Angle measured as	Number of pupils
45°	5
134°	3
135°	4
136°	3

Use the results to decide what each angle is most likely to measure.

Angle **A** is ...... °   Angle **B** is ...... °

How did you decide?   How did you decide?   *2 marks*

4 **a** A spinner has **eight** equal sections.

What is the probability of scoring 4
on the spinner?

1 mark

What is the probability of scoring
an even number on the spinner?

1 mark

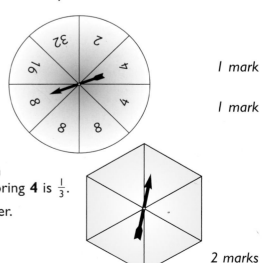

b A different spinner has six equal sections
and **six numbers**.

On this spinner, the probability of scoring an
even number is $\frac{2}{3}$ and the probability of scoring **4** is $\frac{1}{3}$.

Write what numbers could be on this spinner.

2 marks

5 Mark and Kate each buy a family pack of crisps.
Each family pack contains **ten bags** of crisps.

The table shows how many bags of each flavour are in each pack.

flavour	number of bags
plain	5
vinegar	2
chicken	2
cheese	1

a Mark is going to take a bag of crisps at random from his family pack. Complete these sentences.

The probability that the flavour will be .... is $\frac{1}{2}$.

1 mark

The probability that the flavour will be **cheese** is ....

1 mark

b Kate ate **two bags** of **plain** crisps from her family pack of 10 bags. Now she is going to take a bag at random from the bags that are left.

What is the probability that the flavour will be **cheese**?

1 mark

c A shop sells **12 bags** of crisps in a large pack. I am going to take a bag at random from the large pack.

The table shows the probability of getting each flavour.

Use the probabilities to work out **how many bags** of each flavour are in this large pack.

flavour	probability	number of bags
plain	$\frac{7}{12}$	
vinegar	$\frac{1}{4}$	
chicken	$\frac{1}{6}$	
cheese	0	

1 mark

6 The two diagrams show the number of hours of sunshine in two different months.

Number of hours of sunshine in month A

Number of hours of sunshine in month B

number of days with less than 4 hours

number of days with 4 to 8 hours

number of days with more than 8 hours

a How many days are there in **month A**? Tick (✓) the correct box.

28 ☐ 29 ☐ 30 ☐ 31 ☐ not possible to tell ☐

1 mark

b How many days are there in **month B**? Tick (✓) the correct box.

28 ☐ 29 ☐ 30 ☐ 31 ☐ not possible to tell ☐

1 mark

c Which month had more hours of sunshine? Tick (✓) the correct box.

month A ☐ month B ☐

Explain how you know.

1 mark

7 A school has a new canteen.
A special person will be chosen to perform the opening ceremony.
The names of all the pupils, all the teachers and all the canteen staff are put into a box.
One name is taken out at random.

A pupil says:

> There are only three choices.
> It could be a pupil, a teacher or one of the canteen staff.
> The probability of it being a **pupil** is $\frac{1}{3}$.

The pupil is **wrong**. Explain why. *1 mark*

8 In each box of cereal there is a free gift of a card.
You cannot tell which card will be in a box. Each card is equally likely.

There are **four** different cards: A, B, C or D.

a Zoe needs card **A**.
Her brother **Paul** needs cards **C** and **D**.

They buy one box of cereal.

What is the probability that the card is one that **Zoe** needs? *1 mark*

What is the probability that the card is one that **Paul** needs? *1 mark*

b Then their mother opens the box.
She tells them that the card is **not card A**.

Now what is the probability that the card is one that **Zoe** needs? *1 mark*

What is the probability that the card is one that **Paul** needs? *1 mark*

9 **a** There are four people in Sita's family.
Their shoe sizes are 4, 5, 7 and 10.

What is the **median** shoe size in Sita's family? *1 mark*

b There are **three** people in John's family.
The **range** of their shoe sizes is **4**.

Two people in the family wear shoe size 6.
John's shoe size is **not 6** and is **not 10**.

What is John's shoe size? *1 mark*

10 Hannah went on a cycling holiday.

The table shows how far she cycled every day.

Monday	Tuesday	Wednesday	Thursday
32.3 km	38.7 km	43.5 km	45.1 km

Hannah says:

> On average, I cycled **over 40 km** a day.

Show that Hannah is wrong. *2 marks*

Answers are on page 247.

MENTAL ARITHMETIC TEST 1: LEVELS 3 TO 5

The Questions: **Time: 5 seconds**

1   Write the number three thousand and six in figures. | **1** | |

2   What number should you subtract from one hundred | **2** | |
    to get the answer thirteen?

3   What is fifty-eight multiplied by ten? | **3** | |

4   In a survey, one quarter of people liked tennis. | **4** | % |
    What percentage of people liked tennis?

5   What is forty-two divided by six? | **5** | |

6   Change one hundred and thirty millimetres into | **6** | cm |
    centimetres.

7   What is four point seven multiplied by one hundred? | **7** | 4.7 |

The Questions: **Time: 10 seconds**

8   What is double thirty-two? | **8** | |

9   How many five-pence coins make forty-five pence? | **9** | coins |

10 What is seven hundred and fifty-eight to the nearest | **10** | |
    ten?

11 On your answer sheet are two numbers. Write down | **11** | 16   22 |
    the number which is halfway between them.

12 On your answer sheet is a scale. | **12** |
    Estimate the number shown by the arrow.   8   9   10

13 A television programme starts at ten minutes to | **13** | |
    seven. It lasts twenty-five minutes. At what time does
    the programme finish?

14 One third of a number is twelve. What is the number? | **14** | |

15 Gary collects ten-pence coins. Altogether he has | **15** | coins |
    twelve pounds. How many ten-pence coins is that?

16   What number is nine squared?

16	

17   In a group of sixty-three children, twenty-nine are boys. How many are girls?

17	girls

18   What is one-quarter of thirty-two?

18	

19   Subtract one hundred from six thousand and three.

19	

20   The temperature in London was minus three degrees. Barcelona was twenty degrees warmer. What was the temperature in Barcelona?

20	degrees

21   Ten per cent of a number is thirteen. What is the number?

21	

22   Write the number four and a half million in figures.

22	

23   Write eight tenths as a decimal number.

23	

The Questions:

Time: 15 seconds

24   The numbers on your answer sheet show how many children go to a Youth Club on three days. How many is this altogether?

24		18 15 20

25   What is the cost of five cassettes at one pound ninety-nine pence each?

25	£

26   The year is two thousand and four. What year will it be four hundred years from now?

26	

27   A bag of oranges costs one pound forty-nine pence. How many bags could you buy with ten pounds?

27	bags

28   Look at the map on your sheet.
The scale is one centimetre to five kilometres.
Estimate how many kilometres it is by road from town A to town B.

28	km

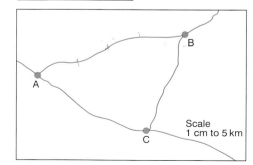

Answers are on page 242.

| # Working with decimals

> • You should be able to order and approximate decimals when solving numerical problems.

PLACE VALUE IN DECIMALS

- The number 234 has 2 hundreds, 3 tens and 4 units. Hundreds, tens and units are like column headings for the digits in the number.
- These column headings describe the place value of the digits in whole numbers.
- Decimal numbers can include fractions or parts of numbers.
- You use a decimal point to separate the fraction from the whole number.
- The decimal point always comes after the units digit.
- Each column heading or place value is ten times as big as the one on the right of it and ten times as small as the one on the left of it.
- The place value for the first digit after the decimal point is ten times as small as the place value for the units digit.
- The first three places of decimals are also called 'tenths', 'hundredths', 'thousandths'.
- These are the place values for the number 362.794:

hundreds	tens	units	decimal point	tenths	hundredths	thousandths
3	6	2	.	7	9	4

Worked example

Give the place value of the underlined digit in each number.

a 5.6<u>5</u>   **b** 0.71<u>4</u>   **c** 23.0<u>6</u>

a 6 tenths or 0.6   **b** 4 thousandths or 0.004
c 6 hundredths or 0.06

Worked example

Put these decimal numbers in order, smallest first.

2.3   2.202   2.32   2.21   2.33

In order the numbers are:

2.202   2.21   2.3   2.32   2.33

What you should already know

- *How to add and subtract decimals with up to two places*
- *How to multiply a decimal with up to two places by a single-digit number*
- *How to round numbers to the nearest whole number or the nearest ten*

Note:

A 1 in the units column is worth 1, so a 1 in the first decimal place is worth $\frac{1}{10}$ or 0.1.

A 1 in the next place is worth $\frac{1}{100}$ or 0.01.

A 1 in the third place is worth $\frac{1}{1000}$ or 0.001.

Hint:

Add zeros to give each decimal number the same number of digits.

2.202   2.210   2.300
2.320   2.330

ROUNDING DECIMALS

- You can estimate the answer to a problem that includes decimals by rounding them.
- Rounding to the nearest whole number will not work for a number such as 0.326 as it would round to zero. You need to round to the first decimal place.
- Use similar rules as before to round to one decimal place (1 d.p.)

Hint:

0.326 rounds to 0.3
0.67 rounds to 0.7
0.458 rounds to 0.5.

> **Worked example**
> **a** Round these numbers to the nearest tenth.
> **(i)** 0.53 **(ii)** 0.189 **(iii)** 0.85
> **b** Round these numbers to the nearest hundredth.
> **(i)** 0.032 **(ii)** 0.089 **(iii)** 0.055
>
> **a (i)** 0.5 (1 decimal place, or 1 d.p.). **(ii)** 0.2 (1 d.p.)
> **(iii)** 0.9 (1 d.p.) Round upwards.
> **b (i)** 0.03 (2 d.p.) **(ii)** 0.09 (2 d.p.)
> **(iii)** 0.06 (2 d.p.) Round upwards.

Hint:

Always show the number of decimal places to which you have rounded, so that an examiner can see the level of accuracy of your working.

MENTAL CALCULATIONS WITH DECIMALS

- After you have rounded the decimals, you can use them to estimate the answers to division and multiplication questions.
- To work out 0.6×0.7, work out $6 \times 7 = 42$ and count the number of decimal places in the whole problem. There are two in the question, so there will be the same number in the answer. The answer is 0.42.

$$0.6 \qquad \times \qquad 0.7 \qquad = 0.42$$
1 decimal place + 1 decimal place = 2 decimal places.

> **Worked example**
> Write down the answers to these.
>
> **a** 0.5×0.7 **b** 0.04×0.08 **c** 0.5×0.03 **d** 0.5×0.6
>
> **a** 0.35 **b** 0.0032 **c** 0.015 **d** 0.3
>
> In (b) and (c) you have to add in zeros to make up the decimal places.
> In (d) the answer is actually 0.30 because $5 \times 6 = 30$ but it is not necessary to write down the final zero.

> **Worked example**
> Work out the answers.
>
> **a** 0.7×40
> **b** 0.06×400
> **c** 500×0.3
> **d** 70×0.08
>
> **a** 28 **b** 24
> **c** 150 **d** 5.6

CALCULATING WITH DECIMALS AND MULTIPLES OF 10

- To calculate answers to questions with whole numbers and decimals, use the techniques you learned at level 5 for multiplying and dividing by tens and hundreds.
- When you multiply a whole number by a decimal, every time you move the digits one place to the left on one number, you must move the digits one place to the right on the other. For example:
$0.8 \times 500 = 8 \times 50 = 400$ $0.06 \times 30 = 0.6 \times 3 = 1.8$

- To divide, move the digits until the number you are dividing by is a whole number. Each time you do this, multiply the other number by 10. For example:

$40 \div 0.5 = 400 \div 5 = 80$

$300 \div 0.06 = 3000 \div 0.6 = 30\,000 \div 6 = 5000$

ESTIMATING WITH DECIMALS

- Use all of the methods described so far to estimate answers to questions.

> **Worked example**
> Estimate answers to these.
>
> **a** 532×0.61 **b** $789 \div 0.39$ **c** $32 \times 0.78/0.25$
>
> **a** Round 532 to 500, round 0.61 to 0.6. The question then becomes $500 \times 0.6 = 50 \times 6 = 300$.
> **b** Round 789 to 800, round 0.39 to 0.4.
>   The question then becomes $800 \div 0.4 = 8000 \div 4 = 2000$.
> **c** Round 32 to 30, round 0.78 to 0.8.
>   The top line is $30 \times 0.8 = 3 \times 8 = 24$.
>   Round 0.25 to 0.3. The question then is $24 \div 0.3 = 240 \div 3 = 80$.

> **Worked example**
> Work out the answers.
>
> **a** $20 \div 0.5$
> **b** $600 \div 0.06$
> **c** $800 \div 0.4$
> **d** $80 \div 0.02$
>
> **a** $200 \div 5 = 40$
> **b** $6000 \div 0.6 =$
> $60\,000 \div 6 =$
> $10\,000$
> **c** $8000 \div 4 = 2000$
> **d** $800 \div 0.2 =$
> $8000 \div 2 = 4000$

CHECK YOURSELF QUESTIONS

Q1 Give the place value of the underlined digit in each number.

a 2.4<u>6</u>   **b** 3.5<u>6</u>7
c 32.0<u>4</u>   **d** 0.97<u>2</u>

Q2 Put these decimals in order, smallest first.

4.02   4.21   4.002   4.202   4.022

Q3 Round these numbers to the nearest tenth.

a 0.73   **b** 0.137
c 0.65   **d** 2.81

Q4 Round these numbers to the nearest hundredth.

a 0.553   **b** 0.235
c 0.816   **d** 2.378

Q5 Write down the answer to each question.

a 0.6×0.7 **b** 0.02×0.08
c 0.3×0.03 **d** 0.5×0.9
e 0.7×50 **f** 0.08×500
g 600×0.6 **h** 70×0.09

Q6 Work out the answers.

a $30 \div 0.5$ **b** $300 \div 0.06$
c $60 \div 0.03$ **d** $200 \div 0.05$

Q7 Estimate the answers.

a 689×0.078 **b** $921 \div 0.27$
c $\dfrac{48 \times 0.029}{0.26}$ **d** $\dfrac{312 \times 0.061}{0.89}$

Answers are on page 231.

Comparing numbers, fractions and percentages

> - **You should be able to compare numbers and evaluate one number as a fraction or percentage of another.**

COMPARING NUMBERS

- You can use a variety of methods to compare numbers. For example, you can compare 6 to 8 by writing 6:8 (the sign : means 'compared to'). This is called a **ratio**. This ratio can be cancelled by a factor of 2 to give 3:4. The ratios 3:4 and 6:8 are the same but 3:4 is the **simplest form**.
- You can also express ratios as 1:n. To do this, divide both numbers by the first number in the ratio. To express 6:8 in the form 1:n divide both numbers by 6. This gives 1:$1\frac{1}{3}$ or 1:1.33.

> **Worked example**
> Write these ratios in their simplest form.
>
> **a** 5:10   **b** 6:9   **c** 15:35   **d** 12:27
>
> **a** 1:2   **b** 2:3   **c** 3:7   **d** 4:9

> **Worked example**
> Write these ratios in the form 1:n.
>
> **a** 6:9   **b** 12:15   **c** 10:35   **d** 8:36
>
> **a** 1:1.5   **b** 1:1.25   **c** 1:3.5   **d** 1:4.5

EXPRESSING ONE NUMBER AS A FRACTION OF ANOTHER

- Suppose that in a class of 30 students, 18 are girls. You can express this as a fraction. There are 18 girls out of 30 pupils, or $\frac{18}{30}$. Cancel top and bottom by 6 to give $\frac{3}{5}$.

> **Worked example**
> A radio is priced at £60. In a sale, £15 is taken off the price. What fraction of the original price is the reduction? Give the fraction in its lowest terms.
>
> The fraction is $\frac{15}{60}$ and cancelling top and bottom by 15 gives $\frac{1}{4}$.

EXPRESSING ONE NUMBER AS A PERCENTAGE OF ANOTHER

- In the same class of 30 pupils, what percentage are girls? What percentage are boys? To change a fraction to a percentage, multiply by 100.
- The calculation is $18 \div 30 \times 100$. Do this on a calculator as $18 \div 30 \times 100$ or $18 \times 100 \div 30$.
- Some calculators also have a percentage button: %
  This does not work the same way on all calculators so make sure you know what your calculator does!
  The answer is 60%. Boys must make up 40% of the class as $60 + 40 = 100$.

Worked example

In a sale, the price of a car is reduced by £120 from £960.
What percentage reduction of the original price is this?

The percentage is $\frac{120}{960} \times 100$ which is $12\frac{1}{2}$%.

CALCULATING PERCENTAGES OF NUMBERS

- You can already calculate percentages such as 10% and 25% but you must be able to calculate any percentage.
- The word **percentage** means 'out of one hundred', so 13% of 90 means 13 hundredths of 90. Work this out as $\frac{13}{100} \times 90$.
- On a calculator you can do this as $13 \div 100 \times 90$. The answer is 11.7% and you can round it to 12%.

Worked example

a Find 12% of £68.   **b** Find 45% of 165 books.

a $12 \div 100 \times 68 = £8.16$ **b** $45 \div 100 \times 165 = 74.25 = 74$ books

CHECK YOURSELF QUESTIONS

Q1 Write each of these ratios in its simplest form.
    a 2:10   **b** 8:20   **c** 5:45   **d** 15:55

Q2 Write these ratios in the form 1 : *n*.
    a 2:10   **b** 8:20   **c** 9:45   **d** 45:9

Q3 What fraction is:
    a 12 of 48   **b** 16 of 40   **c** 8 of 30   **d** 9 of 30?

Give the answers in their simplest form.

Q4 After having a special food, a plant grows from 32 cm tall to 44 cm tall. What fraction of the original height is the increase? Give the fraction in its lowest terms.

Q5 **a** What percentage is 15 of 45?
    b What percentage is 27 of 45?
    c What percentage is 9 of 50?

Q6 After an attack by poachers there were 120 elephants left out of a herd of 150.
    a What percentage decrease is this of the original herd of elephants?
    b What percentage of the original herd is left?

Q7 **a** Find 16% of £78.
    b Find 30% of 190 pupils.
    c Find 18% of £120.
    d Find 35% of 200.
    e Find 52% of £138.
    f Find 48% of 59 desks.

Answers are on page 231.

> • You should understand and be able to use the equivalences between fractions, decimals and percentages.

• From level 5, you know that fractions, decimals and percentages are basically the same. It is a matter of experience and judgement which to use when solving problems. You must know how to convert between them.

CONVERTING BETWEEN PERCENTAGES AND DECIMALS

• To change a decimal to a percentage just multiply by 100.
• To change a percentage into a decimal just divide by 100.

Worked example

Convert these percentages to decimals.

a 33%   **b** 65%   **c** 5%

a $33 \div 100 = 0.33$ **b** $65 \div 100 = 0.65$
c $5 \div 100 = 0.05$

Worked example

Convert these decimals to percentages.

a 0.24   **b** 0.7   **c** 0.625

a $0.24 \times 100 = 24\%$ **b** $0.7 \times 100 = 70\%$
c $0.625 \times 100 = 62.5\%$

CONVERTING BETWEEN FRACTIONS AND PERCENTAGES

• To change a fraction into a percentage, divide the **numerator** (top number) by the **denominator** (bottom number) and multiply by 100.
• To change a percentage into a fraction, write the percentage as a fraction with a denominator (bottom number) of 100 and then cancel if possible.

Worked example

Convert these fractions to percentages.

a $\frac{5}{8}$ **b** $\frac{1}{12}$ **c** $\frac{2}{3}$

a $5 \div 8 \times 100 = 62.5\%$ **b** $1 \div 12 \times 100 = 8.33\%$ (2 d.p.)
c $2 \div 3 \times 100 = 66.7\%$ (1 d.p.)
(b) and (c) are rounded to give sensible answers.

---

number of decimal places	denominator
1	10
2	100
3	1000

CONVERTING BETWEEN FRACTIONS AND DECIMALS

- To change a fraction into a decimal, divide the numerator (top number) by the denominator (bottom number).
- To change a decimal to a fraction, write the decimal, without the decimal point, as a fraction of 10 or 100 (see table), then cancel.

Worked example

Convert these fractions to decimals.

a $\frac{3}{8}$ **b** $\frac{4}{5}$ **c** $\frac{2}{7}$

a $3 \div 8 = 0.375$
b $4 \div 5 = 0.8$
c $2 \div 7 = 0.286$
(3 d.p.)

Worked example

Convert these decimals to fractions.

a 0.3 **b** 0.76 **c** 0.125

a $\frac{3}{10}$ **b** $\frac{76}{100} = \frac{19}{25}$ **c** $\frac{125}{1000} = \frac{1}{8}$

(a) does not cancel, (b) cancels by 4 and (c) cancels by 125.

THE BEST ONE TO USE

- It is easier to spot which method to use in any question if you know your equivalences well. This will also save you time.

Note:

It is not always possible to cancel, but you should if you can.

Worked example

The price of a jacket is reduced from £63 by 33.3%. How much does the jacket now cost?

33.3% is the fraction $\frac{1}{3}$. As 63 divides easily by 3, use the fraction.

$\frac{1}{3}$ of 63 = 21 and £63 − £21 = £42.

Worked example

To convert from miles to kilometres, multiply by $\frac{8}{5}$. How many kilometres is 32 miles?

The fraction $\frac{8}{5}$ is the decimal 1.6.

With a calculator it is easier to multiply by 1.6 than $\frac{8}{5}$.
$32 \times 1.6 = 51.2$ kilometres.

Hint:

In this case there is not much to choose between the different methods.

Worked example

A line 25 centimetres long is increased by a factor of 1.2. How long is the new line?

With a calculator it is easy to work out 25×1.2.
Alternatively, 0.2 is the fraction $\frac{1}{5}$ and $\frac{1}{5}$ of 25 is 5, so the answer is 30.

? CHECK YOURSELF QUESTIONS

Q1 Convert these percentages to decimals.
a 67% b 22% c 8% d 17.5%

Q2 Convert these decimals to percentages.
a 0.44 b 0.4 c 0.875 d 0.66

Q3 Convert these fractions to percentages.
a $\frac{3}{4}$ b $\frac{1}{5}$ c $\frac{2}{7}$ d $\frac{8}{9}$

Q4 Convert these percentages to fractions.
a 28% b 48% c 40% d 66.7% (1 d.p.)

Q5 Convert these fractions to decimals.
a $\frac{1}{10}$ b $\frac{5}{8}$ c $\frac{7}{8}$ d $\frac{11}{32}$

Q6 Convert these decimals to fractions.
a 0.9 b 0.68 c 0.375 d 0.65

Q7 a What percentage is equivalent to the decimal 0.45?
b The size of a 200 g tin of cocoa is increased by factor of 1.45. How much does the new tin weigh?

Q8 a What fraction is the same as 20%?
b The size of a 5 gallon can of paint is increased by 20%. How much paint is in the new tin?

Q9 A survey finds that the number of fish in a pond has increased by about $\frac{9}{20}$. If there were 170 fish in the pond, how many fish are now in the pond?

Answers are on page 232.

Solving ratio problems

What you should already know

- *How to write down a ratio*
- *How to cancel a ratio*
- *How to interpret frequency tables and diagrams*

> • **You should be able to use ratios in appropriate situations.**

CANCELLING RATIOS

- You can already use ratios with only two numbers, but you need to be able to use ratios to compare as many numbers as you like.
- To find the simplest ratio, cancel by the largest number that divides exactly into all of the numbers (this is the **highest common factor**).

Worked example

Michael earns £100 a week. He saves £20, spends £30 on rent, £25 on food and the rest of his money on entertainment.

a How much does he spend on entertainment?
b Express the ratio of savings : rent : food : entertainment in its simplest form.
c Michael decides to save an extra £10 a week. He saves equal amounts on food and entertainment. What is the new ratio savings : rent : food : entertainment in its simplest form?

a $100 - (20 + 30 + 25) = 100 - 75 = 25$
b The ratio is $20 : 30 : 25 : 25$. These numbers have a highest common factor of 5. The ratio cancels to $4 : 6 : 5 : 5$.
c He now spends money in the ratio $30 : 30 : 20 : 20$. These numbers have a highest common factor of 10. The ratio cancels to $3 : 3 : 2 : 2$.

CALCULATING WITH RATIOS

- You can use ratio to solve many everyday problems. Most recipes, for example, give quantities of food for four people. If you needed to feed five people you would use ratios to increase all the quantities to allow for the extra person.

Worked example

Anna's grandmother has an old cookery book. The recipe for pancake batter uses eggs, flour and milk in the ratio 1 egg to 3 ounces of flour to 5 fluid ounces of milk. If Anna follows the recipe and uses 3 eggs, how much flour and milk should she use?

The ratio is $1 : 3 : 5$. If the first number is increased to 3, then all the numbers in the ratio must be multiplied by 3 to give $3 : 9 : 15$.

So Anna needs 9 ounces of flour and 15 fluid ounces of milk.

> **Worked example**
>
> Two people are to share £45 in the ratio 2:3. How much do they get each?
>
> The total number of shares in the ratio 2:3 is 2 + 3 = 5.
>
> One share will be £45 ÷ 5 = £9, so each share is £9.
>
> The first person gets 2 × £9 = £18.
> The second person gets 3 × £9 = £27. (As a check £18 + £27 = £45.)

- The key to solving ratio problems is to work out what one share is worth!

CHECK YOURSELF QUESTIONS

Q1 Cancel each of these ratios to its simplest form.
  - **a** 4:6:8
  - **b** 5:15:25
  - **c** 6:15:18:21
  - **d** 7:14:28
  - **e** 8:14:18:22
  - **f** 12:18:42:60

Q2 In a day, Colin's computer is turned off for 15 hours, used for games for 6 hours and used for his work for 3 hours.

  - **a** Write the ratio of:
    time that Colin's computer is off:playing games:used for work.
  - **b** After his boss finds out Colin has to work 3 more hours each day. He uses this time to work on his computer but still plays games for the same time. What is the new ratio for
    off : playing games : used for work?

Q3
  - **a** Share £28 in the ratio 4:3.
  - **b** Share £30 in the ratio 1:3:6.
  - **c** Share £120 in the ratio 11:13.

Q4 The ratio of paperback books to hardback books in my local library is 2:5. There are 1400 books altogether in the library. How many of them are hardback books?

Q5 In the same library (1400 books) the ratio of fiction books to non-fiction books is 2:3. How many fiction books are there?

Answers are on page 232.

- You should be able to solve cubic equations (that means equations with a cube power) by trial and improvement.

SOLVING EQUATIONS BY TRIAL AND IMPROVEMENT

- To solve an equation by this method, you make a guess at the solution, try it out and then refine your guess until you find an appropriate answer.
- You will usually be given the first and sometimes the second guess. This will be in a table. If it isn't, draw a table to show your results.

Worked example

Solve $x^3 + x = 20$. Give your answer correct to 1 decimal place.

Guess	$x^3 + x$	Comment
2	10	Too low
3	30	Too high
2.5	18.125	Too low
2.6	20.176	Too high
2.55	19.1313	Too low

After trying 2 which is too low and 3 which is too high, try values with 1 decimal place, between 2 and 3.

Once you find the two values either side of the answer, to 1 decimal place, then try the halfway value to check which answer is nearer the real solution. In this case $x = 2.6$ is nearest.

? CHECK YOURSELF QUESTIONS

Use trial and improvement to find the solution to each of these equations, giving answers correct to 1 decimal place.

Q1 $x^3 - x = 15$ (Start with 2 and 3.)

Q2 $x^3 + 4x = 100$ (Start with 4 and 5.)

Q3 $x^3 - 6x = 20$ (Start with 3.)

Answers are on page 232.

> • **You should be able to add and subtract fractions with the same denominators and with different denominators.**

What you should already know

- *How to form equivalent fractions for a given fraction*
- *How to order fractions*
- *How to find common multiples of two or more numbers*
- *How to find the lowest (least) common multiple of two or more numbers*

- To add or subtract fractions, you need to make sure they have the **same denominator** (bottom number).
- You can use **equivalent fractions** to change the fractions you are adding or subtracting so that they have the same denominator.
- This is called finding a **common denominator**.
- It makes the working easier if you find the **lowest common denominator**.
- The lowest common denominator is the **lowest common multiple** of the denominators. This is the smallest number that is a multiple of all of the denominators.

Worked example

Add these fractions.

a $\frac{2}{5} + \frac{1}{3}$ **b** $\frac{7}{9} + \frac{5}{6}$

a First, find the lowest common multiple of 5 and 3. This means the smallest number that they will both divide into exactly, which is 15.

Write both fractions with a denominator of 15.

$\frac{2}{5} = \frac{6}{15}$ Multiply top and bottom by 3.

$\frac{1}{3} = \frac{5}{15}$ Multiply top and bottom by 5.

Add the numerators (top numbers), leaving the denominators the same.

$\frac{6}{15} + \frac{5}{15} = \frac{11}{15}$

b For $\frac{7}{9}$ and $\frac{5}{6}$ the lowest common denominator is 18.

$\frac{7}{9} + \frac{5}{6} = \frac{14}{18} + \frac{15}{18} = \frac{29}{18} = 1\frac{11}{18}$

- The answer to the example above is an **improper fraction** (the numerator is bigger than the denominator). It can be turned into a **mixed number**, which is a whole number and fraction.
- Improper fractions are also known as **top-heavy fractions**.

Subtract these fractions.

a $\frac{3}{4} - \frac{1}{3}$ **b** $\frac{7}{15} - \frac{3}{10}$

Tackle subtraction in the same way as addition, but subtract the numerators instead of adding them.

a For $\frac{3}{4} - \frac{1}{3}$ the lowest common denominator is 12 so the new denominator is 12.

$$\frac{3}{4} - \frac{1}{3} = \frac{9}{12} - \frac{4}{12} = \frac{5}{12}$$

b For $\frac{7}{15} - \frac{3}{10}$ the lowest common denominator is 30 so the new denominator is 30.

$$\frac{7}{15} - \frac{3}{10} = \frac{14}{30} - \frac{9}{30} = \frac{5}{30} = \frac{1}{6}$$

The answer of $\frac{5}{30}$ can be cancelled as 5 and 30 have a common factor of 5.

? CHECK YOURSELF QUESTIONS

Q1 Add these fractions.

   a $\frac{2}{3} + \frac{1}{4}$ **b** $\frac{1}{6} + \frac{3}{8}$ **c** $\frac{2}{5} + \frac{11}{15}$

Q2 Subtract these fractions.

   a $\frac{2}{3} - \frac{1}{6}$ **b** $\frac{3}{5} - \frac{1}{4}$ **c** $\frac{7}{9} - \frac{1}{6}$

Answers are on page 232.

1 a In a magazine there are three adverts on the same page.

Advert 1 uses $\frac{1}{4}$ of the page.

Advert 2 uses $\frac{1}{8}$ of the page.

Advert 3 uses $\frac{1}{16}$ of the page.

In total, what **fraction** of the page do the three adverts use?

Show your working.

2 marks

b Cost of advert: **£10** for each $\frac{1}{32}$ of a page

An advert uses $\frac{3}{16}$ of a page. How much does the advert cost?   *1 mark*

2 a Two numbers **multiply** together to make ⁻15.
They **add** together to make **2**.

What are the two numbers?   *1 mark*

b Two numbers **multiply** together to make ⁻15
but **add** together to make ⁻2.

What are the two numbers?   *1 mark*

c Two numbers **multiply** together to make **8**
but **add** together to make ⁻6.

What are the two numbers?   *1 mark*

d The square of 5 is 25.
The square of another number is also 25.

What is that other number?   *1 mark*

3 Two parts of this square design
are shaded red. Two parts are
shaded yellow.

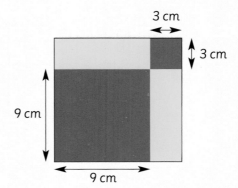

Show that the ratio of red to
yellow is **5 : 3**.

2 marks

4 On a farm **80** sheep give birth.

30% of the sheep gave birth to two lambs.
The rest of the sheep gave birth to just one lamb.

In total, how many lambs were born?

Show your working.

2 marks

5 Fill in the missing numbers in the boxes, using **only negative numbers**.

$\square$ – $\square$ = 5   *I mark*

$\square$ – $\square$ = ⁻5   *I mark*

6 A garden centre sells plants for hedges.
The table shows what they sold in one week.

Plants	Number of plants sold	Takings
Beech	125	£212.50
Leylandii	650	£2437.50
Privet	35	£45.50
Hawthorn	18	£23.40
Laurel	5	£32.25
Total	**833**	**£2751.15**

a What percentage of the total number of plants sold was **Leylandii**?

Show your working.   *2 marks*

b What percentage of the **total takings** was for Leylandii?

Show your working.   *2 marks*

c Which is the **cheaper** plant, Beech or Privet?

Show working to explain how you know.   *2 marks*

7 Here are six number cards. $\boxed{1}\ \boxed{2}\ \boxed{3}\ \boxed{4}\ \boxed{5}\ \boxed{6}$

a Arrange these six cards to make the calculations below.
The first one is done for you.

939 = $\boxed{4}\ \boxed{2}\ \boxed{3}$ + $\boxed{5}\ \boxed{1}\ \boxed{6}$

1164 = $\square\ \square\ \square$ + $\square\ \square\ \square$

                                                                          I mark

750 = $\square\ \square\ \square$ + $\square\ \square\ \square$

                                                                          I mark

b Now arrange the six cards to make a difference of 115.

115 = $\square\ \square\ \square$ – $\square\ \square\ \square$

                                                                          I mark

8 A drink from a machine costs **55p**.

The table shows the coins that were put into the machine one day.

Coins	Number of coins
50p	31
20p	22
10p	41
5p	59

How many cans of drink were sold that day?

Show your working.

3 marks

9 A company sells and processes films of two different sizes.

The tables show how much the company charges.

Film size: **24** photos	
Cost to **buy** each film	£2.15
Postage	free

Cost to **print** each film	£0.99
Postage for each film	60p

Film size: **36** photos	
Cost to **buy** each film	£2.65
Postage	free

Cost to **print** each film	£2.89
Postage for each film	60p

I want to take **360** photos.

I need to buy the film, pay for the film to be printed and pay for the postage.

Is it cheaper to use all films of size 24 photos or all films of size 36 photos?

How much cheaper is it?

Show your working.

4 marks

Answers are on page 248.

7 Finding the *n*th term

- *How number patterns built up*
- *How to find next terms by writing down each term*

- You should be able to give a rule for the *n*th term of a number pattern where the pattern increases by a fixed amount each time.

INDUCTIVE RULES – FINDING THE *n*TH TERM

- When you look at a number pattern and you can say, 'The numbers go up by 3 each time', this is an **inductive** rule.
- In an inductive rule, you use the previous term to find the next one.

Worked example
A teacher writes this number pattern on the board.

3, 7, 11, 15, 19, …

a Describe how this number pattern is building up.
b Find the   **(i)** 6th term   **(ii)** 10th term   **(iii)** 100th term.

a The pattern is going up by 4 each time.
b **(i)** $19 + 4 = 23$ **(ii)** $19 + 4 + 4 + 4 + 4 + 4 = 39$
   (iii) The 100th term is 95 terms more than the 5th term so it is $19 + 95 \times 4 = 399$.

ALGEBRAIC RULES

- In the last example, finding the answer to b(iii) was quite difficult. You can find the 10th term by 'counting on' but you cannot find the 100th. It is easier to use an **algebraic rule**.
- An algebraic rule for the terms in a number pattern is based on the term number. You do not need to know the previous term.
- The algebraic rule for the last worked example is:
  nth term $= 4n - 1$
  This means that the value of each term is equal to $4 \times n - 1$ where n is the number of the term.
  The 10th term is $4 \times 10 - 1$ which is $40 - 1$ which equals 39.
  The 100th term is $4 \times 100 - 1 = 400 - 1 = 399$.
- You can find the algebraic rule for a number pattern by using the **difference method**.

THE COMMON DIFFERENCE

- You can take away one term in the number pattern from the term following it to find the difference between them. This gives you the number you need to add on each time.

3   7   11   15   19   23
   4   4   4   4   4

- In the worked example the difference is 4, so the algebraic rule will use the 4 times table
- This means it will have $4n$ in it. Write down the 4 times table next to the number pattern.

$4n$	4	8	12	16	20	24
$4n - 1$	3	7	11	15	19	23

Now it is obvious what to add on or take away. In this case each term in the original number pattern is 1 less than the corresponding number in the 4 times table. So the rule is $4n - 1$.

Worked example

Find the nth term of each of these number patterns.

a 7, 12, 17, 22, 27, ...   **b** 1, 4, 7, 10, 13, ...

a The difference is 5 so the algebraic rule will use the 5 times table and will have $5n$ in it. Comparing the pattern and the 5 times table:

$5n$	5	10	15	20	25	....
?	7	12	17	22	27	....

So each term in the pattern is 2 more than the corresponding number in the 5 times table. The rule to find the nth term is therefore $5n + 2$.

b The difference is 3 so the algebraic rule will be related to the 3 times table and will have $3n$ in it. Comparing the pattern and the 3 times table:

$3n$	3	6	9	12	15	....
?	1	4	7	10	13	....

So each term in the pattern is 2 less than the corresponding number in the 3 times table. The rule to find the nth term is therefore $3n - 2$.

Worked example

These are the first three patterns of John's matchstick patterns.
How many matches (m) will he need for the nth pattern?
Using the letters m and n to write your rule.

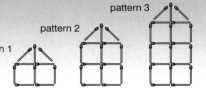

pattern 1   pattern 2   pattern 3

Writing down the numbers of matches as a number pattern gives:
10, 15, 20, ...

The number goes up by 5 each time, so the difference is 5.
Comparing the pattern to the 5 times table gives:

$5n$	5	10	15
?	10	15	20

The pattern is 5 more than the 5 times table.
The rule is $m = 5n + 5$.

Note:
You write this as $m = 5n + 5$ because this is a rule connecting the number of matches (m) and the pattern number (n) so you must use the equals sign.

CHECK YOURSELF QUESTIONS

Q1 Find the *n*th term of each of these number patterns.
- **a** 3, 6, 9, 12, 15, ...
- **b** 1, 3, 5, 7, 9, ...
- **c** 2, 5, 8, 11, 14, 17, ...
- **d** 2, 8, 14, 20, 26, 32, ...

Q2 Look at each series of pictures and answer the questions.

(i)

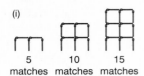

| 5 | 10 | 15 |
| matches | matches | matches |

(ii)

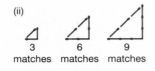

| 3 | 6 | 9 |
| matches | matches | matches |

(iii)

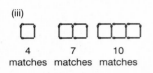

| 4 | 7 | 10 |
| matches | matches | matches |

(iv)

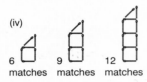

| 6 | 9 | 12 |
| matches | matches | matches |

- **a** How many matches are needed for the *n*th pattern?
- **b** Write down a rule connecting the number of matches needed (*m*) and the pattern number (*n*).

Q3 These are the lockers at the local sports centre.

Row E	5	10	15	20	25
Row D	4	9	14	19	24
Row C	3	8	13	18	23
Row B	2	7	12	17	22
Row A	1	6	11	16	21

- **a** Explain why the locker number in the *n*th column of Row A is given by the rule $5n - 4$.
- **b** Find a similar rule for the locker number in the *n*th column of each of the rows B, C, D and E.
- **c** Adding up the columns of locker numbers gives 15, 40, 65, 90, 115, ... Find a rule for the *n*th term of this number pattern.

Answers are on page 232.

Linear equations

> • You should be able to set up and solve linear equations with whole-number coefficients.

What you should already know

• *How to use a number machine*

• *How to find the inverse function*

• *How to solve simple equations*

SETTING UP AND SOLVING LINEAR EQUATIONS

• A **linear equation** is an equation that only has single letters in it (no squared terms).
• Solving an equation means finding the value of the letter.
• Letters often stand for numbers in maths. Most problems can be solved using common sense.

> **Worked example**
> Find the number missing from each box to make these true.
>
> **a** ☐ + 5 = 11   **b** 3 × ☐ + 1 = 10   **c** ☐ ÷ 2 + 5 = 7   **d** 2 × ☐ − 7 = 13
>
> **a** The number in the box is 6 because 6 + 5 = 11.
> **b** The number in the box is 3 because 3 × 3 + 1 = 10.
> **c** The number in the box is 4 because 4 ÷ 2 + 5 = 7.
> **d** The number in the box is 10 because 2 × 10 − 7 = 13.

• The questions in the worked example are all equation problems. They could have been written using a letter, instead of the empty box, to stand for the unknown number.

• It is usual to use *y* or *x* as the unknown, but you can use any letter.

Hint:

a $y + 5 = 11$

b $3y + 1 = 10$

c $\dfrac{y}{2} + 5 = 7$

d $2y - 7 = 13$

SOLVING EQUATIONS

• To solve an equation, you need to 'undo' steps in the equation.
• You must know how the equation was set up. The basic rule that governs how equations are set up is BODMAS, which stands for: Brackets, Of (or pOwer), Divide, Multiply, Add, Subtract. This is the order in which you must do the parts of the equation.
• To solve $2x - 3 = 9$, take the number *x*, multiply it by 2 and then subtract 3. This flow diagram shows the steps.

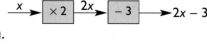

• The three methods shown in this table all solve this equation.

1 Reverse flow diagram	2 Doing the same thing to both sides	3 Reverse operations
Set up the flow diagram, then reverse it and change all the operations in the boxes to the inverse operations. Run the number through and the answer comes out on the left.	$2x - 3 = 9$ $2x - 3 + 3 = 9 + 3$ $2x = 12$ $\dfrac{2x}{2} = \dfrac{12}{2}$ $x = 6$	$2x - 3 = 9$ $2x = 12 \ (+ 3)$ $x = 6 \ (\div 2)$

6 ← [÷ 2] ← 12 ← [+ 3] ← 9

- There are lots of rules for solving equations, such as 'Change sides, change signs' and 'What you do to one side you do to the other'. The third method is used in these examples.
- Whatever method you use, always check your answer works! If you do that then it will show you if you have made a mistake.

Worked example

Solve these equations.

a $4a - 7 = 8$ **b** $\dfrac{b-2}{4} = 7$ **c** $\dfrac{c}{2} + 5 = 3$

a $4a = 15 \ (+ 7)$ **b** $b - 2 = 28 \ (\times 4)$ **c** $\dfrac{c}{2} = {}^-2 \ (- 5)$

       $a = 3.75 \ (\div 4)$ $b = 30 \ (+ 2)$ $c = {}^-4 \ (\times 2)$

Check: Check: Check:

$4 \times 3.75 - 7$ $30 - 2 = 28,$ ${}^-4 \div 2 + 5 = 3 \ \checkmark$

$= 15 - 7 = 8 \ \checkmark$ $28 \div 4 = 7 \ \checkmark$

EQUATIONS WITH MORE THAN ONE LETTER TERM

- At level 6, equations with two letter terms are the most difficult that you will be asked to solve.
- Follow the rule: 'Get rid of the letter term with the smallest coefficient by moving it to the other side of the equals sign'. When you do this, its sign changes. If it was plus, it becomes minus; if it was minus it becomes plus. Then solve the equation in the normal way.

Worked example

Solve these equations.

a $4c - 28 = 2c + 4$ **b** $2d + 3 = 13 - 3d$

a $2c$ is the smallest letter term. To 'get rid' of it, move it from the right-hand side to the left-hand side to give:
$4c - 2c - 28 = 4$
Collect the letter terms together.
$4c - 2c = 2c$

$2c - 28 = 4$
$\quad 2c = 32 \ (+ 28)$
$\quad\ c = 16 \ (\div 2)$
Check:
$4 \times 16 - 28 = 2 \times 16 + 4$
$64 - 28 = 32 + 4$
$36 = 36 \ \checkmark$

b ${}^-3d$ is the smallest letter term. Move it from the right-hand side to the left-hand side to give:
$2d + 3d + 3 = 13$
Collect the letter terms.
$2d + 3d = 5d$

$5d + 3 = 13$
$\quad 5d = 10 \ (- 3)$
$\quad\ d = 2 \ (\div 5)$
Check: $2 \times 2 + 3 = 13 - 3 \times 2$
$4 + 3 = 13 - 6$
$7 = 7 \ \checkmark$

CHECK YOURSELF QUESTIONS

Q1 Find the number missing from the box to make each of these correct.

    a $\Box - 6 = 13$ **b** $2 \times \Box - 1 = 15$

    c $\Box \div 4 - 5 = 5$ **d** $3 \times \Box + 7 = 4$

Q2

> I am thinking of a number. I have multiplied it by 3 and then subtracted 5 from the answer. The final answer is 19. What number did I start with?

Q3 Solve these equations.

    a $3a + 5 = 14$ **b** $\dfrac{b + 3}{4} = 7$ **c** $\dfrac{c}{4} - 5 = 3$

Q4 Mr Wilson needs 27 bulbs for his garden. He buys two packets of bulbs and seven single bulbs. There are the same number of bulbs in each of the packets.

    a Set up an equation to represent this situation.

    b Use your equation to find the number of bulbs in each packet.

Q5 Solve these equations.

    a $3c - 21 = c + 5$

    b $2e - 3 = 15 - 4e$

    c $3d + 8 = 5d - 2$

    d $4f - 7 = 20 + f$

Q6 Four pupils hold up cards with algebraic expressions.

    a Show that $b = 1$ gives the cards held up by Alex and Bob the same value.

    b Find the value of b that gives the cards held by Bob and Cath the same value.

    c Find the value of b that gives the cards held by Bob and Denise the same value.

    d Two pupils have cards that can never have the same value. Which two pupils are they? Explain your answer.

$3b - 4$	$4b - 5$	$3b + 2$	$b + 4$
Alex	Bob	Cath	Denise

Answers are on page 232.

Mappings and graphs

- You should be able to express a mapping algebraically and interpret the general features of it.

NUMBER MACHINES AND MAPPING DIAGRAMS

- This number machine is for the simple rule $y = 2x + 3$.

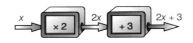

In (x)	Out (y)
⁻2	⁻1
0	3
1	5
⁻1	1

- The table next to the number machine shows the numbers that come out of the machine (the y-values) when various numbers are put into it (the x-values).
- You can write these pairs of numbers as coordinates (x, y).
- In coordinates the first number is the x-value and the second is the y-value.
- In the table above the coordinate pairs are: (⁻2, ⁻1), (0, 3), (1, 5) and (⁻1, 1).
- You can also show this rule on a mapping diagram.

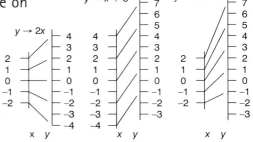

- The first two diagrams are the same as the boxes in the number machine above. They break the rule down into two parts.
- The third diagram does the whole rule in one go.
- The numbers at each end of an arrow make a pair of coordinates.
- The coordinate pairs in the diagram are (2, 7), (1, 5), (0, 3), (⁻1, 1) and (⁻2, ⁻1).

GRAPHS

- You can plot all coordinate pairs on a graph.
- There is no need to do a mapping diagram, a number machine *and* a graph to show a rule. They are just different ways of showing the same thing.

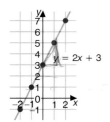

$y = 2x + 3$

Worked example

Use the number machine with inputs of $^-2, ^-1, 0, 1$ and 2 to complete the graph of $y = 4x - 1$.

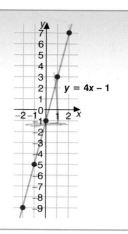

$y = 4x - 1$

The coordinate pairs are $(^-2, ^-9), (^-1, ^-5), (0, ^-1), (1, 3), (2, 7)$.

Worked example

Use the mapping diagram starting with $4, 2, 0, ^-2, ^-4$ to complete the graph of $y = \frac{x}{2} + 1$.

The coordinate pairs are $(^-4, ^-1), (^-2, 0)$, $(0, 1), (2, 2), (4, 3)$.
The inputs were chosen as even numbers so that they would easily divide by 2.

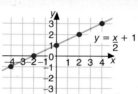

$y = \frac{x}{2} + 1$

GRADIENT

- Every graph has a measure of its steepness, called the **gradient**.
- You can find the gradient of a line by making the line the sloping part of a right-angled triangle.

  You can find the gradient using the equation:

  $$\text{gradient} = \frac{y\text{-step}}{x\text{-step}}$$

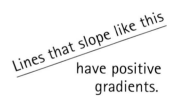

Lines that slope like this have positive gradients.

Lines that slope like this have negative gradients.

Worked example

Find the gradient of each of these lines.

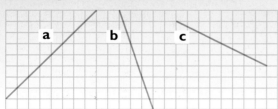

Drawing right-angled triangles anywhere on the grid will give answers that cancel to give the gradients in their simplest terms.

a 1   **b** $^-3$ **c** $^-\frac{1}{2}$ or $^-0.5$

Note that lines **b** and **c** have negative gradients.

Worked example

Draw lines with these gradients.

a 2   **b** $\frac{1}{3}$ **c** $^-4$

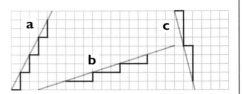

a If a line has a gradient of 2 there is a y-step of 2 for every x-step of 1. You can repeat this as much as you like.

b If a line has a gradient of $\frac{1}{3}$ there is a y-step of 1 for every x-step of 3.

c If a line has a gradient of $^-4$ there is a y-step of $^-4$ for every x-step of 1. This is a negative gradient so the y-step goes down.

CHECK YOURSELF QUESTIONS

Q1 Use the number machine with inputs of $^-2$, $^-1$, 0, 1 and 2 to complete the graph of $y = 3x + 3$.

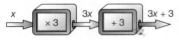

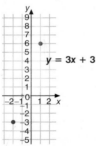

Q2 Complete the mapping diagram and use it to complete the graph of $y = \dfrac{x}{3} - 1$.

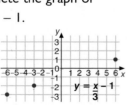

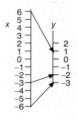

Q3 Calculate the gradient of each of these lines.

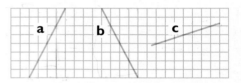

Q4 Draw lines with these gradients.

     a $^-1$ **b** $-\frac{1}{3}$

Answers are on page 233.

> • You should be able to express a mapping algebraically and interpret the general features of it.

What you should already know

• *How to measure a gradient*

• *How to find coordinate pairs from a rule written as a mapping diagram, a number machine, or an algebraic rule*

LINEAR GRAPHS

- A linear graph is a **straight-line graph**.
- You can draw linear graphs by:
  - plotting the points
  - using a gradient-intercept
  - using the cover-up rule.
- Typical equations for linear graphs are $y = 3x - 1$ and $2x + 5y = 10$. The graph of the first equation can be drawn by plotting the points or doing a gradient intercept. The graph of the second equation can be drawn using the cover-up rule.

PLOTTING POINTS

- You can draw a straight line by plotting just two points but it is better always to use three.
- The numbers that go into the number machine or algebraic rule are the x-values. What comes out are the y-values.
- The x-value is always the first number in a pair of coordinates, the y-value is always the second number in a pair of coordinates.
- Sometimes you are told what x-values to use. If not you can choose them. Choose sensible values such as $^-2$, $^-1$, 0, 1 and 2.
- In a graph, the horizontal line through the origin (0, 0) is the x-axis and the vertical line through the origin is the y-axis.

Worked example

Draw the line $y = 3x - 1$ for values of x between $^-3$ and 3. This can be written as $^-3 \leqslant x \leqslant 3$.

In this question you are given a range of values for x. Use $x = ^-3$, $x = 0$ and $x = 3$ as the three starting values and work out $y = 3x - 1$ for each of them.

If $x = ^-3$, $y = 3 \times ^-3 - 1 = ^-10$ so the coordinates are $(^-3, ^-10)$.

If $x = 0$, $y = 3 \times 0 - 1 = ^-1$ so the coordinates are $(0, ^-1)$.

If $x = 3$, $y = 3 \times 3 - 1 = 8$ so the coordinates are $(3, 8)$.

Put these results into a table.

This gives the graph on the right.

x	$^-3$	0	3
y	$^-10$	$^-1$	8

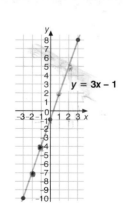

GRADIENT INTERCEPT

- The gradient of the line in the worked example is 3. The line crosses the y-axis at $y = {}^-1$. The equation for this graph is: $y = 3x - 1$.
- The number in front of x is the **coefficient** of x. This is also the gradient of the line. The gradient for the equation $y = 3x - 1$ is 3.
- The number on its own in the equation is the **intercept** on the y-axis. The y-intercept for the equation $y = 3x - 1$ is ${}^-1$.
- You can use these rules for any straight-line graph, to write the general equation:
  $$y = mx + c$$
  where m is the gradient and c is the intercept on the y-axis.

Worked example

x	$^-3$	0	3
y	1	2	3

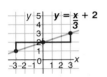

Draw the line $y = \dfrac{x}{3} + 2$.

The intercept, the point where the line crosses the y-axis, is $^+2$.

The line has a gradient of $\frac{1}{3}$. This means for an x-step of 3, there is a y-step of 1.

Draw as many triangles as you like or do a table and join up the points.

FINDING THE EQUATION OF A LINE FROM THE GRAPH

- You can look at a graph and work out the gradient of the line. This gives the value of m in the general equation:
  $$y = mx + c$$
- You find the value of c by looking where the line crosses the y-axis.

Worked example

Find the equations of these lines.

a 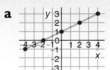   **b**   **c**

a $y = \frac{1}{2}x + 1$ **b** $y = x + 2$ **c** $y = 4x + 1$

Check that the gradients and intercepts are correct. Note that in part **b** the gradient is 1, which does not need to be written in front of x.

SPECIAL LINES

- You need to know some special lines.

  - The equation for a line that is vertical and so parallel to the y-axis, is $x = a$, where a is a number.
  - The equation for a line that is horizontal and so parallel to the x-axis is $y = a$, where a is a number.
  - The equation for the line that starts bottom left and goes at an angle of 45° to the top right, passing through the origin $(0, 0)$, is $y = x$.
  - The equation for the line that starts bottom right and goes at an angle of 45° to the top left, passing through the origin $(0, 0)$, is $y = ^-x$.

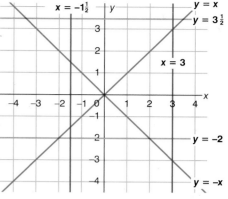

- You can soon check that these rules are true by taking some points on these lines and showing that they obey the rules.
- The x-axis is the line $y = 0$ and the y-axis is the line $x = 0$.

THE COVER-UP RULE

- You can use the gradient–intercept method to draw lines such as $2x + 5y = 10$ but you have to rearrange the equation first.
- It is easier to think about the point where this line crosses the x-axis, where the value of y is zero. Then the y-term disappears so you can cover it up (or ignore it). Solve the simple equation that is left, to find where the line crosses the x-axis.
  $2x + 0 = 10$, so when $y = 0$, $x = 5$.
- When the line crosses the y-axis the x-value is zero. Use the same rule.
  $0 + 5y = 10$, so when $x = 0$, $y = 2$.
- The line crosses the x-axis at 5 and the y-axis at 2. Plot these points and join them up.
- Normally you should find another point to check but, for now, settle for just two.

> **Note:**
>
> This is level 8 algebra, which you would not be expected to do yet.

Worked example
Draw these lines.

a $3x + 4y = 12$ **b** $2x - 7y = 14$

a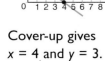

b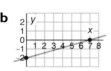

Cover-up gives
$x = 4$ and $y = 3$.

Cover-up gives
$x = 7$ and $y = ^-2$.

CHECK YOURSELF QUESTIONS

Q1 By measuring the gradient of each of these lines and finding where they cross the *y*-axis, give the equations of these lines.

a 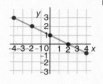 **b** 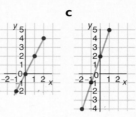 **c**

In the next five questions, use a grid like this.

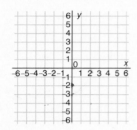

Q2 Plot points to draw the graphs of these equations.

a $y = \dfrac{x}{3} - 3$ **b** $y = 2x - 4$

Q3 Use the gradient–intercept method to draw these lines.

a $y = 3x - 2$ **b** $y = \dfrac{x}{3} + 3$

Q4 Use the cover-up rule to draw these lines.

a $3x - 5y = 15$ **b** $x + y = 5$

Q5 **a** Draw these two lines on the same axes.
    (i) $y = x - 2$ **(ii)** $x + y = 4$
b Where do the lines meet?

Q6 **a** Draw these two lines on the same axes.
    (i) $y = 2x + 1$ **(ii)** $y = 4x - 1$
b Where do the lines meet?

Answers are on page 233.

1 **a** The diagram shows a rectangle **18 cm** long and **14 cm** wide.
It has been split into **four smaller rectangles**.
Write the **area** of each **small rectangle** on the diagram.
One has been done for you.

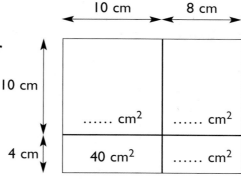

1 mark

What is the area of the whole rectangle?   *1 mark*

What is 18×14?   *1 mark*

b The diagram shows a rectangle **(n + 3) cm** long and **(n + 2)** cm wide.
It has been split into **four smaller rectangles**.
Write a **number** or an **expression** for the **area** of **each small rectangle** on the diagram.
One has been done for you.

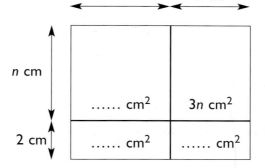

1 mark

2 These straight-line graphs all pass through the point (10, 10).

Fill in the gaps to show which line has which equation.

line ...... has equation $x = 10$

line ...... has equation $y = 10$

line ...... has equation $y = x$

line ...... has equation $y = \frac{3}{2}x - 5$

line ...... has equation $y = \frac{1}{2}x + 5$

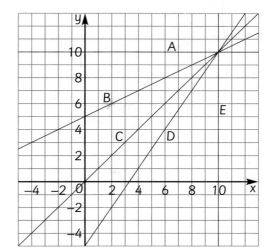

3 Write each expression in its simplest form.

$7 + 2t + 3t$ *1 mark*

$b + 7 + 2b + 10$ *1 mark*

$(3d + 5) + (d - 2)$ *1 mark*

$3m - (-m)$ *1 mark*

4 **a** Solve this equation.

$7 + 5k = 8k + 1$ $k = $ ....   *1 mark*

b Solve this equation. Show your working.

$10y + 23 = 4y + 26$ $y = $ ....   *1 mark*

5 **a** When $x = 5$, work out the values of the expressions below.

$2x + 13 = $

$5x - 5 = $

$3 + 6x = $ ......   *1 mark*

b When $2y + 11 = 17$, work out the value of y.
Show your working.   *1 mark*

c Solve the equation $9y + 3 = 5y + 13$.
Show your working.   *1 mark*

6 You can often use algebra to show why a number puzzle works.

Fill in the missing expressions.

Example: Algebra:

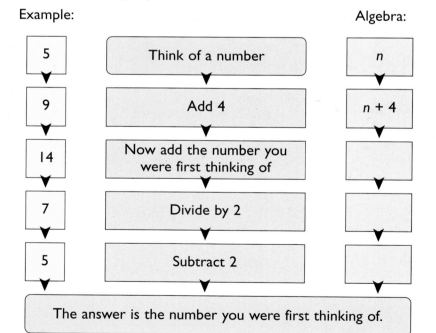

The answer is the number you were first thinking of.

2 marks

7 The graph shows my journey in a lift.

I got in the lift at floor number 10.

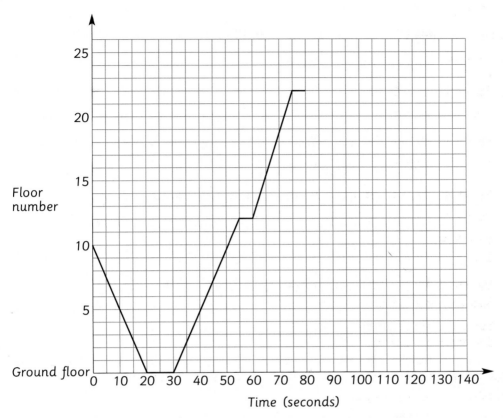

Time (seconds)

a The lift stopped at two different floors before I got to floor number 22. What floors were they?

1 mark

b For how long was I in the lift while it was moving?

1 mark

c After I got out of the lift at floor number 22, the lift went directly to the ground floor. It took **45 seconds**.

On the graph, show the journey of the lift from floor number 22 to the ground floor.

1 mark

8 Look at the equations.

$3a + 6b = 24$

$2c - d = 3$

a Use the equations to work out the values of the expressions below.
The first one is done for you.

$8c - 4d = $ ..12..

$a + 2b = $ ...... *I mark*

$d - 2c = $ ...... *I mark*

b Use one or both of the equations to write an expression that has a value of **21**.

.... = 21 *I mark*

9 I went for a walk.

The distance–time graph shows
information about my walk.

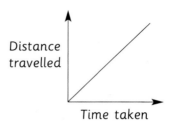

Distance
travelled

Time taken

Tick (✓) the statement below that describes my walk.

I was walking faster and faster. ☐

I was walking more and more slowly. ☐

I was walking north-east. ☐

I was walking at a steady speed. ☐

I was walking uphill. ☐ *I mark*

10 Each point on the straight line **x + y = 12** has an x-coordinate and a y-coordinate that **add together** to make **12**.

Draw the straight line $x + y = 12$.

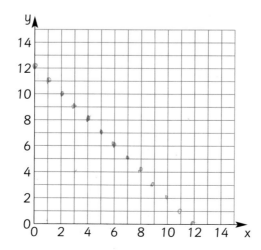

I mark

REVISION SESSION 11 Isometric drawings

What you should already know

- *How to make 3-D models by drawing a net*
- *How to recognise front, side and top elevations for a 3-D shape*

- You should recognise common 2-D representations of 3-D objects.

ISOMETRIC PROJECTIONS
- It can be difficult to draw a 2-D representation of a 3-D shape because of the **perspective** of the drawing.
- It can be easier to draw 3-D shapes on **isometric paper** (triangular dotty paper).
- Shapes drawn on isometric paper are **isometric projections**.

Worked example
Draw the front, side and top elevations, and the isometric projection for the triangular prism.

  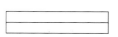

| front
elevation | side
elevation | top elevation
(or plan) | isometric
projection |

Worked example
Draw an isometric projection for this letter 'T' when it is standing upside down.

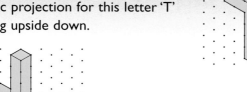

? CHECK YOURSELF QUESTION

Q1 Draw an isometric projection for this cuboid when it is standing on its face BCGF.

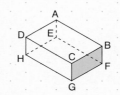

Answers are on page 233.

What you should already know

• *The language associated with angles and line and rotational symmetry for 2-D shapes*

• You should know the properties of quadrilaterals and be able to recognise quadrilaterals from their properties.

• You should be able to use angle and symmetry properties of polygons and properties of intersecting and parallel lines to solve problems.

• You should be able to explain these properties.

DESCRIBING GEOMETRIC SHAPES

• Each corner of a quadrilateral is called a **vertex**. The quadrilateral ABCD has four vertices. Each side is described by the two letters at the vertices at each end. The quadrilateral has four sides: AB, BC, CD and AD. Each angle can be described in three different ways.

For the angle at A you could use:
 – a small italic letter, a.
 – the vertex letter with a 'hat' over it $\hat{A}$.
 – the two sides that form the angle – $D\hat{A}B$ or $B\hat{A}D$.

PROPERTIES OF SPECIAL QUADRILATERALS

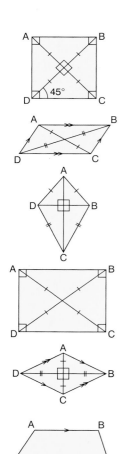

• Learn the basic geometrical facts about these quadrilaterals.

Square   The two diagonals AC and BD bisect each other at right angles. The right angles at the vertices are bisected by the diagonals at these vertices.

Parallelogram Opposite sides are equal and parallel. The diagonals AC and BD bisect each other but are not equal. Opposite angles are equal. $\hat{A} = \hat{C}$ and $\hat{B} = \hat{D}$.

Kite   Two pairs of adjacent sides are equal to each other. The diagonal AC bisects the diagonal BD at right angles.

Rectangle   The diagonals AC and BD are equal in length (AC = BD). The diagonals bisect each other.

Rhombus   All sides are equal and opposite sides are parallel. The diagonals AC and BD bisect each other at right angles but are not equal. The diagonals bisect the angles at the vertices.

Trapezium   One pair of parallel sides.

In the rectangle ABCD, AB = 8 cm, BC = 6 cm and AC = 10 cm.
Write down the lengths of these sides.

a CD   **b** BD   **c** DX

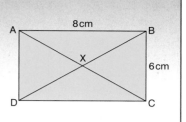

a 8 cm (opposite side)
b 10 cm (diagonals are equal)
c 5 cm (diagonals bisect each other)

a In the kite ABCD, BÂD = 84°. Write down the sizes of these angles.
    (i) AX̂B   **(ii)** BÂX
b Explain why B̂ = D̂.

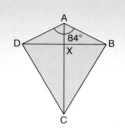

a (i) AX̂B = 90° (diagonals intersect at right angles)
    (ii) BÂX = 42° (diagonal AC bisects the angle at A)
b The diagonal AC is a line of symmetry.

ANGLE PROPERTIES OF POLYGONS

- You can find the angles in any polygon if you know that the sum of the angles in a quadrilateral is 360°.
  $a + b + c + d = 360°$

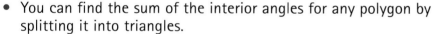

- You can find the sum of the interior angles for any polygon by splitting it into triangles.
- The sum of the angles in all three triangles equals the sum of the five interior angles in the pentagon.
  The sum of the interior angles in a pentagon is $3 \times 180° = 540°$.

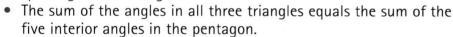

- In the same way any hexagon can be split into four triangles, so the sum of the interior angles of a hexagon is $4 \times 180° = 720°$.
- For any n-sided polygon, the sum, S, of its interior angles is given by the formula:
  $S = 180(n - 2)°$

INTERIOR AND EXTERIOR ANGLES OF POLYGONS

- A pentagon has five interior angles which add up to 540°. The pentagon also has five exterior angles. From the diagram, $a + b = 180°$.

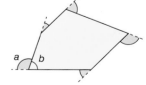

- For any polygon, interior angle + exterior angle = 180°.
- The sum of all the exterior angles is 360°. (Imagine walking around the shape – you will have turned through 360°.)
- A regular hexagon has six equal exterior angles (marked x on the diagram). The sum of the exterior angles is 360°. So, $6x = 360°$, and $x = 60°$. Therefore each of the interior angles is 120°.

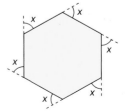

- For any n-sided regular polygon:

  $\text{exterior angle} = \dfrac{360°}{n}$ $\text{interior angle} = 180° - \dfrac{360°}{n}$

Worked example

Calculate the missing angle in each of these diagrams.

a

b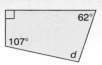

a Let third interior angle = x
$x = 180° - (49° + 72°) = 59°$
$c = 180° - x$
$c = 121°$

b $d + 90° + 107° + 62° = 360°$
$d + 259° = 360°$
$d = 101°$

Worked example

a Calculate the sum of the interior angles in an octagon.
b In an octagon, three of the interior angles are 132°, 158° and 124° and three of the exterior angles are 45°, 71° and 18°. The remaining two interior angles are equal. Calculate the size of each of the remaining interior angles.

a Use $S = 180(n - 2)°$ with $n = 8$.
$S = 180 \times 6° = 1080°$

b Three interior angles are given. The other three interior angles are 135°, 109° and 162°.
Let each remaining interior angle = x.
So, $2x + 132° + 158° + 124° + 135° + 109° + 162° = 1080°$
$2x + 820° = 1080°$
$2x = 260°$
$x = 130°$

Hint:

You can find these interior angles as they are on the same straight lines as the exterior angles.

INTERSECTING LINES AND PARALLEL LINES

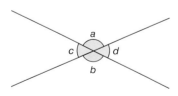

- When two lines intersect, four angles are formed.
- In the diagram, a and b are **vertically opposite** angles or opposite angles and are equal. c and d are also opposite angles. In the diagram $a = b$ and $c = d$.
- A line AB that crosses a pair of parallel lines is a **transversal**.
- Learn these facts.

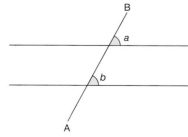

$a = b$
a and b are **corresponding** angles.
(Look for the letter F.)

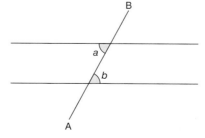

$a = b$
a and b are **alternate** angles.
(Look for the letter Z.)

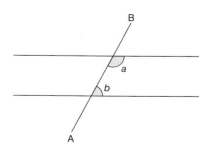

$a + b = 180°$
a and b are **allied** or **interior** angles.
(Look for the letter U.)

Calculate the missing angles in each of these diagrams.

a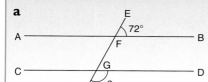

b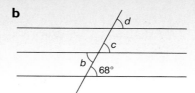

c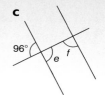

a FĜD=72° (corresponding angles)
   $a = 180° - 72° = 108°$ (angles on a line)
b $b = 68°$ (alternate angles)
   $c = 68°$ (opposite angles)
   $d = 68°$ (corresponding angles)
c $e = 96°$ (opposite angles)
   $f = 180° - 96° = 84°$ (allied angles)

CHECK YOURSELF QUESTIONS

Q1 Calculate the missing angles in each diagram.

a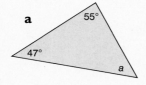

b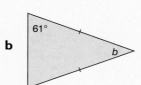

c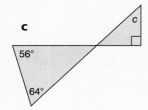

d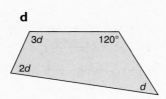

Q2 **a** Calculate the sum of the interior angles in a heptagon.
   b Find the missing angle x in the diagram.

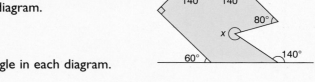

Q3 Calculate the size of the missing angle in each diagram.

a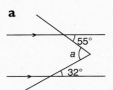

b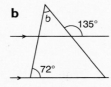

Answers are on page 234.

REVISION SESSION 13 Transformation geometry

What you should already know

- *The symmetrical properties of 2-D shapes*
- *How to find the exterior angle of a polygon*
- *How to plot coordinates*

- **You should be able to devise instructions for a computer to generate and transform shapes and paths.**
- **You should be able to enlarge shapes by a positive whole-number scale factor.**

USING COMPUTER INSTRUCTIONS TO GENERATE SHAPES

- You can use a computer language such as LOGO to draw 2-D shapes, by giving a list of instructions or writing a **program** for the computer to follow.
- You need to know these instructions.
  - FORWARD a given distance of units
  - LEFT TURN a given number of degrees
  - RIGHT TURN a given number of degrees
  - REPEAT an instruction a given number of times

Worked example

Write a LOGO program to draw a square of side 100 units.

START
FORWARD 100
RIGHT TURN 90
FORWARD 100
RIGHT TURN 90
FORWARD 100
RIGHT TURN 90
FORWARD 100

Note that FORWARD 100, RIGHT TURN 90 occurs three times.
It can be written as REPEAT 3 [FORWARD 100 RIGHT TURN 90].

The computer drawing is shown on the left.

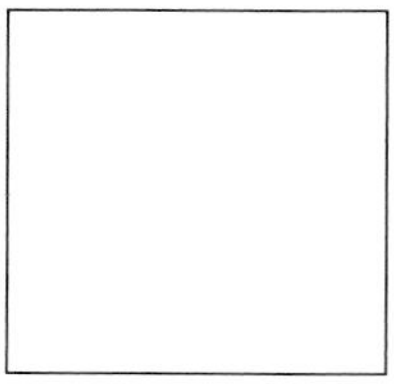

Worked example

Write a LOGO program to draw the parallelogram.

START
REPEAT 2 [FORWARD 140
RIGHT TURN 65
FORWARD 100
RIGHT TURN 115]

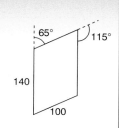

ROTATION

- A shape can be rotated **through an angle** about a **centre of rotation**.
- You need to know how to rotate a shape clockwise or anticlockwise through 90° or 180°.
- Remember that you can use tracing paper to help you.

Worked example
Rotate the flag through 90° clockwise about the point A.

Use tracing paper.

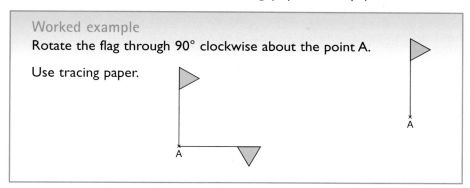

ENLARGEMENT

- You can enlarge a shape to make it bigger by multiplying the lengths of its sides by a **scale factor**.
- The shape is enlarged about a **centre of enlargement**.
- You need to know how to enlarge a shape by using the ray method or by drawing a shape on a coordinate grid and enlarging it about the origin.

Worked example
Enlarge triangle ABC about the point O by a scale factor of 2.

Draw rays OA, OB and OC.
Measure the lengths of these three rays and multiply each length by 2.
Draw the rays for these three new lengths as OA', OB' and OC'.
Join A', B' and C' to obtain the enlarged triangle A'B'C'.

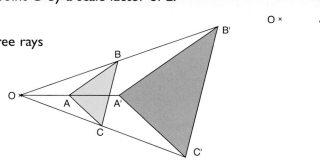

Worked example
Plot the points A(1, 1), B(3, 1), C(3, 2) and D(1, 2) and join them to make a rectangle ABCD. Enlarge the rectangle about the origin by a scale factor of 3.

For an enlargement about the origin, the numbers in each coordinate pair are just multiplied by the scale factor. So plot the points A'(3, 3), B'(9, 3), C'(9, 6), D'(3, 6) and join them to make the enlarged rectangle A'B'C'D'.

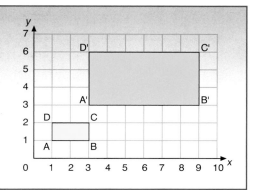

CHECK YOURSELF QUESTIONS

Q1 Write a LOGO program to draw this shape.

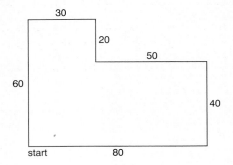

Q2 Rotate the letter T through 90° anticlockwise about the point A.

Q3 Rotate the letter L through 90° clockwise about the origin.

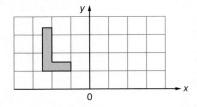

Q4 On a grid plot the points A(0, 1), B(2, ⁻1) and C(⁻2, ⁻1). Join them to make a triangle ABC. Enlarge the triangle about the origin by a scale factor of 2. Label the enlarged triangle A'B'C'.
What are the coordinates of A', B' and C'?

Q5 Use the ray method to enlarge the rectangle about the point A by a scale factor of 3.

A

Answers are on page 234.

> • You should understand and be able to use the formulae for finding the circumference and area of circles.
>
> • You should be able to find the area of plane figures and the volumes of cuboids.

What you should already know

• *The idea of perimeter, area and volume*

• *The metric units of length, area and volume*

PERIMETER
• You need to know how to use these formulae to solve problems.

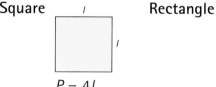

Square

$P = 4l$

Rectangle

$P = 2l + 2w$ or $P = 2(l + w)$

Circle

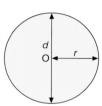

r = radius
d = diameter
perimeter = circumference (C)
$C = 2\pi r = \pi d$

• $\pi = 3.14$ or 3.142 or use the calculator value $\pi = 3.141\,592\,654$.
• Remember to use the correct units for perimeter: mm, cm, m, km.

Worked example

Mr Peters was planting flower bulbs around the edge of a lawn 10 metres long and 8 metres wide.
a Find the perimeter of the lawn.
b How many bulbs did he need, if he planted them 50 cm apart?

a $P = 2(l + w) = 2 \times 18 = 36\,m$
b $50\,cm = \frac{1}{2}\,m$ So the number of bulbs $= 36 \div \frac{1}{2} = 72$.

Worked example

Jon's mountain bike wheels have a radius of 30 cm.
a Find the circumference of a wheel.
b Jon goes on a 10 km ride. Find how many times a wheel turns.

a $C = 2\pi r = 2 \times \pi \times 30 = 188.5\,cm$ (correct to one decimal place and using the calculator value for π)
Remember to use the **Min** or **Sto** button on your calculator.
You need this answer for the next part.
b $10\,km = 10\,000\,m = 1\,000\,000\,cm$.
The wheel turns $1\,000\,000 \div 188.450 = 5305$ times (to the nearest whole number).
Remember to use the **MR** or **RCL** button on your calculator.

AREA

- You need to know how to use these formulae to solve problems.

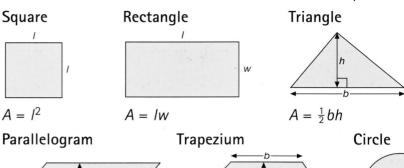

Square	Rectangle	Triangle
$A = l^2$	$A = lw$	$A = \frac{1}{2}bh$

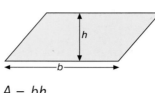

Parallelogram	Trapezium	Circle
$A = bh$	$A = \frac{1}{2}h(a + b)$	$A = \pi r^2$

- Remember to use the correct units for area: mm^2, cm^2, m^2, km^2.

Worked example

Find the area of each of these shapes.

a 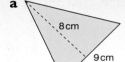 **b** 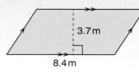 **c** 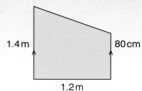 **d**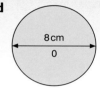

a $A = \frac{1}{2} \times 9 \times 8 = 36\,cm^2$

b $A = 8.4 \times 3.7 = 31.08\,m^2$

c Change 80 cm to m. 80 cm = 0.8 m.

$A = \dfrac{(1.4 + 0.8) \times 1.2}{2} = 1.32\,m^2$

d $d = 8\,cm$ so $r = 4\,cm$ and $A = \pi \times 4^2 = \pi \times 16 = 50.3\ cm^2$ (to one decimal place)

Worked example

Calculate the area of the road sign as you enter 'Mathsville'.

The sign is made up of a rectangle with sides of 80 cm and 30 cm and a semicircle with diameter 80 cm.

The area of the rectangle is $80 \times 30 = 2400\,cm^2$.

The area of a circle with a radius of 40 cm is

$\pi \times 40^2 = \pi \times 1600 = 5026.55$.

So the area of the semicircle is

$5026.55 \div 2 = 2513\,cm^2$ (to the nearest whole number).

Total area of the sign is $2400 + 2513 = 4913 = 4910\,cm^2$ (to 3 s.f.).

VOLUME

- You need to know this formula for the volume of a cuboid.
  $V = lwh$
- Remember to use the correct units for volume: mm^3, cm^3, m^3.

Cuboid

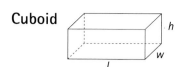

Worked example
Find the volume and total surface area of this cuboid block.

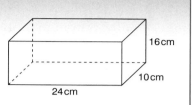

$V = 24 \times 10 \times 16 = 3840\, cm^3$

Find the surface area by adding together the areas of the six faces of the cuboid. There are three pairs of rectangles with equal areas.

$A = 2(24 \times 10) + 2(24 \times 16) + 2(10 \times 16) = 480 + 768 + 320$
$\quad = 1568\, cm^2$

CHECK YOURSELF QUESTIONS

Q1 Find the area of these shapes.

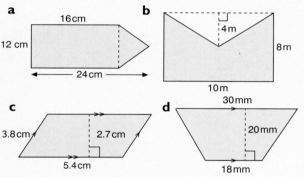

Q2 The diagram shows the spectator area around a rectangular sports field.

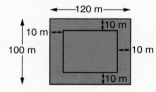

a Find the area of the field.
b Find the area for the spectators.

Q3 Mr Gleeson wanted to paint one side of his garden shed. The diagram shows the dimensions of the side to be painted. Calculate the area Mr Gleeson will have to paint.

Q4 Find the circumference area of each of these circles. Give your answers correct to one decimal place.

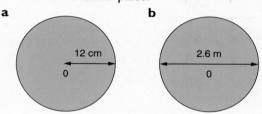

Q5 Anna makes a clown's mask out of card. Calculate the area of the card used, giving your answer correct to one decimal place.

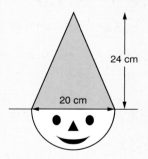

Answers are on page 234.

1 The diagram shows two isosceles triangles inside a parallelogram.

Not drawn accurately

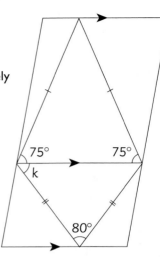

a On the diagram, mark another angle that is 75°.

I mark

b Calculate the size of the angle marked *k*. Show your working.

2 marks

2 a A circle has a radius of 15 cm.

Calculate the **area** of the circle. Show your working.

2 marks

b A different circle has a **circumference** of **120 cm**. What is the **radius** of the circle? Show your working.

2 marks

3 a Any quadrilateral can be split into two triangles.

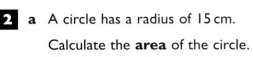

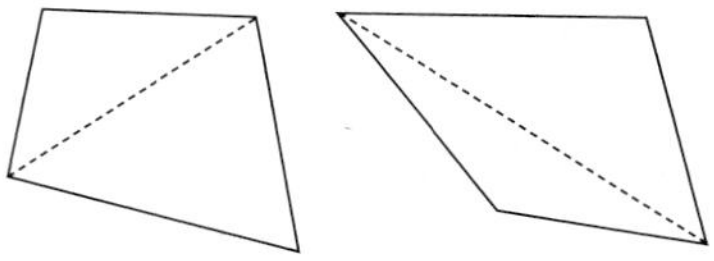

Explain how you know that the angles inside the **quadrilateral** add up to 360°.

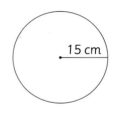

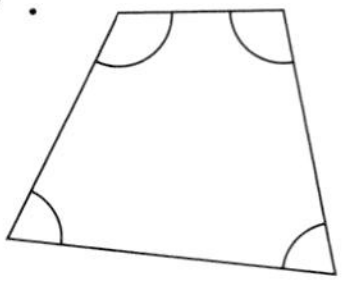

I mark

b What do the angles inside a **pentagon** add up to?

I mark

c What do the angles inside a **heptagon** (seven-sided shape) add up to? Show your working,

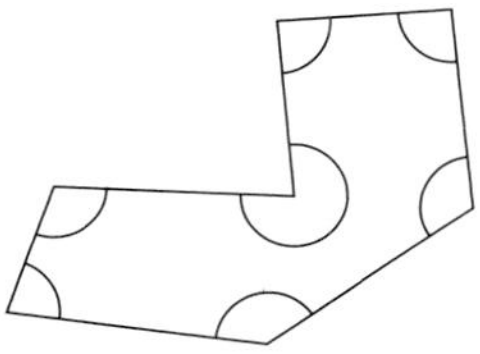

I mark

4 A trundle wheel is used to measure distances.
Imran makes a trundle wheel of diameter 50 cm.

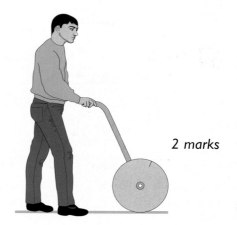

a Calculate the **circumference** of
Imran's trundle wheel.

Show your working,

2 marks

b Imran uses his trundle wheel to measure the
length of the school car park.
His trundle wheel rotates **87 times**.
What is the **length** of the car park, to the
nearest metre?

I mark

5 **a** On the cm³ grid below, draw a **right-angled triangle** with an area of **12 cm²**.
Use the line AB as one side of the triangle.

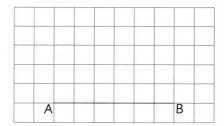

I mark

b Now draw an **isosceles triangle** with an area of **12 cm²**.
Use the line AB as one side of the triangle.

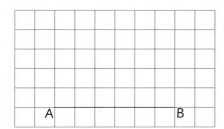

I mark

6 The drawing shows two cuboids that have the **same volume**.

Cuboid A

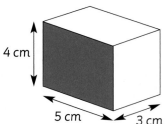

4 cm

5 cm   3 cm

Cuboid B

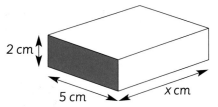

2 cm

5 cm   x cm

Not drawn accurately

a What is the volume of cuboid A?
Remember to state your units.

1 mark

b Work out the value of the length marked *x*.

2 marks

7 The diagram shows a rectangle.

Work out the size of angle *a*.
You **must** show your working.

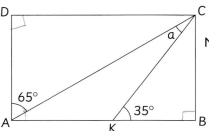

Not drawn accurately

1 mark

8 The information in the box describes three different squares, A, B and C.

The **area** of square A is **36 cm²**

The **side length** of square B is **36 cm**

The **perimeter** of square C is **36 cm**

Put squares A, B and C in order of size, starting with the smallest.
You **must** show calculations to explain how you work out your answer.

.... *2 marks*

smallest   largest

Answers are on page 249.

HANDLING DATA   LEVEL 6

REVISION SESSION 15   Frequency diagrams

- You should be able to collect and record continuous data, choosing appropriate class intervals, and create frequency diagrams.

What you should already know

- *How to collect and record data*
- *How to read and interpret statistical graphs and diagrams*

CONTINUOUS DATA

- Data that you collect by measuring, for example, length, height, weight, time is called **continuous** data.
- You must round measurements accurately and place continuous data into a **grouped frequency table** with suitable **class intervals**.
- Class intervals should all be of equal width with no overlap.
- Class intervals are usually written as inequalities or open intervals.

Worked example

These are the weights of 24 boys in a fitness club, recorded to the nearest kilogram. Make a grouped frequency table to show the data.

65 61 62 48 58 71 47 64 59 60 64 68
59 68 73 70 68 63 70 65 71 62 67 56

The range of the weights is 73 − 47 = 36 kg. Choose four class intervals of width 10 kg. Write the intervals in an open form 40–, 50–, 60– , 70– , where 40– means a weight from 40 kg up to but not including 50 kg.

Weight (kg)	Tally	Frequency
40–	II	2
50–	IIII	4
60–	JHT JHT III	13
70–	JHT	5

REPRESENTING GROUPED DATA IN DIAGRAMS

- **Group frequency diagrams** are similar to bar charts for discrete data but the horizontal axis is labelled to show the lower and upper limits of the class intervals.
- **Frequency polygons** are line graphs with the points plotted in the middle of each class interval.

Worked example

The frequency diagram shows the distribution of the maths SATs marks for the boys and girls in a school. Comment on the results.

The boys' results are more spread out as there are more boys than girls at the top and bottom of the range of marks. The girls did better overall, because more of them had marks in the 90–100 and 100–110 ranges.

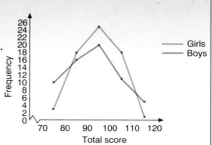

The grouped frequency table shows the ages of all the staff who work at Erinsburgh High School. From the table of data, draw:

Age	Frequency
20–	14
30–	18
40–	22
50–	12
60–	6

a a grouped frequency diagram

b a frequency polygon.

a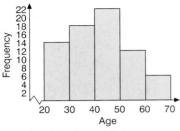

b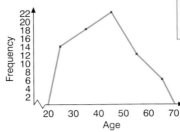

Notice the labelling of the age axis: the jagged line shows that there are no values between 0 and 20. The numbers are the boundaries of the class intervals.

The points are plotted at the halfway point for each of the class intervals. The polygon starts and finishes on the age axis, at the lowest and highest possible age.

CHECK YOURSELF QUESTIONS

Q1 Mr Beetone's telephone bill was far more than he had expected. So during the next week he kept a record of the times that he spent on the phone and rounded all the times up to the nearest minute. The times were:

2 5 7 10 3 1 2 6 7 11 4 6 4 3 8
12 3 5 1 3 2 7 4 6 10 3 1 5 8 12

  a Make a grouped frequency table of his results, using class intervals
    $0 < t \le 2, 2 < t \le 4, \dots$.

  b Draw a grouped frequency diagram.

Q2 Constable FitzGerald was using radar speed check equipment to monitor the speeds of vehicles on a dual carriageway. This is his frequency table.

Speed (mph)	20–	30–	40–	50–	60–	70–
frequency	14	23	28	35	52	8

  a Draw a grouped frequency diagram for the data.

  b How many vehicles did he check?

  c Can you find the mean speed for the vehicles? Explain why.

Q3 Sam was carrying out a survey on the heights of boys and girls in Year 9. He took a sample of 30 boys and 30 girls and made a grouped frequency table.

Height (cm)	No of boys	No of girls
140–	1	3
150–	6	8
160–	10	12
170–	11	7
180–	2	0

  a Draw a frequency polygon, showing both sets of data on the same diagram.

  b What is the most common height for all pupils?

  c Compare the distribution of the heights of the boys with the heights of the girls.

Answers are on page 234.

> • You should be able to construct pie charts.

What you should already know

• *How to calculate fractions of a quantity*

• *How to measure and draw angles*

• *How to interpret a pie chart*

WHEN TO USE PIE CHARTS

• You cannot always draw frequency diagrams to display data, especially when there are large differences in the frequencies or when the data is just used for illustration, as in advertising.
• In these cases, it is better to use **pie charts**.
• To draw a pie chart you need to be able to calculate fractional amounts of 360°.
• A pie chart only shows **proportions**, not individual frequencies.

Worked example

Mo asked 30 pupils in her class: 'Where did you go for your last holiday?' The frequency table shows her results. Draw a pie chart to show the data.

England	Scotland	Wales	Europe	America
12	4	2	9	3

The table shows how to calculate the angle for each sector of the pie chart.

Draw a vertical radius. Put in the 'England' sector first. Then work round clockwise. You need not show the angles or frequencies.

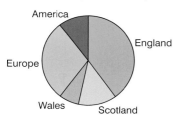

Remember to check that the angles total 360°.

Place	Frequency	Calculation	Angle
England	12	$\frac{12}{30} \times 360 = 144$	144°
Scotland	4	$\frac{4}{30} \times 360 = 48$	48°
Wales	2	$\frac{2}{30} \times 360 = 24$	24°
Europe	9	$\frac{9}{30} \times 360 = 108$	108°
America	3	$\frac{3}{30} \times 360 = 36$	36°
Totals	30		360°

❓ CHECK YOURSELF QUESTIONS

Q1 This is how form 9MP voted for four candidates to stand on the School Council. Draw a pie chart to show how the form voted.

Z. Freeman	I. Knapp	A. Clouns	D. Best
10	7	8	11

Q2 Sara had £50 to buy Christmas presents. This is what she spent.

£11.00 on a table decoration for Mum
£11.50 on a pullover for Dad
£7.50 on perfume for her sister Sue
£8.00 on a model car for her brother Andrew
£12.00 on a CD for her boyfriend Philip.

Draw a pie chart to show the proportion she spent on each person's present.

Answers are on page 235.

Scatter diagrams

What you should already know

- *How to read and interpret statistical graphs and diagrams with one set of data or one variable*

> • **You should be able to draw scatter diagrams and understand correlation.**

COMPARING TWO SETS OF DATA – CORRELATION

- You often need to find out if there is a connection between two variables, for example, do tall children always have tall parents? This connection is known as **correlation**.
- You need to know the terms **positive correlation**, **negative correlation** and **no correlation**.
- A scatter diagram shows whether there is a connection between two variables. Like any graph, it has two perpendicular axes.

Worked example

The scatter diagram shows the marks of 30 pupils for Papers 1 and 2 in their Key Stage 3 Maths tests. Describe what the diagram tells you.

The scatter diagram shows a positive correlation. This means that many of the pupils who had a high mark on Paper 1 also had a high mark on Paper 2.

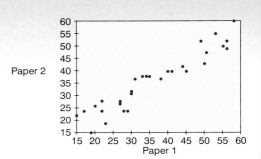

- Positive correlation tells you that as one variable increases, so does the other.

Worked example

The scatter diagram shows the relationship between the number of hours spent on homework and the number of hours spent watching TV on a particular weekday evening for a group of Year 9 pupils.

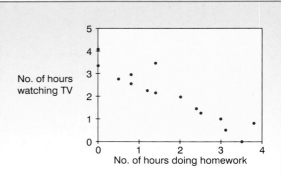

a Describe what the diagram tells you.

b Sanjay spent $1\frac{1}{2}$ hours working on his Geography project that evening. How much TV did he probably watch?

a The scatter diagram shows a negative correlation. This means that the more time pupils spend on homework, the less time they spend watching TV.

b Going up from the horizontal axis at $1\frac{1}{2}$ and looking where the points are nearby, you can see that Sanjay probably spent about $2\frac{1}{2}$ hours watching TV.

Worked example

Martha thought that the further you lived from school, the earlier you needed to get up in a morning. To test this statement, she carried out a survey on 10 of her school friends, then drew this scatter diagram.

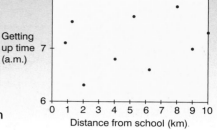

a Describe what the diagram tells Martha.
b Make another statement comparing distance from school with another variable that might show positive correlation.

a The scatter diagram shows no correlation. There seems to be no connection between the distance from school and getting-up time.
b An example to show positive correlation might be: 'The distance from school and the time it takes to get to school'.

? CHECK YOURSELF QUESTIONS

Q1 The scatter diagram shows the heights and weights of 12 people.
  a Describe what the diagram tells you.
  b Eric is one of the people on the scatter diagram. He weighs 62 kg. Is he likely to be as tall as the other 11 people on the same diagram?

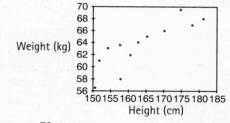

Q2 Mr Reneé owns a café at Bridpool and keeps a record of the number of cups of tea and coffee he sells on certain days of the summer holidays. He also records the midday temperature on these days. This data is shown on the scatter diagram.
  a Describe what the diagram tells you.
  b Give a reason for your answer.

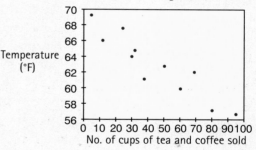

Q3 The table shows the end of year examination marks for French and History for 10 friends in Year 9.
  a Plot the data on a scatter diagram.
  b Describe what you notice from the diagram.

Name	French mark (%)	History mark (%)
Ant	23	47
Bill	50	68
Cath	29	67
Den	60	26
Edith	85	42
Flora	68	70
Gary	34	80
Helen	88	91
Iris	55	78
Jack	95	40

Answers are on page 235.

What you should already know

- *How to use the formula to find the probability of an event*

- *About equally likely outcomes*

- When dealing with two experiments, you should be able to identify all the outcomes and show them in diagrammatic or tabular form.

- You should know that the total probability of all the mutually exclusive events of an experiment is 1 and use this to solve problems.

COMBINED EVENTS

- If an event or experiment is carried out more than once, or if one is done straight after another, this is a **combined event**.
- To calculate the probabilities for a combined event you need to know how to use lists, tables or diagrams to identify all the possible outcomes.
- You should know the probability formula is

$$P(outcome) = \frac{\text{number of favourable outcomes}}{\text{total number of possible outcomes}}$$

Worked example

a Find all the possible outcomes when you throw two coins.

b Find: **(i)** P(2 heads) **(ii)** P(1 head) **(iii)** P(0 heads).

c What do you notice about these three probabilities?

a Method 1.
List all the outcomes: HH, HT, TH, TT.
Method 2.
Draw a sample space diagram.
In both cases there are four equally likely outcomes.

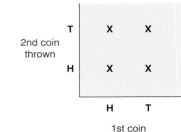

b Using the probability formula:

  (i) P(2 heads) = $\frac{1}{4}$

  (ii) P(1 head) = $\frac{2}{4}$ = $\frac{1}{2}$

  (iii) P(0 heads) = $\frac{1}{4}$

c The three probabilities add up to 1. This is because every possible outcome has been included only once for the three different events. The three events are mutually exclusive since none of them includes any common outcomes.

Worked example

A box contains three balls; one is red, one is green and one is blue. A ball is drawn out at random, its colour is noted and then it is replaced. The box is shaken and again one ball is drawn at random.

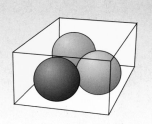

a Find all the possible outcomes for the colours of the two balls.

b Find: **(i)** P(2 reds)

(ii) P(the 2 balls are the same colour)

(iii) P(the 2 balls are of different colours).

a Method 1: List all the outcomes.

RR, GR, BR, RG, GG, BG, RB, GB, BB

Method 2: Draw a sample space diagram.

There are nine equally likely outcomes.

b (i) P(2 reds) = $\frac{1}{9}$

(ii) P(same colour) = P(2 reds or 2 greens or 2 blues) = $\frac{3}{9}$ = $\frac{1}{3}$

(iii) P(same colour) and P(not the same colour) are mutually exclusive events, since they do not have any common outcomes, and add up to 1.

P(2 different colours) = $1 - \frac{1}{3} = \frac{2}{3}$

B	X	X	X
G	X	X	X
R	X	X	X
	R	G	B

Worked example

In the game of Backgammon two dice are used and it is an advantage if you get a double or a high score. (A double means both dice show the same number and the score is the total of both numbers.)

a Draw a sample space diagram to show all the possible scores when throwing two dice.

b Find: **(i)** P(double 6)   **(ii)** P(any double)

(iii) P(no double)   **(iv)** P(a score of 9).

a On the sample space you can either put Xs for the scores or write in the scores as numbers. There are 36 equally likely outcomes.

b (i) P(double 6) = P(a score of 12) = $\frac{1}{36}$

(ii) P(any double) = $\frac{6}{36} = \frac{1}{6}$ (The six outcomes are ringed on the sample space diagram.)

(iii) P(no double) = $1 - \frac{1}{6} = \frac{5}{6}$ (Mutually exclusive events)

(iv) P(A score of 9) = $\frac{4}{36} = \frac{1}{9}$ (The four outcomes are ringed on the sample space diagram.)

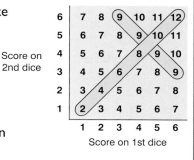

Score on 2nd dice

Score on 1st dice

Worked example

Maggie wants to find all the outcomes when three coins are thrown together. She decides to make a table to help her find all the possible outcomes. This is how she started the table.

a Complete the table.
b Use the table to find:
   (i) P(3 heads) **(ii)** P(2 heads)
   (iii) P(1 head) **(iv)** P(0 heads).
c How can you check your answer to part (b)?

1st coin	2nd coin	3rd coin
H	H	H
H	H	T
H	T	H

a

1st coin	2nd coin	3rd coin
H	H	H
H	H	T
H	T	H
H	T	T
T	H	H
T	H	T
T	T	H
T	T	T

b There are eight equally likely outcomes.
   (i) P(3 heads) = $\frac{1}{8}$ **(ii)** P(2 heads) = $\frac{3}{8}$
   (iii) P(1 head) = $\frac{3}{8}$ **(iv)** P(0 heads) = $\frac{1}{8}$
c The four probabilities must add up to 1. The events are mutually exclusive and all possible outcomes have been included.

CHECK YOURSELF QUESTIONS

Q1 Stan is playing a game using the four letters I R O N. He shuffles the letters and places them face-down. Then Stan takes a letter, keeps it, and then takes a second letter.
   a List all possible outcomes for the two letters Stan can choose.
   b Find P(making a proper two-letter word).

Q2 Barbara, Ian, Linda and Mike played as a team in an inter-class quiz in Year 9. The team won and two of them were then invited to play in an inter-year quiz. The team decided to select the pair by putting their names into a hat and choosing the first two names that came out.
   a List all the possible pairs of names that could be chosen.
   b Find P(the pair chosen will be a boy and a girl).

Q3 A coin and a dice are thrown together. Draw a sample space diagram to show all the possible outcomes.

Q4 In the game 'Tetra', two four-sided dice with faces numbered 1 to 4 are thrown and the numbers on the bases of the dice are multiplied together to find the score.
   a Draw a sample space diagram to show all the possible scores for the game.
   b Find: **(i)** P(the score is even) **(ii)** P(the score is odd).

Answers are on page 236.

1   **a**   A bag has **20** cubes in it. **6** of the cubes are green.

You take one cube out of the bag at random.

Which values below show the **probability** that you take out a cube that is green?

Circle the correct **four** values.

$\frac{6}{14}$ 30%   0.6 $\frac{3}{10}$

6% $\frac{3}{5}$ $\frac{6}{20}$ 0.03

0.3 $\frac{6}{10}$ 60% $\frac{6}{26}$ *2 marks*

  b   A box has **20** counters in it. **11** of the counters are red.

You take one counter out of the box at random.
What is the probability that the counter you take out is **not** red?

Write your answer as a fraction.   *1 mark*

Now write your answer as a percentage.   *1 mark*

2   There are some cubes in a bag.
The cubes are either **red** (R) or **black** (B).

The teacher says:

If you take a cube at random out of the bag the probability that it will be **red** is $\frac{1}{5}$.

  a   What is the probability that the cube will be black?   *1 mark*

  b   A pupil takes one cube out of the bag.
It is red.

What is the **smallest** number of
black cubes there could be in the bag?   *1 mark*

  c   Then the pupil takes another cube out of the bag.
It is also red.

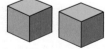

From this new information, what is the
smallest number of **black** cubes there could be in the bag?   *1 mark*

  d   A different bag has **blue** (B), **green** (G) and **yellow** (Y) cubes in it.
There is at least one of each of the three colours.

The teacher says:

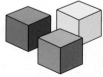

If you take a cube at random out of the bag the probability
that it will be **green** is $\frac{3}{5}$.

There are **20** cubes in the bag.

What is the **greatest** number of yellow cubes there could be in the bag?

Show your working.   *2 marks*

2 The scatter diagram shows the heights and masses of some horses.
The scatter diagram also shows a line of best fit.

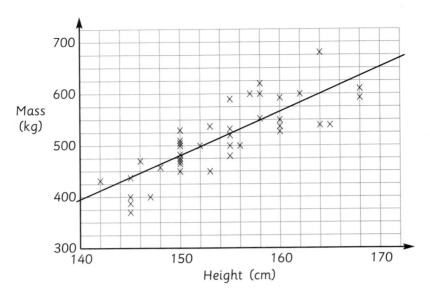

Height (cm)

a What does the scatter diagram show about the **relationship** between
the height and mass of horses?   *1 mark*

b The **height** of a horse is **163 cm**.
Use the line of best fit to estimate the mass of the horse.   *1 mark*

c A different horse has a **mass of 625 kg**.
Use the line of best fit to estimate the height of the horse.   *1 mark*

d A teacher asks his class to investigate this statement:

'The length of the **back leg** of
a horse is always less than the length
of the **front leg** of a horse.'

What might a scatter graph
look like if the statement is
correct? Use the axes to
show your answer.

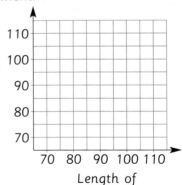

Length of
front leg (cm)   *1 mark*

4 Here are three number cards.
The numbers are hidden.

The **mode** of the three numbers is **5**.

The **mean** of the three numbers is **8**.

What are the three numbers?
Show your working.

2 marks

5 There are **60 pupils** in a school. **6** of these pupils wear glasses.

a The pie chart is not drawn accurately.
What should the angles be?
Show your working.

Wear glasses

Do not
wear glasses

2 marks

b Exactly **half** of the 60 pupils in
the school are boys.

From this information, what percentage of boys in this school wear glasses? Tick (✓)
the correct box below.

5% ☐   6% ☐   10% ☐   20% ☐   50% ☐   not possible to tell ☐   *1 mark*

6 Three types of mouse might come into our homes.

Some mice are more likely to be found in homes far from woodland. Others are more
likely to be found in homes close to woodland.

The bar charts show the **percentages of mice** that are of each type.

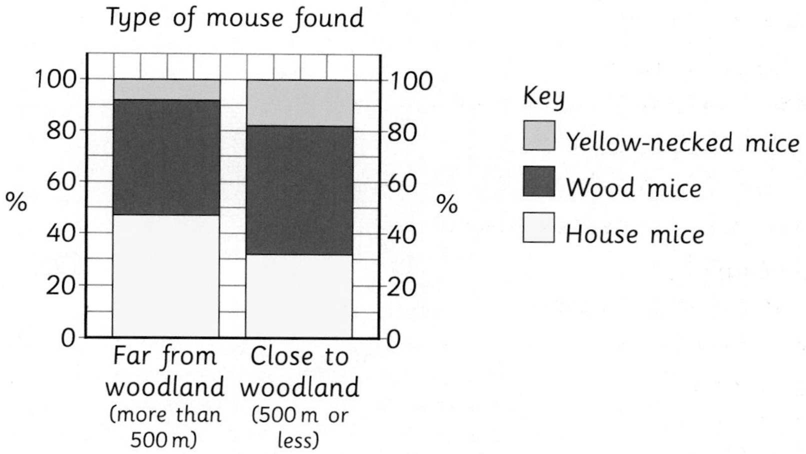

Type of mouse found

Key

☐ Yellow-necked mice

■ Wood mice

☐ House mice

Far from
woodland
(more than
500 m)

Close to
woodland
(500 m or
less)

Use the bar charts to answer these questions.

a About what percentage of mice in homes **close to woodland** are **wood mice**?

1 mark

b About what percenatge of mice in homes **far from woodland** are **not** wood mice?

1 mark

c The **black** bars show the percentages for house mice.
One of the bars is taller than the other.

Does that mean there **must be more** house mice in homes far from
woodland than in homes close to woodland?

Tick (✓) Yes ☐ or No ☐

Explain your answer.

1 mark

7 This advert was in a newspaper.

It does not say how the advertisers know that 93% of people drop litter every day.

Some pupils think the percentage of people who drop litter every day is much lower than 93%. They decide to do a survey.

93% of us drop litter every day. Do your bit. Use a bin.

a Jack says:

We can ask 10 people if they drop litter every day.

Give two **different** reasons why Jack's method might not give very good data.

First reason: *1 mark*

Second reason: *1 mark*

b Lisa says:

We can go into town on Saturday morning.
We can stand outside a shop and record how many people walk past and how many of those drop litter.

Give two **different** reasons why Lisa's method might not give very good data.

First reason: *1 mark*

Second reason: *1 mark*

8 Ann, Ben, Carl, Donna and Eric are friends.

They have four tickets for a concert.
The order in which they sit at the concert does not matter.

Ben must go to the concert.
If Eric goes, Donna must go too.

List all the possible groups of four who could go to the concert.
Remember, order does not matter. *2 marks*

9 **a** Paula played four games in a competition.
In **three** games, Paula scored **8** points each time.
In the other game she scored **no** points.

What was Paula's **mean** score over the **four** games? *1 mark*

b Jessie only played **two** games.
Her **mean** score was **3** points.
Her **range** was **4** points.

What points did Jessie score in her two games? *1 mark*

c Ali played **three** games.
His **mean** score was also **3** points.
His **range** was also **4** points.

What points might Ali have scored in his three games?
Show your working. *1 mark*

Answers are on page 250.

Rounding to significant figures and estimating

> • You should be able to round to one significant figure and multiply and divide mentally.

SIGNIFICANT FIGURES

• The number 287 has three significant figures. This is how the digits would look if they were drawn to scale depending on their place value.

$$2\,8\,_7$$

• Compared to the 2, the 7 does not seem very important.
• Rounding 287 to the nearest 10 gives 290. This has two significant figures (2 s.f.).
• Rounding 287 off to the nearest hundred gives 300. This number has one significant figure (1 s.f.).
• Although it might seem that the rule for significant figures is just 'Count the non-zero digits', zero is significant if it is between two numbers. So 307, for example, has three significant figures.

Worked example

How many significant figures do these numbers have?

a 458   **b** 3400   **c** 203   **d** 1000   **e** 304 500

a 3 s.f.   **b** 2 s.f. Zeros do not count.
c 3 s.f. The zero does count because it is between two other digits.
d 1 s.f.
e 4 s.f. The first zero counts but the last two do not.

DECIMALS AND SIGNIFICANT FIGURES

• Zeros at the start or end of a number are not significant figures but zeros between digits are significant figures.

Worked example

How many significant figures do these numbers have?

a 0.0045   **b** 0.2045   **c** 0.8900   **d** 0.070 09

a 2 s.f. Zeros do not count.   **b** 4 s.f.
c 2 s.f. Zeros at the end do not change the value of the number but you do not actually know if they are there for a reason. They might be significant, so the answer could be 4 s.f.
d 4 s.f.

Hint:

3783 would be 4000 to 1 s.f., 3800 to 2 s.f. and 3780 to 3 s.f.
0.0906 would be 0.09 to 1 s.f. and 0.091 to 2 s.f.

Hint:

Part (c) is unusual because 0.599 rounds to 0.60. You must include the extra zero as it counts as a significant figure. This is why the answer to part (c) of the last example could have been 2 s.f. or 4 s.f. Halfway numbers, like part (b), round upwards.

ROUNDING TO SIGNIFICANT FIGURES

- Generally, you only have to round to one significant figure, to make estimates of the answers to calculations.
- You can round numbers to any number of significant figures. For example

Worked example
Round each number to the number of significant figures in the brackets.

a 3567 (2 s.f.) **b** 0.0965 (2 s.f.) **c** 0.599 (2 s.f.)

a 3600 **b** 0.097 **c** 0.60

ESTIMATING

- To estimate, you round numbers to values that you can work out in your head (i.e. without a calculator). One significant figure is usually close enough.

Worked example
Estimate the answers to these. **a** $\dfrac{325.7 + 40.7}{24.9}$ **b** $\dfrac{52.1 \times 0.783}{(53.6 + 17.6)}$

a Round the numbers to 1 s.f. (or 2 s.f. for easy numbers such as 25).

$$\frac{300 + 40}{25} \approx \frac{340}{25} \approx \frac{350}{25} = 14$$

Change 340 to 350 to make the calculation easy to do in your head.

b $\dfrac{50 \times 0.8}{50 + 20} \approx \dfrac{40}{70} \approx \dfrac{40}{80} = \dfrac{1}{2}$

CHECK YOURSELF QUESTIONS

Q1 How many significant figures are there in:
  a 246 **b** 3567
  c 3204 **d** 9700?

Q2 How many significant figures are there in:
  a 0.06 **b** 0.567
  c 30.04 **d** 0.0320?

Q3 Round these numbers to 1 significant figure.
  a 246 **b** 3967
  c 3204 **d** 0.0804

Q4 Round these numbers to 2 significant figures.
  a 246 **b** 2417
  c 2294 **d** 0.0842

Q5 Round these numbers to 3 significant figures.
  a 2462 **b** 2417
  c 2294 **d** 0.08427

Q6 Estimate the answers.
  a 0.72×53 **b** 0.076×489
  c 612×0.63 **d** 72×0.087

Q7 About how many 28p postage stamps can you get for £10.00?

Q8 Petrol is 79.7p per litre. About how much will 51 litres cost?

Q9 An athlete can run a mile in 6 minutes and 10 seconds.
  a About how long will it take her to run a marathon of 26 miles?
  b Will your answer be an overestimate or an underestimate? Explain why.

Answers are on page 236.

REVISION SESSION 2 — Multiplying by numbers between 0 and 1

> • You should understand the effects of multiplying by a number between 0 and 1.

What you should already know

• *How to to multiply and divide with decimals*

• Some people think that when you multiply something it has to get bigger and that when you divide something it has to get smaller. This is only true if you multiply and divide by numbers bigger than 1.
• When you multiply by numbers between 0 and 1 the answer is smaller than the number you started with. When you divide by numbers between 0 and 1 the answer is bigger!
• 1 is a special number because multiplying and dividing any number by 1 does not change the value of the number.

Note:

If you want to catch someone out ask them, 'What is a half times a half?' They will usually say 1. But if you ask them what a half of a half is they will say a quarter.

Worked example
Choose five numbers bigger than 1. Put them through each of these function machines.

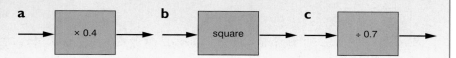

a → × 0.4 →   **b** → square →   **c** → ÷ 0.7 →

For each function decide if it:
• always gives an answer bigger than the number you start with
• always gives an answer smaller than the number you start with
• leaves the number the same
• does none of the above.

a This function always makes any number bigger than 1 smaller.
b This function always makes any number bigger than 1 bigger.
c This function always makes any number bigger than 1 bigger.

Worked example
Repeat the last example for the number 1.

a This function makes 1 smaller.
b This function leaves 1 the same.
c This function makes 1 bigger.

> Worked example
>
> Repeat the first worked example for five numbers between 0 and 1.
>
> **a** This function always makes any number between 0 and 1 smaller.
> **b** This function always makes any number between 0 and 1 smaller.
> **c** This function always makes any number between 0 and 1 bigger.

CHECK YOURSELF QUESTIONS

Q1 Consider these expressions.

$$0.5n \qquad n^2 \qquad \sqrt{n} \qquad n \div 0.5 \qquad \frac{1}{n}$$

 a If $n = 3$, which give a value greater than 3?
 b If $n = 5$, which give a value less than 5?
 c If $n = 0.4$, which give a value greater than 0.4?
 d If $n = 0.7$, which give a value less than 0.7?

Q2 Use the same expressions as in Question 1, and take n as a positive number.
 a Which of them always gives a value greater than n?
 b Which of them always gives a value less than n?

Q3 Complete the table using always $> n$, always $< n$ or always $= n$ (n is positive).

	$n > 1$	$n < 1$	$n = 1$
n^3	Always $> n$		
$\sqrt{n}$			Always $= n$
$\frac{1}{n}$			

Answers are on page 236.

- You should be able to solve numerical problems involving multiplication and division with numbers of any size.

- You should be able to use a calculator efficiently and appropriately.

What you should already know

- *What a bracket does in a calculation*

- *How to use the square root and square button on your calculator*

THE ORDER OF OPERATIONS
- BODMAS stands for Brackets, Of (pOwer), Division, Multiply, Addition and Subtraction. This is the order in which calculations should be done: brackets should be done first, then powers, then multiplications and so on.
- Asked to work out the sum $2 + 3 \times 4$ in their heads, many people will give the answer as 20. In fact it is 14. Check with a scientific calculator. According to BODMAS, the multiplication should be done first. This means 3×4 is done before $2 + ...$ so the problem becomes $2 + 12$ which is 14.

Note:

A calculator works out complicated expressions almost instantly, but it only does what it is told to. It will give a correct answer if you put the numbers into it correctly. Make sure you know how calculations are structured and how to use your calculator to work them out.

Worked example

The sum below has four operations in it (and a set of brackets). The operations are square, add, times and subtract. What order should they be done in? Do them and check that you get an answer of 91.

$(2 + 3)^2 \times 4 - 9$

Do the bracket first (addition):	$5^2 \times 4 - 9$
Do the power second:	$25 \times 4 - 9$
Do the multiplication third:	$100 - 9$
Do the subtraction fourth:	91

Worked example
Put brackets into these calculations to make them true.

a $2 + 4^2 \div 3 - 2 = 10$ **b** $2 + 4^2 \div 3 - 2 = 18$

a $(2 + 4)^2 \div 3 - 2 = 10$ **b** $2 + 4^2 \div (3 - 2) = 18$

Hint:

Try brackets in various places until you get it right.

THE BRACKET KEYS
- You can use brackets to make sure you remember (and the calculator knows) to work out that bit before the others.
- You can have more than one bracket operation going on at once (nesting brackets).
- There must always be the same number of left-hand as right-hand brackets in a calculation or you will get an error message.

Note:

Scientific calculators have two bracket keys – a left-hand bracket **(** and a right-hand bracket **)**.

- Usually, you can just key in calculations that have brackets 'as they read' on the page. For example to work out $(3 + 5) \times (9 - 2)$, key in:

(3 + 5) × (9 – 2) =

- The brackets together work like an equals sign. As soon as a left-hand bracket is joined by a right-hand bracket the calculator works outs everything between them.
- On some calculators you can key in $2(3 + 4)$. On others you may need to type $2 \times (3 + 4)$. Check your calculator. If you are not sure, put the multiplication sign in anyway.

> **Worked example**
> Use the bracket keys on your calculator to work these out.
>
> **a** $(16 + (8 - 3)) \div 7$ **b** $(3^2 + 7) \div 4$
>
> **a** 3 **b** 4

THE MEMORY KEYS
- If you use brackets properly, you won't need to write down parts of sums as you go along. If you need to keep a number to use later, you can do it by using the memory keys.
- The memory keys on your calculator should:
  - put a number into the memory, replacing anything already in there. (This is [Min] or [STO] on most calculators.)
  - add (or subtract) the number in the display to the number in the memory (This is [M+] ([M–]) on most calculators.)
  - recall the number from the memory and put it in the display. (This is usually [MR] or [RCL].)

THE DIVIDING LINE IN A FRACTION
- This means 'divide the top by the bottom'. It also acts like brackets for both the expressions on the top and the bottom. So $\frac{63 + 57}{26 - 16}$ can be read as $\frac{(63 + 57)}{(26 - 16)}$ or $(63 + 57) \div (26 - 16)$.
- You can use the bracket keys or the memory keys to do calculations like these.

> **Worked example**
> Work out $\dfrac{36.8 + 57.7}{17.9 - 7.4}$ by using: **a** brackets keys **b** memory keys.
>
> **a** (3 6 . 8 + 5 7 . 7) ÷
> (1 7 . 9 – 7 . 4) =
>
> **b** 1 7 . 9 – 7 . 4 = Min 3 6
> . 8 + 5 7 . 7 = ÷ MR =

COMMON ERRORS

- Calculate the mean of 3, 5, 6, 7, 8. You should get 5.8.
  If a whole class did the sum, some people would get an answer
  of 22.6 because they keyed in 3 + 5 + 6 + 7 + 8 ÷ 5 =, so did
  not add up all the numbers before they divided by 5. They should
  have used a bracket or pressed = after the 8.
- Another common error is forgetting to press = at the end of the
  sum. For example, 3 × (22 − 6) = 48 but if you only key in 3 ×
  (22 − 6) but forget to press =, the display will show 16. You need
  to press = to get the correct answer of 48.

Worked example

What errors have been made in these calculations? Work out the
correct answer.

a 6 + 9 ÷ 3 = 5   **b** (6 + 4) × (2 + 5) = 7

a The equals sign has been pressed after 9, giving the answer 15,
which has then been divided by 3 to give 5. To do the calculation
correctly, use brackets and key in 6 + (9 ÷ 3) = to give the correct
answer of 9.

b The equals sign has not been pressed after the second bracket, so 7
is shown in the display. To do the calculation correctly, key in (6 + 4)
× (2 + 5) = to give the correct answer of 70.

? CHECK YOURSELF QUESTIONS

Q1 Circle the operation that must be done first, then work out the
answer.

    a $5 + 5 \times 3 =$ **b** $8 + 6 \div 2 =$ **c** $3 + 4^2 =$

    d $(3 + 4)^2 =$ **e** $2 \times 5^2 =$ **f** $4 \times 3 - 6 =$

Q2 Put brackets into these sums to make them true.

    a $4 + 4 \times 4 \div 4 = 8$ **b** $4 \div 4 + 4 + 4 = 4.5$

    c $4 + 4 \div 4 + 4 = 1$ **d** $4 + 4 + 4 \div 4 = 3$

Q3 Write down the order of operations for these calculations and then
work them out.

    a $2 + 3^2 \times 4 - 9 \div 3$ **b** $(2 + 4)^2 \div (3 - 2)$

Q4 Work these out using, the brackets keys on your calculator.

    a $\dfrac{87.3 - 21.9}{4.7 - 1.7}$ **b** $\dfrac{17.2 + (98.5 - 16.9)}{3.4 + 0.6}$

Q5 Work these out, using the memory keys on your calculator.

    a $\dfrac{37.6 - 18.4}{3.2 + 1.8}$ **b** $\dfrac{8 + (98.5 - 18.5)^2}{98.5 - 18.5}$

Q6 Work this out, using **a** bracket keys **b** memory keys.

    $\dfrac{12.4 \times 4.5}{3.3 - 1.8}$

Answers are on page 237.

Proportional changes

What you should already know

- *How to use ratios to solve problems*
- *How to work out percentages of quantities*

- **You should understand and use proportional changes.**

REVERSE PERCENTAGE
- Most prices of goods in shops include value added tax (VAT).
- Some companies do not have to pay VAT on everything they buy so they may want to know the price without VAT.
- This means they start with the price including VAT and have to work backwards, to solve a **reverse percentage** problem.

Hint:

There are many ways to do this. Two are shown here.

Method 2 is actually exactly the same as Method 1, but Method 1 goes through the calculation more slowly, so use this at first.

Worked example

The price of a cooker is listed as £446.50, including 17.5% VAT. What is the price of the cooker without VAT?

Method 1: Set up a table comparing percentage and price.

100% + 17.5% = 117.5%. The price of the cooker is therefore equivalent to 117.5%.
Work out 1% by dividing by 117.5.
This gives 3.8.
Work out 100% by multiplying by 100.
This gives the price without VAT as £380.

%	Price
117.5	446.50
1	3.8
100	380

Method 2: Divide by 117.5 and multiply by 100.
446.5 ÷ 117.5 × 100 = 380

Worked example

The price of a burger meal has been reduced by 15%. It now costs £2.72. What did it cost before?

£2.72 is a reduction of 15%, so it is 85%. Divide by 85 to get 1%.

2.72 ÷ 85 = 0.032. Multiply by 100 to get 100%.
0.032 × 100 = 3.20. The original price was £3.20.

COMPOUND INTEREST
- When you put money into a savings account in a bank or building society you are paid **interest** on your money.
- The amount of interest paid varies but is always expressed as a percentage. This is the **interest rate**. Interest is paid at regular intervals (usually every 6 or 12 months).
- After a year, you still have the money you originally put in and the interest is added to this.
- This total amount is used to calculate the interest for the next year and so on. This is called **compound interest**.

Worked example

I put £300 into a bank that pays 7% interest each year.

a If I leave my money there and don't take any out, how much will I have after **(i)** 1 year **(ii)** 3 years?

b How many years will it be before I have over £400 in the bank?

a (i) £321

Interest for the first year is 7% of £300 = £21 (7 × 300 ÷ 100).
The amount in the bank after 1 year is £300 + £21 = £321.

(ii) £367.51

The interest for the second year is 7% of £321 = £22.47.
The amount after 2 years is £321 + £22.47 = £343.47.
The interest for the second year is 7% of £343.47 = £24.04.
The amount after 3 years is £343.47 + £24.04 = £367.51.

b 5 years

You could use the first method and see how many years it takes to get to over £400 but using the decimal method:
$300 × (1.07)^4 = 393.24$, $300 × (1.07)^5 = 420.76$.

Note:

You may see 'every year' referred to as per annum or p.a.

These can also be done using decimals. 7% is 0.07, which can be added to the original amount (100%) to give 1.07. $300 × 1.07 = 321$, $321 × 1.07 = 343.47$, $343.07 × 1.07 = 367.51$ (nearest penny).
This can be done as $300 × (1.07)^3$.

CHECK YOURSELF QUESTIONS

Q1 Find the original quantity (100%) if:
   a 40% is £60   **b** 23% is £57.50
   c 117.5% is £305.50 **d** 120% is 78 kg.

Q2 Last year 16 pupils at a school got level 8 in their SATs. This represents 6.4% of the year. How many were in the year group?

Q3 After a pay rise of 3.2%, Brian's pay went up to £237.36 a week. How much did he get before the pay rise?

Q4 In a garden 24% of the plants are shrubs, 56% are flowers. The remaining 20% are trees. There are 60 shrubs in the garden. How many trees are there?

Q5 I saved up to buy a computer that was priced at £1000. Just as I had saved enough the price went up by 20%. The company then had a sale and reduced the price of the computer by 20%. Did I have enough money to buy the computer?

Q6 Find the amount of money in the bank if:
   a £250 is invested for 2 years at 4% p.a.
   b £2000 is invested for 4 years at 7% p.a.

Q7 Ivy grows by 35% per week. I planted an ivy that was 20 cm tall.
   a How tall was it after
       (i) 1 week **(ii)** 3 weeks?
   b How many weeks did it take to reach a height of 1 metre?

Q8 I want to buy a new car that costs £12 000. My buyers' guide tells me that it will lose 20% of its value each year.
   a How much is it worth after
       (i) 1 year
       (ii) 4 years?
   b Once the value of the car falls below £3000 I will sell it. How many years will this take?

Q9 A grandmother puts £1000 in the bank on the birth of her granddaughter. She gets 7% interest p.a. The money will be paid out when the granddaughter is 21 years old. How much will she get?

Answers are on page 237.

1 **a** Look at these numbers.

1^6 2^5 3^4 4^3 5^2 6^1

Which is the **largest**? *1 mark*

Which is equal to 9^2? *1 mark*

b Which **two** of the numbers below are **not** square numbers?

2^4 2^5 2^6 2^7 2^8 *1 mark*

2 **a** Circle the **best** estimate of the answer to

$72.32 \div 8.91$

6   7   8   9   10   11 *1 mark*

b Circle the **best** estimate of the answer to

32.7×0.48

1.2   1.6   12   16   120   160 *1 mark*

c Estimate the answer to $\dfrac{8.62 + 22.1}{5.23}$

Give your answer to **1 significant figure**. *1 mark*

d **Estimate** the answer to $\dfrac{28.6 \times 24.4}{5.67 \times 4.02}$. *1 mark*

3 Look at these number cards.

0.2   2   10   0.1   0.05   1

a Choose two of the cards to give the **lowest possible answer**.
Fill in the cards below and work out the answer.

 $\times$ ☐ = ... *2 marks*

b Choose two of the cards to give the answer **100**.

☐ $\div$ ☐ = 100 *1 mark*

4 Look at these expressions.

$$n - 2 \quad 2n \quad n^2 \quad \frac{n}{2} \quad \frac{2}{n}$$

  a Which expression gives the greatest value when *n* is **between 1 and 2**?

1 mark

  b Which expression gives the greatest value when *n* is **between 0 and 1**?

1 mark

  c Which expression gives the greatest value when *n* is **negative**?

1 mark

5 The ship *Queen Mary* used to sail across the Atlantic Ocean.

The ship's usual speed was **33 miles per hour**.

On average, the ship used fuel at the rate of **1 gallon** for every **13 feet** sailed.

Calculate how many gallons of fuel the ship used in one hour of travelling at the usual speed. (There are 5280 feet in one mile.)

Show your working and write down the **full calculator display**.

2 marks

Now write your answer correct to **2 significant figures**.

1 mark

6 **a** Write the values of *k* and *m*.

    $64 = 8^2 = 4^k = 2^m$

2 marks

  b Complete the following.

    $2^{15} = 32\,768$

    $2^{14} = \ldots\ldots$

1 mark

7 A groundsman marks out a football pitch.

a He makes the pitch 93 metres long, to the nearest metre.

What is the **shortest possible** length of the pitch?

1 mark

b He makes the pitch 50 metres wide, to the nearest metre.

What is the **shortest possible** width of the pitch?

1 mark

c Des wants to know how many times he should run around the outside of this pitch to be sure of running **at least 3 km**.

Use your answers to parts (a) and (b) to find out how many times Des should run around the pitch.

You **must** show your working.

1 mark

8 The table shows the average weekly earnings for men and women in 1956 and 1998.

	1956	1998
Men	£11.89	£420.30
Women	£6.16	£303.70

a For **1956**, calculate the average weekly earnings for women as a percentage of the average weekly earnings for men.

Show your working and give your answer to 1 decimal place.

2 marks

b For **1998**, show that the average weekly earnings for women were a **greater proportion** of the average weekly earnings for men than they were in 1956.

2 marks

9 **a** One calculation below gives the answer to the question:

What is 70 increased by 9%?

Tick (✓) the correct one.

70×0.9 ☐ 70×1.9 ☐ 70×0.09 ☐ 70×1.09 ☐

1 mark

Choose one of the other calculations.

Write a question **about percentages** that this calculation represents.

1 mark

Now do the same for one of the remaining two calculations.

1 mark

b Fill in the missing decimal number.

To decrease by 14%, multiply by _____ .

1 mark

Answers are on page 251.

Finding the *n*th term when the rule is quadratic

> • You should be able to give a rule for the next term or the **n**th term of a number pattern where the rule is quadratic.

LINEAR RULES

- Rules for sequences that increase or decrease by a fixed amount each time are **linear rules** and have the form $an \pm b$.

QUADRATIC RULES

- Sequences that do not increase or decrease by the same amount each time may have **quadratic** rules.
- The sequence 2, 6, 12, 20, 30, ... goes up by 4, then by 6 then by 8, then by 10, then by 12 and so on. Rules for series that increase in this way involve a term in n^2. There are two ways to try to find the pattern.
- **Finding a multiplication sum**
  Some series like the one above may be written as a series of multiplication sums. For example you could write the series as:
  $1 \times 2, 2 \times 3, 3 \times 4, 4 \times 5, 5 \times 6, ...$
  Each part of the multiplication can be expressed as a linear term in n. The first numbers in each multiplication form the series 1, 2, 3, 4, 5, ... which is just n. The second numbers for the series 2, 3, 4, 5, 6, ... which is just $n + 1$.
  This gives the nth term as $n(n + 1)$.
  This can also be written as $n^2 + n$.
- **Differencing**
  You cannot write the series 3, 7, 12, 18, 25, ... as a set of multiplications that gives any sort of pattern. When this happens you can use differencing.
  Write the series as a list and calculate the differences between consecutive terms.

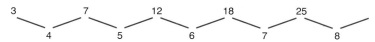

The differences go up by 1 each time. Now find the differences of the differences (called the **second differences**).

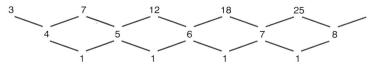

Try this. As the second difference is odd, multiply the original series by 2. This gives 6, 14, 24, 36, 50, ... Now look for a series of multiplications. Try:

$1 \times 6, 2 \times 7, 3 \times 8, 4 \times 9, 5 \times 10$

- This is a nth term of $n(n + 5)$. As you doubled the original series you need to write down the nth term as $\frac{1}{2}n(n + 5)$. Check it and see if it works!

Worked example

Find the nth term of this series.

6, 12, 20, 30, 42, 56, ...

First look for a series of multiplications.

$2 \times 3 \quad 3 \times 4 \quad 4 \times 5 \quad 5 \times 6 \quad 6 \times 7$

Each part of this can be expressed as a linear series in n. For example, the first numbers in the multiplications are 2, 3, 4, 5, 6, ... which is $n + 1$. The second numbers are 3, 4, 5, 6, 7, ... which is the series $n + 2$. This gives the nth term as $(n + 1)(n + 2)$ which can be written as $n^2 + 3n + 2$.

Worked example

Martin is making triangles with marbles. These are his first four patterns.

1 marble   3 marbles   6 marbles   10 marbles

How many marbles will there be in the nth triangle?

Write the pattern out as a list and carry it on a bit.

1, 3, 6, 10, 15, 21, 28, 36, ...

The second difference is odd (1) so double the series.

2, 6, 12, 20, 30, 42, 56, 72, ...

Now look for a multiplication series:

$1 \times 2, 2 \times 3, 3 \times 4, 4 \times 5, 5 \times 6, 6 \times 7, 7 \times 8, 8 \times 9, ...$

Now you can see that this series is $n(n + 1)$. So the nth term of the original series is $\frac{1}{2}n(n + 1)$.

CHECK YOURSELF QUESTIONS

Q1 Find the *n*th term of each of these number patterns.
You will be able to find a multiplication sum for each of them.

   a 3, 8, 15, 24, 35, ...   **b** 2, 6, 12, 20, 30, ...
   c 0, 3, 8, 15, 24, ...   **d** 4, 12, 24, 40, 60, ...

Q2 4, 11, 21, 34, 50, 69, ...

   a Work out the second differences for the series above.
   b Multiply the original series by 2.
   c Find a multiplication series for your answer to (b).
      Hint: it starts $1 \times 8, 2 \times 11$.
   d Write down the *n*th term of the series
      8, 11, 14, 17, 20, ...
   e Write down the *n*th term of the original series.

Q3 Find the *n*th term of each of these number patterns.
You will need to double each series and look for a multiplication
sum of the doubled series.

   a 2, 5, 9, 14, 20, ...
   b 7, 12, 18, 25, 33, ...

Q4 Find how many matches are needed for the *n*th pattern for the
series of pictures below.

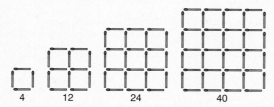

4   12   24   40

Answers are on page 237.

Solving simultaneous equations by algebra

What you should already know

- *How to solve a linear equation*

- *How to substitute into algebraic expressions*

- *How to do simple algebraic operations such as $2 \times 3x = 6x$ and $6y - 4y = 2y$*

- You should be able to solve simultaneous equations algebraically.

THE SIX STEPS
- There are six steps in solving simultaneous equations.
- These are **balancing, eliminating, solving, substituting, solving again** and **checking.**
- The equation $2x + y = 5$ has an infinite number of solutions. For example $x = 2$, $y = 1$ is one solution; $x = {}^{-}1$, $y = 7$ is another. The equation $3x - 2y = 4$ also has an infinite number of solutions. For example $x = 2$, $y = 1$ and $x = 6$, $y = 7$ both work. However only one solution fits both equations at the same time (simultaneously).

Worked example

Solve: $2x + 3y = 30$
$\qquad 5x + 7y = 71$

$2x + 3y = 30$	**1**
$5x + 7y = 71$	**2**
$\mathbf{1} \times 5$	
$10x + 15y = 150$	**3**
$\mathbf{2} \times 2$	
$10x + 14y = 142$	**4**

Step 1: Balancing Multiply equation **1** by 5 and equation **2** by 2. This gives two more equations but they have the same coefficient for x. Call them **3** and **4**.

$\mathbf{3} - \mathbf{4}$
$$10x + 15y = 150$$
$$\underline{10x + 14y = 142}$$
$$\qquad\quad y = \quad 8$$

Step 2: Elimination Equation **3** and equation **4** now have the same number of xs and they are both positive. Subtract equation **4** from equation **3** to eliminate the x-terms.

Step 3: Solving You are left with a simple equation involving y. Solve this to find y. (This is already done!)

Substitute in **1**
$2x + 3 \times 8 = 30$

Step 4: Substituting Substitute the value of y into one of the original equations.

$2x = 6$ (subtract 24)
$\ x = 3$ (divide by 2)

Step 5: Solving again You have a linear equation in x. Solve this to find x.

$2 \times 3 + 3 \times 8 = 30$ ✓
$5 \times 3 + 7 \times 8 = 71$ ✓

Step 6: Checking Put the values of x and y into both of the original equations to check that they work.

SOLVING PROBLEMS

- Solving simultaneous equations can be useful in real-life situations.

Worked example

When Mr Walsh goes to the garage he always buys petrol and some cans of cola. Last week he bought four gallons of petrol and three cans of cola. His bill was £11.75. Yesterday he bought five gallons of petrol and four cans of cola. His bill was £14.80. Today he has just bought two gallons of petrol and one can of cola. Assuming the prices of petrol and cola haven't changed, what is his bill today?

Call the cost of a gallon of petrol p and a can of cola c, and work in pence, to form two equations.

$$4p + 3c = 1175 \quad \mathbf{1}$$

$$5p + 4c = 1480 \quad \mathbf{2}$$

$\mathbf{1} \times 5 \qquad 20p + 15c = 5875 \quad \mathbf{3}$

$\mathbf{2} \times 4 \qquad 20p + 16c = 5920 \quad \mathbf{4}$

$\mathbf{4} - \mathbf{3} \qquad\qquad 1c = 45 \qquad \mathbf{4} - \mathbf{3}$ keeps everything positive.

Substitute in $\mathbf{1}$ $\quad 4p + 3 \times 45 = 1175$

(Subtract 135) $\qquad\qquad 4p = 1040$

(Divide by 4) $\qquad\qquad p = 260$

Check: $4 \times 260 + 3 \times 45 = 1175$ ✓ and $5 \times 260 + 4 \times 45 = 1480$ ✓

His bill today will be $2 \times £2.60 + £0.45 = £5.65$.

? CHECK YOURSELF QUESTIONS

Q1 Solve these simultaneous equations. (They are already balanced.)

  a $x - y = 8$ **b** $2x + 3y = 1$
      $x + 2y = 14$ $2x + y = 3$
  c $3x - y = 7$ **d** $4a + 5b = 6$
      $2x + y = 8$ $7a + 5b = 3$

Q2 Solve these simultaneous equations. (Multiply one to balance the equations.)

  a $3x - y = 8$ **b** $5x + 3y = 7$
      $2x + 2y = 8$ $4x - y = 9$
  c $3x - 4y = 7$ **d** $3a + b = 13$
      $x + 2y = 9$ $7a + 5b = 9$

Q3 Solve these simultaneous equations. (Multiply both of them to balance them.)

  a $5x - 3y = 18$ **b** $2x + 3y = 1$
      $3x + 2y = 7$ $5x + 2y = 8$
  c $3x - 5y = 0$ **d** $4a + 5b = 4$
      $2x + 7y = 31$ $6a + 4b = 20$

Q4 Mr Li buys two bags of tulip bulbs and seven bags of daffodils, and pays £13.10. His wife buys three bags of tulips and four bags of daffodils, for £9.90.

  a Set up a pair of simultaneous equations. (Use t for tulips and d for daffodils.)

  b Use them to find the cost of each bag.

Q5 The Mays buy three cups of tea and five sticky buns, for £6.30. The Lees buy four cups of tea and three sticky buns, for £5.10. The Hills buy two cups of tea and two sticky buns. How much do they pay?

Q6 Six teachers and 48 pupils pay £138 to see *Hamlet*. Five teachers and 22 pupils pay £70. Teachers' tickets cost £x each and pupils' tickets cost £y each. Form two simultaneous equations and solve them to find what three teachers and 35 pupils pay.

Answers are on page 238.

Using graphs to solve simultaneous equations

- **You should be able to solve simultaneous equations graphically.**

THE POINT OF INTERSECTION

- Equations such as $y = 2x + 3$ and $2x - y = 4$ can be represented by **linear** (straight-line) graphs. Each point on the line represents one of the infinitely-many solutions for the equation of that line.
- Unless two lines are parallel they must cross at some point. This **point of intersection** is the solution of both lines. In other words it is the one solution that is true for both lines simultaneously.
- The coordinates of point of intersection give the solution to the problem.

Worked example

Use a graph to solve $y = 2x - 1$
$$x + y = 8$$

Use the gradient-intercept method to draw the first graph. The line crosses the y-axis at $^-1$ and has a gradient of 2.

Use the cover-up method to draw the second graph. The line crosses the x-axis at **8** and the y-axis at **8**.

The two graphs cross at $x = 3$, $y = 5$ so the solution of the original equations is $x = 3$ and $y = 5$.

Check these values in the original equations

$5 = 2 \times 3 - 1$ ✓
$3 + 5 = 8$ ✓

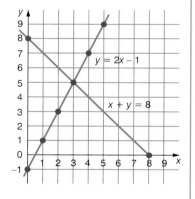

Worked example

Use a graph to solve $2x + y = 5$
$$3x - 2y = 4$$

Use the cover-up method to draw both of these graphs. The first graph crosses the x-axis at 2.5 and the y-axis at 5. The second graph crosses the x-axis at 1.33 and the y-axis at $^-2$.

They cross at $x = 2$, $y = 1$, giving the solution $x = 2$ and $y = 1$.

Check these values in the original equation.

$2 \times 2 + 1 = 5$ ✓
$3 \times 2 - 2 \times 1 = 4$ ✓

Worked example

Use a graph to solve $y = \dfrac{x}{2} - 3$

$\qquad\qquad\qquad y = 2x - 5$

Use the gradient-intercept method to draw both graphs.

They appear to cross at $(1.3, ^-2.3)$.

Check: $^-2.3 = 1.3 \div 2 - 3 = {}^-2.35$ (close)

$\qquad\ ^-2.3 = 2 \times 1.3 - 5 = {}^-2.4$ (close)

This result is good enough, as it was read from a graph.

The actual answer is $x = 1\frac{1}{3}, y = {}^-2\frac{2}{3}$.

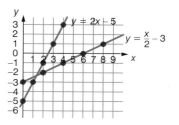

CHECK YOURSELF QUESTIONS

Q1 Draw graphs to solve these simultaneous equations.

   a $2x + 3y = 12$ **b** $3x - y = 7$

       $2x - y = 4$ $2x + y = 8$

Q2 The line $y = x$ is already drawn on the grid.

   a Use this table to help you draw the line $y = 2x - 1$.

   b Solve the pair of simultaneous equations $y = x$ and $y = 2x - 1$.

x	0	1	2
y			

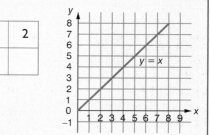

Q3 Draw graphs to solve these equations.

   $y = 2x + 1$

   $x - 2y = 1$

Q4 The line $y = \frac{1}{2}x - 3$ is drawn on the grid.

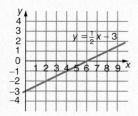

   a On the same grid draw the line $x + y = 4$.

   b Find the point of intersection of the graph.

       Check that your answer works for both lines.

Answers are on page 238.

Solving inequalities

What you should already know

- *How to solve simple linear equations*
- *How to substitute into formulae that use powers*

Note:

You have used inequalities in expressions such as $^-3 \leqslant x \leqslant 3$, when drawing linear graphs. This expression means x is bigger than or equal to $^-3$ but smaller than or equal to 3.

TYPES OF INEQUALITY

- There are two types of inequality.
- **Strict inequalities** use the signs $<$ (less than) and $>$ (greater than).
- **Inclusive inequalities** use the signs $\leqslant$ (less than or equal to) and $\geqslant$ (greater than or equal to).
- In inclusive inequalities, the limiting number or boundary is included.

> **Worked example**
>
> x is an integer. What values can x take if $^-3 < x \leqslant 2$?
>
> Integers are positive or negative whole numbers. The value $^-3$ is not included as x is greater than $^-3$. 2 is included as x is less than or equal to 2. So x can take the values $^-2, ^-1, 0, 1$ and 2.

THE NUMBER LINE

- Inequalities can be represented on number lines.
- Strict inequalities are shown by open circles to indicate that the boundary is not included.
- Inclusive inequalities are shown by solid circles to indicate that the limiting point is included.

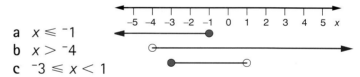

a $x \leqslant {}^-1$
b $x > {}^-4$
c $^-3 \leqslant x < 1$

SOLVING INEQUALITIES

- If $x + 4 < 6$, then x can take a range of values up to but not including 2. For example, $1 + 4 = 5 < 6$, $^-5 + 4 = {}^-1 < 6$, $1.99 + 4 = 5.99 < 6$.
- The solution would be written as $x < 2$ and could be shown on a number line.

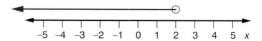

- Remember: 'Treat an inequality like an equation'.

Worked example

Solve these inequalities.

a $\dfrac{x}{2} - 3 > 5$

b $5x - 3 \leqslant 2x + 9$

a $\dfrac{x}{2} > 8$ (add 3)

$\quad x > 16$ (multiply by 2)

b $3x - 3 \leqslant 9$ (subtract $2x$)
$\quad 3x \leqslant 12$ (add 3)
$\quad\quad x \leqslant 4$ (divide by 3)

NEGATIVE COEFFICIENTS FOR THE VARIABLE

- The rule does not work with negative values. There are two ways to deal with this.
  - Move the letter term over the inequality to make it positive.
  - Reverse all the signs and reverse the inequality sign.

Worked example

Solve these inequalities.

a $3 - 2x < 7$

b $4 - \dfrac{x}{3} \geqslant 2$

a Move the x-term across
inequality sign.
$\quad 3 < 7 + 2x$ (add $2x$)
$\quad ^-4 < 2x$ (subtract 7)
$\quad ^-2 < x$ (divide by 2)
$\quad\; x > ^-2$ (write 'backwards')

b $-\dfrac{x}{3} \geqslant {}^-2$ (subtract 4)

$\quad ^-x \geqslant {}^-6$ (multiply by 3)
$\quad\; x \leqslant 6$ (change all signs,
$\qquad\qquad$ including the inequality
$\qquad\qquad$ sign)

? CHECK YOURSELF QUESTIONS

Q1 n is an integer. What values can n take for these ranges?
   a $^-2 < n < 5$ **b** $0 \leqslant n < 6$
   c $^-3 \leqslant n \leqslant 4$

Q2 Draw these inequalities on a number line.
   a $x > {}^-1$ **b** $x \leqslant 5$
   c $^-1 \leqslant x < 4$

Q3 What inequalities are represented on these number lines?

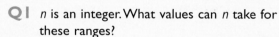

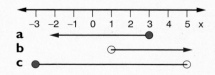

a
b
c

Q4 Solve these inequalities.
   a $x - 6 < 7$ **b** $\dfrac{x}{2} \geqslant 4$

Q5 Solve these inequalities.
   a $2x + 4 \leqslant x - 5$
   b $3x - 2 \geqslant 4(5 - 2x)$

Q6 Solve these inequalities.
   a $3 - x < 9$ **b** $2 - \dfrac{x}{4} \leqslant 6$

Q7 If $x^2 \leqslant 9$ explain why x can take any value between $^-3$ and 3 inclusive.

Q8 **a** What integers obey the inequality
       $^-4 \leqslant x < 3$?
   b What is the largest value x^2 can take?

Answers are on page 238.

Expanding brackets

What you should already know

- *How to multiply out brackets*
- *How to simplify expressions and collect like terms*

- **You should be able to expand an expression such as $(x + 2)(x + 3)$.**

FOIL

- The best way to recall how to expand an expression such as $(x + 2)(x + 3)$ is to remember **FOIL** which stands for First, Outer, Inner, Last.
- You must multiply *each* of the two terms in the first bracket by each of the two terms in the second bracket.
  - Multiply together the **first** terms in each bracket.
    $(x + 2)(x + 3)$ $x \times x = x^2$
  - Multiply together the **outer** terms in each bracket.
    $(x + 2)(x + 3)$ $x \times 3 = 3x$
  - Multiply together the **inner** terms in each bracket.
    $(x + 2)(x + 3)$ $2 \times x = 2x$
  - Multiply together the **last** terms in each bracket.
    $(x + 2)(x + 3)$ $2 \times 3 = 6$
  - Now combine the terms.
    $x^2 + 3x + 2x + 6 = x^2 + 5x + 6$

Worked example
Expand **a** $(x + 4)(x - 2)$ **b** $(x - 3)(x - 5)$

Using FOIL:

a $(x + 4)(x - 2) = x^2 - 2x + 4x - 8 = x^2 + 2x - 8$
b $(x - 3)(x - 5) = x^2 - 5x - 3x + 15 = x^2 - 8x + 15$

❓ CHECK YOURSELF QUESTIONS

Expand the brackets.

Q1 a $(x + 3)(x + 5)$ **b** $(x + 6)(x + 3)$ **c** $(x + 4)^2$

Q2 a $(x - 1)(x + 5)$ **b** $(x + 2)(x - 5)$ **c** $(x - 3)(x + 3)$

Q3 a $(x - 1)(x - 4)$ **b** $(x - 5)(x - 6)$ **c** $(x - 3)^2$

Answers are on page 239.

1 Each term of a number sequence is made by adding 1 to the numerator and 2 to the denominator of the previous term.

Here is the beginning of the number sequence:

$\frac{1}{3}, \frac{2}{5}, \frac{3}{7}, \frac{4}{9}, \frac{5}{11}, \ldots$

  a Write an expression for the **nth term** of the sequence.   *1 mark*

  b The *n*th term of a different sequence is $\frac{n}{n^2 + 1}$.

     The **first term** of the sequence is $\frac{1}{2}$.

     Write down the **next three** terms.   *2 marks*

2 Look at this graph.

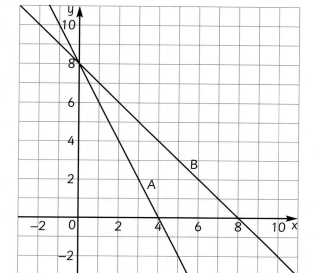

  a Show that the equation of line **A** is $2x + y = 8$.   *1 mark*

  b Write the equation of line **B**.   *1 mark*

  c On the graph, draw the line with equation $y = 2x + 1$.
     Label your line **C**.   *1 mark*

  d Solve these simultaneous equations.

     $y = 2x + 1$
     $3y = 4x + 6$

     Show your working.   *1 mark*

3 Solve these equations. Show your working.

  a $4 - 2y = 10 - 6y$ *2 marks*

  b $5y + 20 = 3(y - 4)$ *2 marks*

4 **a** Two of the expressions below are **equivalent**.
     Circle them.

     $5(2y + 4)$ $5(2y + 20)$ $7(y + 9)$ $10(y + 9)$ $2(5y + 10)$ *1 mark*

  b One of the expressions below is **not** a correct factorisation of $12y + 24$.
     Which one is it? Put a cross (**✗**) through it.

     $12(y + 2)$ $3(4y + 8)$ $2(6y + 12)$ $12(y + 24)$ $6(2y + 4)$ *1 mark*

  c Factorise this expression.

     $7y + 14$ *1 mark*

  d Factorise this expression as fully as possible.

     $6y^3 - 2y^2$ *1 mark*

5 a m is an **odd** number.

Which of the numbers below must be even, and which must be odd?
Write 'odd' or 'even' under each one.

$2m$ $\qquad$ m^2 $\qquad$ $3m - 1$ $\qquad$ $(m - 1)(m + 1)$

...... $\qquad$ ...... $\qquad$ ...... $\qquad$ ......

2 marks

b m is an **odd** number.

Is the number $\dfrac{m + 1}{2}$ odd or even, or it is impossible to tell?

Tick (✓) the correct box.

odd ☐ $\quad$ even ☐ $\quad$ impossible to tell ☐

1 mark

Explain your answer.

6 Here are six different equations, labelled A to F.

A $y = 3x - 4$ $\qquad$ **B** $y = 4$ $\qquad$ **C** $x = {}^-5$

D $x + y = 10$ $\qquad$ **E** $y = 2x + 1$ $\qquad$ **F** $y = x^2$

Think about the graphs of these equations.

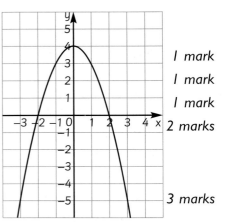

a Which graph goes through the point **(0, 0)**? $\qquad$ *1 mark*

b Which graph is parallel to the y-axis? $\qquad$ *1 mark*

c Which graph is **not** a **straight line**? $\qquad$ *1 mark*

d Which **two** graphs pass through the point **(3, 7)**? $\qquad$ *2 marks*

e The diagram shows the graph of the equation
$y = 4 - x^2$. What are the coordinates of the points
where the graph of this equation meets the graph
of equation **E**? $\qquad$ *3 marks*

7 For each part of the question, tick (✓) the statement that is true.

a When x is even, $(x - 2)^2$ is even. ☐

When x is even, $(x - 2)^2$ is odd. ☐

Show how you know it is true for **all** even values of x. $\qquad$ *1 mark*

b When x is even, $(x - 1)(x + 1)$ is even. ☐

When x is even, $(x - 1)(x + 1)$ is odd. ☐

Show how you know it is true for **all** even values of x. $\qquad$ *1 mark*

8 The subject of the equation below is p.

$p = 2(e + f)$

Rearrange the equation to make f the subject. $\qquad$ *2 marks*

9 The simplified graph shows the flight details of an aeroplane travelling from London to Madrid, via Brussels.

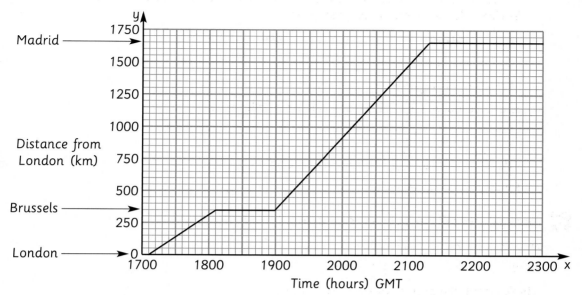

a What is the aeroplane's average speed from **London** to **Brussels**?   *1 mark*

b How can you tell from the graph, **without calculating**, that the aeroplane's average speed from Brussels to Madrid is **greater** than its average speed from London to Brussels?   *1 mark*

c A different aeroplane flies **from** Madrid **to** London, via Brussels. The flight details are shown below.

Madrid		
Brussels	*depart*	1800
	arrive	2000
	depart	2112
London	*arrive*	2218

On the graph, show this aeroplane's journey from Madrid to London, via Brussels. (Do not change the labels on the graph.)
Assume constant speed for each part of the journey.   *2 marks*

d At what time are the two aeroplanes the same distance from London?   *1 mark*

Answers are on page 251.

REVISION SESSION 10 — Pythagoras' theorem

> • You should understand and be able to apply Pythagoras' theorem when solving problems in two dimensions.

USING PYTHAGORAS' THEOREM

- You can use Pythagoras' theorem to calculate the third side in a right-angled triangle if you know the other two sides.
- The longest side c is called the **hypotenuse** and is always opposite the right angle.
- Make sure that you are familiar with the x^2 and $\sqrt{}$ buttons on your calculator.
- When you use Pythagoras' theorem, remember this table.

Pythagoras' theorem: for any right-angled triangle:

$$a^2 + b^2 = c^2$$

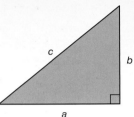

To calculate the hypotenuse	To calculate a short side
1 Square both numbers.	1 Square both numbers.
2 Add the two numbers together.	2 Subtract the smaller number from the larger number.
3 Take the square root.	3 Take the square root.

Worked example

Find the value of x on the diagram.

Try this on your calculator.

You may not have to press the = button at the end. You should get the answer 5.

x is the hypotenuse.
$x^2 = 3^2 + 4^2$
$x^2 = 9 + 16 = 25$
$x = \sqrt{25}$
$x = 5\,\text{cm}$

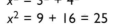
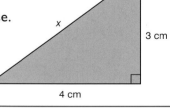

Worked example

Find the value of x on the diagram.

Try this on your calculator.

You may not have to press the = button at the end. You should get the answer 12.

x is one of the shorter sides.
$x^2 = 13^2 - 5^2$
$ = 169 - 25 = 144$
$x = \sqrt{144}$
$x = 12\,\text{cm}$

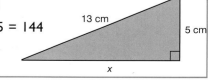

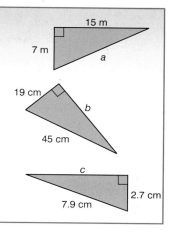

Worked example

Calculate the length of the missing side in each of these right-angled triangles. Give your answers correct to 3 significant figures.

a a is the hypotenuse.

$a^2 = 15^2 + 7^2 = 274$

$a = \sqrt{274}$

$a = 16.6\,m$ (to 3 s.f.)

b b is a short side.

$b^2 = 45^2 - 19^2 = 1664$

$b = \sqrt{1664}$

$b = 40.8\,cm$ (to 3 s.f.)

c c is a short side.

$c^2 = 7.9^2 - 2.7^2 = 55.12$

$c = \sqrt{55.12} = 7.42\,cm$ (to 3 s.f.)

Worked example

Abigail and Simon are on a day's hike over the moors. They set off from the car park and walk 7 km due east before stopping for a coffee break. They then continue walking due north for a further 6.5 km when they stop for lunch. After lunch they decide to go directly back to the car park. How far will they have to walk? Give your answer to a suitable degree of accuracy.

Using Pythagoras' theorem:

$x^2 = 7^2 + 6.5^2 = 91.25$

$x = \sqrt{91.25}$

$x = 9.6\,km$ (to 1 d.p.)

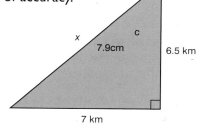

Hint:

Draw a diagram which includes the right angle and the distances. Label the unknown distance x.

Since the original distances are no more accurate than 1 decimal place, it makes sense to give the answer to the same degree of accuracy.

? CHECK YOURSELF QUESTIONS

Q1 Calculate the length of the missing side in each of these right-angled triangles. Give your answers correct to 2 decimal places.

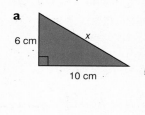

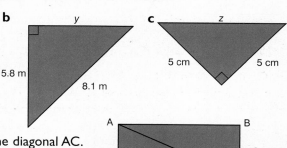

Q2 ABCD is a rectangle. Calculate the length of the diagonal AC. Give your answer correct to 2 significant figures.

Q3 XYZ is an isosceles triangle with XY = XZ = 16 cm and YZ = 12 cm.

    a Calculate the perpendicular height h. Give your answer to the nearest centimetre.

    b Hence calculate the area of triangle XYZ.

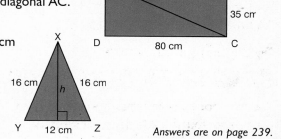

Answers are on page 239.

Areas of compound shapes and volumes of prisms

- You should be able to calculate lengths, areas and volumes in plane shapes and right prisms.

FINDING AREAS OF COMPOUND SHAPES

- A **compound** shape is any shape made up from two or more basic shapes.
- You can find the area of a compound shape by breaking it down into basic shapes and then using the standard area formulae for each one.
- You find the total area by addition or subtraction.

Worked example

Mr Slack wanted to find the area of his garden patio so that he could pave it. He drew a sketch first and made the measurements shown. He saw that he needed to know the length x on the diagram.

a Why does Mr Slack need this measurement?

b Calculate the length x.

c Find the area of the patio.

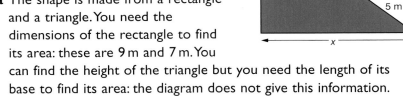

a The shape is made from a rectangle and a triangle. You need the dimensions of the rectangle to find its area: these are 9 m and 7 m. You can find the height of the triangle but you need the length of its base to find its area: the diagram does not give this information.

b The height of the triangle = $9 - 6 = 3$ m.
Let the base of the triangle = y.
It is a right-angled triangle, so use Pythagoras' theorem.
$y^2 = 5^2 - 3^2 = 25 - 9 = 16$ so $y = 4$ m
$x = 7 + y = 11$ m

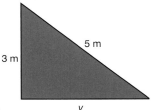

c The area of the rectangle = $9 \times 7 = 63$ m^2.
The area of the triangle = $\frac{1}{2} \times 4 \times 3 = 6$ m^2.
The area of the patio = $63 + 6 = 69$ m^2.

Draw a grid with x and y axes labelled from 0 to 10. Plot the points
A(6, 2), B(7, 4), C(7, 8), D(8, 10), E(9, 8), F(9, 4), G(10, 2). Join the
points to form a 'rocket' shape.

a Find the area of the rocket.
b Enlarge the rocket by a scale factor $\frac{1}{2}$ about the origin.
c Find the area of the enlarged rocket.
d Find the ratio of the areas of the two rockets.

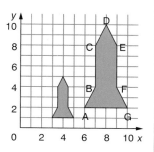

a The rocket is made of three shapes.
Area of triangle CDE = $\frac{1}{2} \times 2 \times 2 = 2$
Area of rectangle BCEF = $4 \times 2 = 8$
Area of trapezium ABFG = $\frac{1}{2}(4 + 2) \times 2 = 6$
Area of rocket = 16

b To enlarge a shape about the origin, you multiply each number in
the coordinates by the scale factor. If the scale factor is $\frac{1}{2}$, this will
mean halving all the numbers. So the new coordinates to be plotted
are: (3, 1), $(3\frac{1}{2}, 2)$, $(3\frac{1}{2}, 4)$, (4, 5), $(4\frac{1}{2}, 4)$, $(4\frac{1}{2}, 2)$, (5, 1).

c Area of small triangle = $\frac{1}{2} \times 1 \times 1 = \frac{1}{2}$
Area of small rectangle = $2 \times 1 = 2$
Area of small trapezium = $\frac{1}{2}(2 + 1) \times 1 = 1\frac{1}{2}$
Area of 'enlarged' rocket = 4
d Ratio of areas of rockets = 16 : 4 = 4 : 1

Notice that the
enlarged shape is $\frac{1}{2}$
the size of the
original and so is
actually made smaller.
You still call this an
'enlargement' in
mathematics.

VOLUME OF A PRISM

- A **prism** is a 3-D shape with a **uniform cross-section**. This means
  that both ends of a prism are the same shape.
- To find the volume of a prism, use the formula $V = Al$, where
  A is the area of the cross-section and l is the length or height.
- Learn how to use the formulae for the volumes of these prisms.

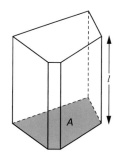

The triangular prism   The trapezoidal prism   The cylinder

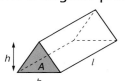

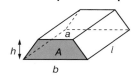
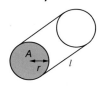

$V = Al = \frac{1}{2}bhl$ $V = Al = \frac{1}{2}(a + b)hl$ $V = Al = \pi r^2 l$

The diagram shows the dimensions of a doorstop that is in the shape
of a wedge. Find its volume.

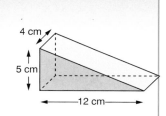

The cross-section of the wedge is a right-angled triangle with area A.
$A = \frac{1}{2} \times 12 \times 5 = 30$
The length of the wedge is 4 cm.
The volume of the wedge = $V = 30 \times 4 = 120 \text{ cm}^3$.

Worked example

A waste skip is used for removing rubble from a building site. The diagram shows the dimensions of the skip. Its cross-section is a trapezium. Find its volume.

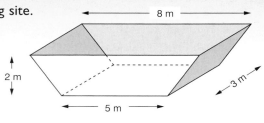

The area of the trapezium = $A = \frac{1}{2}(5 + 8) \times 2 = 13$.
The length of the skip is 3 m.
The volume of the skip = $V = 13 \times 3 = 39$ m³.

Worked example

Joey has been on holiday to Torquay. The diagram shows a stick of rock he brought back as a present. Its length is 30 cm and its diameter is 3 cm. Calculate the volume of the stick of rock. Give your answer to 1 decimal place. (Use calculator value for π.)

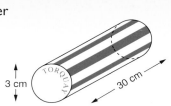

The diameter of the stick of rock is 3 cm so its radius is 1.5 cm.
Using the formula $V = \pi r^2 l$:
$V = \pi \times 1.5^2 \times 30 = 212.058$.
The volume of the stick of rock = 212.1 cm³ (1 d.p.).

CHECK YOURSELF QUESTIONS

Q1 Calculate the areas of these compound shapes.

a
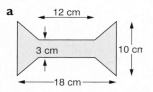

b

c
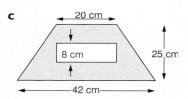

d
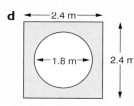

Q2 Find the volume of the tent in the diagram.

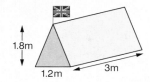

Q3 The diagram shows the dimensions of a swimming pool.

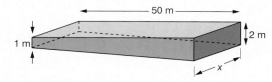

When full the pool holds 900 m³ of water. Find the width x.

Answers are on page 239.

> • You should be able to determine the locus of an object moving according to some rule.

What you should already know

• *How to use a pair of compasses to draw circles*

• *How to draw scale diagrams*

THE LOCUS OF A SET OF POINTS

• A **locus** is a path. It shows all the points that satisfy a certain description or rule on a diagram. For example, a jet aircraft leaves a vapour trail in the sky. This trail is the locus of the aircraft as it moves in the atmosphere.

• You must always show **boundary lines** accurately and shade **regions** correctly.

• If you want to include a boundary, use a solid line. If you don't want to include a boundary, use a dotted line.

Note:

The plural of locus is loci.

Worked example

Draw the locus of a point which is:

a exactly 5 cm from a fixed point A
b 5 cm or less from a fixed point A
c less than 5 cm from a fixed point A.

The circles must be accurately drawn, with a pair of compasses.

a All the points on the circle are exactly 5 cm from A.

b All the points inside and on the circle are 5 cm or less from A. Use a solid line for the boundary.

c Only the points that are inside the circle are less than 5 cm from A. Points on the boundary are not, so use a dotted line.

Worked example

Draw the locus of a point that is equidistant from two points A and B that are 8 cm apart.

All the points on the line XY are the same distance, or equidistant, from the points A and B. The line XY bisects the line AB at right angles (and is infinitely long!). The line XY is the perpendicular bisector of AB and is easy to construct with a pair of compasses.

Try it for yourself. This is the shape you should get.

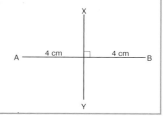

Worked example

Draw the locus of a point that is always less than 3 cm from the line AB.

The drawing must be accurate: the two semicircles must each have a radius of 3 cm. Try it for yourself. The diagram shows the shape you should get. The shaded region shows the locus of all the points that are less than 3 cm from AB. The boundary line should not be included, so it is drawn as a dotted line.

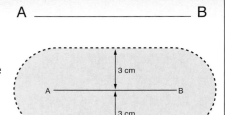

Worked example

Lighthouse A and Lighthouse B are 10 miles apart on the coast. Lighthouse A can be seen by ships from up to 6 miles away and Lighthouse B can be seen by ships from up to 8 miles away. Draw a scale diagram to show the region for which a ship can see both lighthouses. Use a scale of 1 cm to represent 2 miles.

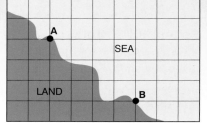

The diagram must be accurately drawn.

Draw a circle with radius 3 cm centred at A and a circle with radius 4 cm centred at B. The locus is the region that lies inside both circles but does not include the land. The boundary lines should be included.

Try it for yourself. The diagram shows the shape you should get.

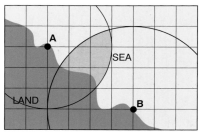

CHECK YOURSELF QUESTIONS

Q1 Draw the locus of a point that is equidistant from a pair of parallel lines.

Q2 Draw the locus of a point which is:
   a exactly 3 cm from a fixed point A
   b between 3 cm and 5 cm from a fixed point A.

Q3 In a game of bowls, the ideal position for the jack to stop is less than 2 m from the line AB and less than 4 m from the point X which is itself 5 m from AB. Draw a scale diagram to show the ideal region for the jack to stop. Use a scale of 1 cm to represent 1 m.

Q4 Liam is behind the shed. He is hiding from his father who is reading his newspaper in the garden.
Copy the diagram and show the region in the garden where Liam cannot be seen by his father.

Answers are on page 239.

Accuracy of measurement and compound measures

> • You should know that measurement is continuous and that measures given to the nearest whole number can be in error by up to one half a unit.
>
> • You should be able to use compound measures such as speed.

What you should already know

• *How to round numbers*

UPPER AND LOWER BOUNDS FOR MEASUREMENT

• When you measure quantities such as height, weight, distance and time, the measurement is often given to the nearest unit.

• You need to know that any measurement you make is inaccurate by up to half a unit in either direction. For example, if you say that your height is 162 cm to the nearest centimetre, you must remember that the smallest number that can be rounded up to 162 is 161.5 and the largest number that can be rounded down to 162 is just less than 162.5 (since 162.5 would be rounded up to 163).

• The measurement for 162 cm can be shown on a number line.

| 161 | 161.5 | 162 | 162.5 | 163 |

• ● means that 161.5 is included. It is the **lower bound** for the measurement.
  ○ means that 162.5 is not included. It is the **upper bound** for the measurement.

• The interval in which the true height, h, can lie is a number between 161.5 and 162.5 and includes 161.5. This can be written as 161.5 cm $\leqslant h <$ 162.5 cm.

Worked example

Helen says that her weight is 58 kg to the nearest kilogram. Write down the interval in which her true weight, w, must lie.

The lower bound for her weight is 57.5 kg and the upper bound for her weight is 58.5 kg. Her true weight must lie in the interval 57.5 kg $\leqslant w <$ 58.5 kg.

Worked example

Steve runs a 100 m race in 15.2 seconds, to the nearest tenth of a second. Write down the interval in which his true time, t, must lie.

The lower bound for his time is 15.15 s and the upper bound is 15.25 s. His true time must lie in the interval 15.15 s $\leqslant t <$ 15.25 s.

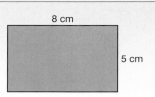

8 cm

5 cm

Worked example

The sides of this rectangle have been rounded to the nearest centimetre.

a Find the interval in which the true length, l, must lie.
b Find the interval in which the true width, w, must lie.
c Find the interval in which the true area, A, must lie.

a The lower bound for l is 7.5 and the upper bound is 8.5.
  The interval is $7.5\,\text{cm} \leqslant l < 8.5\,\text{cm}$.
b The lower bound for w is 4.5 and the upper bound is 5.5.
  The interval is $4.5\,\text{cm} \leqslant w < 5.5\,\text{cm}$.
c The lower bound for the area is the product of the lower bounds for l and w. This is $7.5 \times 4.5 = 33.75$. The upper bound is the product of the upper bounds for l and w. This is $8.5 \times 5.5 = 46.75$.

  The true area must lie in the interval $33.75\,\text{cm}^2 \leqslant A < 46.75\,\text{cm}^2$.

COMPOUND MEASURES

- Some quantities, such as speed and density, must be expressed in terms of two measures. You need to take two measurements to express these quantities correctly.
- Speed is a measure of distance and time. The units of speed are:
  - miles per hour (mph)
  - kilometres per hour (km/h)
  - metres per second (m/s).
- Density is a measure of mass and volume. The units of density are:
  - kilograms per cubic metre (kg/m^3)
  - grams per cubic centimetre (g/cm^3).
- The formula connecting speed (s), distance (d) and time (t) is: $d = st$. You can remember this by using the speed formula triangle. This shows that:

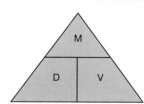

$$d = st \qquad s = \frac{d}{t} \qquad t = \frac{d}{s}$$

- The formula connecting density (D), mass (M) and volume (V) is: $M = DV$. You can remember this by using the density formula triangle. This shows that:

$$M = DV \quad D = \frac{M}{V} \quad V = \frac{M}{D}$$

Worked example

A train leaves London Euston at 8.00 am and arrives at Manchester Piccadilly at 10.30 am. Find the average speed of the train if the distance travelled by the train is 200 miles.

Use the formula $s = \dfrac{d}{t}$ with $d = 200$ and $t = 2\frac{1}{2}$.

$s = 200 \div 2\frac{1}{2} = 80$ mph

Worked example

A Jumbo Jet travels at an average speed of 420 km/h. Find the distance it travels on a $3\frac{1}{2}$ hour flight.

Use the formula $d = st$ with $s = 420$ and $t = 3\frac{1}{2}$.

$d = 420 \times 3\frac{1}{2} = 1470$ km

Worked example

A 1 kg bag of sugar has a volume of 880 cm³. Find the density of the sugar in g/cm³.

Use the formula $D = \dfrac{M}{V}$ with $M = 1000$ g and $V = 880$ cm³.

$D = 1000 \div 880 = 1.1$ g/cm³ (to 1 d.p.)

Worked example

The wooden block has a density of 0.8 g/cm³.

a Find the volume of the block.
b Hence calculate the mass of the block, in grams.

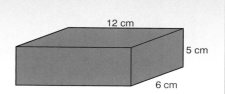

a $V = 12 \times 6 \times 5 = 360$ cm³
b Use the formula $M = DV$ with $D = 0.8$ and $V = 360$.
  $M = 0.8 \times 360 = 288$ g

CHECK YOURSELF QUESTIONS

Q1 The distance by road between London and Edinburgh is given as 410 miles to the nearest 10 miles. Write down the interval in which the true distance, d, must lie.

Q2 The volume of a bottle of wine is 70 cl to the nearest cl. Write down the interval in which the true volume, V, must lie.

Q3 Andy is taking part in a swimming gala and his time for the 400 m freestyle is timed at 4 minutes and 10 seconds. Calculate his average speed in m/s.

Q4 In outer space, light travels at 186 000 miles per second. How far does a ray of light travel in a day?

Q5 An ingot of gold has a volume of 300 cm³. Find the mass of the ingot in kilograms if the density of gold is 19.3 g/cm³.

Q6 A sheet of aluminium foil on a kitchen roll is 10 m long, 45 cm wide and 0.08 mm thick. Calculate the density of aluminium in g/cm³ if the sheet has a mass of 972 g.

Answers are on page 240.

Enlargement by a fractional scale factor

- *How to enlarge a shape by a whole-number scale factor*

- *How to enlarge a shape relative to a given centre of enlargement*

- You should know how to enlarge a shape by a scale factor between 0 and 1.
- You should know how to find the scale factor that produces an enlargement that is smaller than the original shape.

- Enlarging a shape by a fractional scale factor that is less than 1 produces an image that is smaller than the original shape.
- Shape B is an enlargement of shape A, with a scale factor $\frac{1}{2}$ about the centre O.

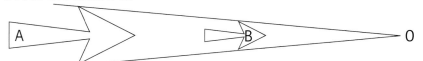

- An enlargement must always be described by stating the **centre of enlargement** and the **scale factor**.

Worked example
Enlarge the shaded shape:

a about (0, 0) by scale factor $\frac{1}{2}$

b about (10, 2) by scale factor $\frac{1}{2}$.

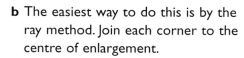

a This can be done by counting squares. For example, the coordinates of the top left corner are (2, 10). Scaling these coordinates by $\frac{1}{2}$ gives the coordinates of the top left corner of the image as (1, 5). The process is repeated for the other corners.

b The easiest way to do this is by the ray method. Join each corner to the centre of enlargement.

As the scale factor of the enlargement is $\frac{1}{2}$, find the midpoint of each of the lines and then join them up.

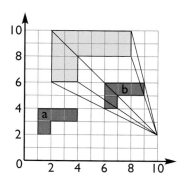

Q1 Describe the enlargement of shape A to shape B in each case.

a

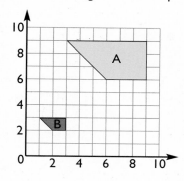

b

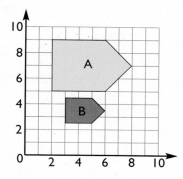

Q2 Copy this diagram three times and enlarge the shaded pentagon:

a about (0, 0) by scale factor $\frac{1}{2}$

b about (6, 0) by scale factor $\frac{1}{3}$

c about (12, 2) by scale factor $\frac{1}{2}$.

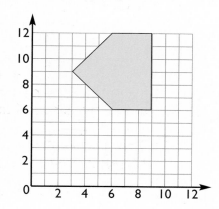

Answers are on page 240.

1 **a** Look at this triangle.

10 cm
8 cm
x°
6 cm
Not to scale

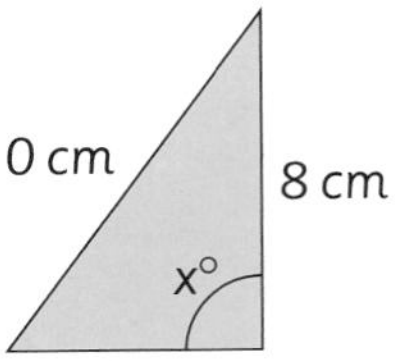

Show working to explain why angle x **must** be a right angle.

1 mark

b What is the **volume** of this prism?

10 cm
6 cm
8 cm
7 cm
Not to scale

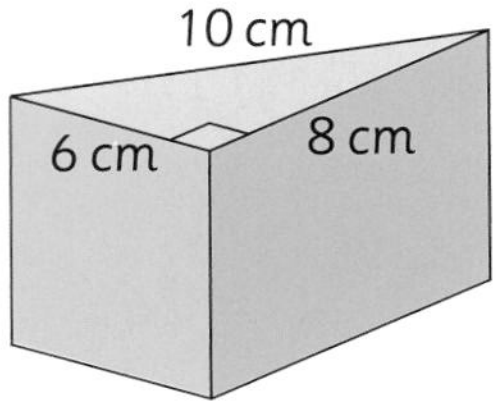

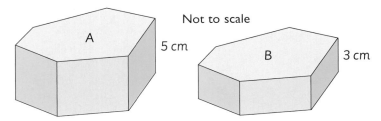

You **must** show **each step** in your working.

2 marks

c Prisms A and B have the same cross-sectional area.

Not to scale
A
5 cm
B
3 cm

Complete the table.

	Prism A	Prism B
height	5 cm	3 cm
volume	200 cm^3	…… cm^3

1 mark

2 The diagram shows a **rectangle** that just touches an **equilateral triangle**.

Not drawn accurately
x
straight line
20°

a Find the size of the angle marked x.

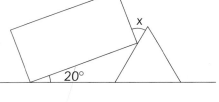

2 marks

Show your working.

b Now the rectangle just touches the equilateral triangle so that **ABC** is a **straight line**.

Not drawn accurately
A
B
D
E
C

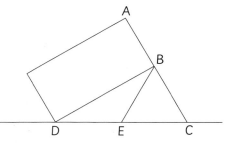

Show that **triangle BDE** is **isosceles**.

2 marks

3 The plan shows the position of three towns, each marked with a **X**.
The scale of the plan is **1 cm to 10 km**.

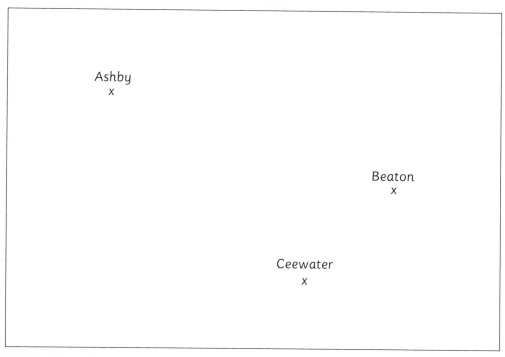

The towns need a new radio mast.

The new radio mast must be:

   nearer to Ashby than Ceewater, and
   less than 45 km from Beaton.

Show on the plan the region where the new radio mast can be placed.

Leave in your construction lines.

3 marks

4 Ramps help people
going into buildings.

A ramp that is **10 m long** must not have a **height** greater than **0.83 m**.

Here are the plans for a ramp.

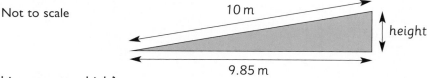

Is this ramp too high?
You **must** show calculations to explain your answer.

2 marks

5 A gardener wants to plant a tree.

She wants it to be **more than 8 m** away from the **vegetable plot**.
She wants it to be **more than 18 m** away from the **greenhouse**.

The plan below shows part of the garden. The scale is **1 cm** to **4 m**.

Show accurately on the plan the region of the garden where she can plant the tree.

Label this region **R**. *3 marks*

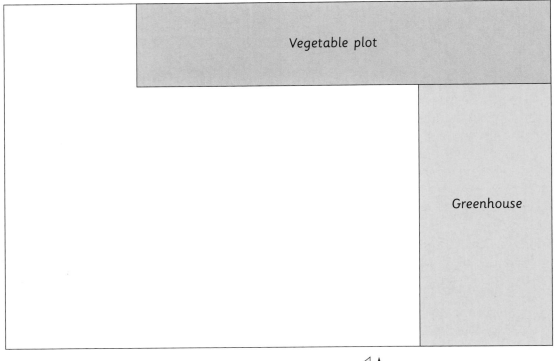

Vegetable plot

Greenhouse

6 **a** Calculate the length of the unknown side of this right-angled triangle.

Show your working.

12 cm

Not drawn accurately

17 cm

2 marks

b Calculate the length of the unknown side of the right-angled triangle below.

5 cm

Not drawn accurately

Show your working. *2 marks*

11 cm

7 The diagram shows a square and a circle.
The circle touches the edges of the square.

What **percentage** of the diagram is shaded?
Show your working.

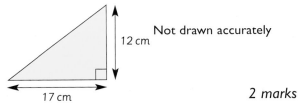

6 cm

3 marks

Answers are on page 252.

> - You should be able to specify an hypothesis and test it by designing an appropriate survey sheet or experiment that takes into account bias.

What you should already know

- *How to collect data and construct frequency tables*

- *How to round numbers, using decimal places or significant figures*

QUESTIONNAIRES

- There is always a purpose for collecting data, whether it is to test an idea or to check if a particular theory is true or false.
- Before collecting any data you need to know what you hope to achieve: you make a statement that you want to test. This statement is called a **hypothesis**. Examples of hypotheses are:
  - Boys do better than girls in science at school.
  - Young people do not listen to classical music.
  - Parents prefer to send their children to a school that has a uniform.
- When you have chosen the hypothesis, you need to design a suitable **questionnaire**. Any questions you ask should help you come to a decision about your hypothesis.
- You can then use the data you collect to draw diagrams or produce averages to support your decision.
- For data to be reliable, you should always try to give your questionnaire to a random sample of at least 30 people.
- When designing a questionnaire:
  - It should not have too many questions – a maximum of 10 is about right.
  - All questions should be relevant.
  - Questions should be easy to understand and require only one answer.
  - Provide alternative answers where possible, for example YES/NO, or ✓ ✗, or Male ☐ Female ☐.
  - Use multi-choice answers to cover all possibilities: 0 ☐ 1 ☐ 2 ☐ 3 ☐ 4 ☐ more than 4 ☐.
  - Avoid vague, misleading or embarrassing questions.
  - Avoid bias in the questions – people may not always want to tell you the truth.
  - If possible, use a computer database to store the data so that it can be regularly amended or updated.
  - Questionnaires look better if they are produced on a word-processor.

Note:

These are all sample answers: there are many more correct possibilities.

Worked example

These are poor questions to give on a questionnaire. Replace them by more suitable questions.

a How old are you?
b How many girl/boyfriends do you have?
c Have you read a magazine recently?
d Do you like fast cars?

a Which age group are you in? Put a ✓ in the box.
under 21 ☐ 21–30 ☐ 31–40 ☐ 41–50 ☐ over 50 ☐
b Do you have a girl/boyfriend at the moment? YES ☐ NO ☐
c How many magazines have you read in the last week?
None ☐ 1 ☐ 2 ☐ 3 ☐ 4 ☐ more than 4 ☐
d What type of car do you drive?
saloon ☐ hatchback ☐ estate ☐ 4-wheel drive ☐ sports ☐ other ☐

Worked example

Design a questionnaire to test the hypothesis: 'Tall pupils tend to weigh more than short pupils.'

A sample questionnaire is shown below.

Please answer these questions by putting a ✓ in the correct box.

Sex: Male ☐ Female ☐

Year group: 7 ☐ 8 ☐ 9 ☐ 10 ☐ 11 ☐

Height: Less than 140 cm ☐ 140–149 cm ☐
150–159 cm ☐ 160–169 cm ☐ 170–179 cm ☐
180–189 cm ☐ Over 189 cm ☐

Weight: Less than 30 kg ☐ 30–39 kg ☐
40–49 kg ☐ 50–59 kg ☐ 60–69 kg ☐
70–79 kg ☐ 80–89 kg ☐ over 89 kg ☐

Worked example

For a maths investigation, Dennis wanted to know people's views on adverts on TV.

He gave this questionnaire to 20 pupils in his class. The questions he chose were poorly-worded and ambiguous. Rewrite the questionnaire in a more suitable format.

For more reliable results, Dennis should ask at least 30 people from a wider age range. Also, the person completing the questionnaire usually remains anonymous.

Here is a sample questionnaire to find people's views on adverts on TV.

NAME: _____ FORM: _____

1 Do you think there are too many adverts on TV?

2 Do you find some of the adverts amusing?

3 What do you do when the adverts are on?

4 Do you ever buy any of the products that are advertised? Which ones?

5 Do you think that advertising on TV is a waste of money?

Which age group are you in?
Under 21 ☐ 21–30 ☐ 31–40 ☐ 41–50 ☐ over 50 ☐

Please underline the response or responses that are closest to your views.

1 What do you think about the amount of time that is devoted to adverts on TV? Is there:
far too much / should be less / about right / should be more / far too little

2 Why do you watch adverts on TV? Because they:
are informative / introduce new products / promote offers / are amusing / never watch / other.

3 What do you usually do when the adverts are on the TV? Do you:
always watch them / do odd jobs / read / change channels / ignore them / other.

4 Do you ever buy any of the products that are advertised on TV? Always / frequently / sometimes / rarely / never.

5 Adverts are a waste of a company's money.
Do you agree with this statement?
Strongly agree / agree / no comment / disagree / strongly disagree.

CHECK YOURSELF QUESTIONS

1 Write more suitable questions to replace these.
   a Do you like going to exotic restaurants?
   b Do you do your Maths homework when it is set?

2 Year 9 are planning to go on a school visit at the end of the year. Mrs White, their Year Head, decides to give 50 pupils a questionnaire to find out where they would like to go. Design a suitable questionnaire for Mrs White.

Answers are on page 240.

What you should already know

- *How to find the mean, median, mode and range for a set of data*

- *How to record continuous data using class intervals*

Note:

Σ is the Greek letter sigma; it means 'the sum of', which means you add up all the values.

- You should be able to find the modal class and estimate the mean, median and range of sets of grouped data.

- You should be able to select the most appropriate statistic for your line of enquiry.

- You should be able to compare two distributions using the measures of average and range and draw the associated frequency polygons.

FINDING AVERAGES FOR A FREQUENCY DISTRIBUTION

- For any set of data, the **mean**, $\bar{x}$, can be calculated as

$$\bar{x} = \frac{\text{the sum of all the values}}{\text{the total number of values}}$$

- For a frequency distribution, the mean can be calculated using the formula:

$$\bar{x} = \frac{\Sigma fx}{\Sigma f}$$

Worked example
The frequency table shows the numbers of people in 20 families.

a Find the mean.
b Find the mode.
c Find the median.
d Which of the three averages is it best to use? Why?

No. (x)	Frequency (f)	fx
3	9	27
4	8	32
5	3	15
Totals	20	74

You can also work this out on a scientific calculator by first setting the calculator in the STAT mode or SD mode.

Then enter

On some calculators DATA is ×.

To find the mean press INV x̄ . The answers should be 3.7.

a Add up all the numbers in the fx column and all the numbers in the frequency column and put the numbers into the formula:

$$\bar{x} = \frac{\Sigma fx}{\Sigma f} = \frac{74}{20} = 3.7$$

b The mode is the value with the highest frequency. The mode is 3.
c The median is the exact middle value. This is the number between the 10th and 11th value when the values are put in order. The 9th value is 3 and the 10th and 11th values are both 4. The median is therefore 4.
d The mean is the best average to use here since it takes all the values into account.

ESTIMATING AVERAGES FOR A GROUPED FREQUENCY DISTRIBUTION

- The mean for data collected by means of a grouped frequency table cannot be calculated exactly because the individual values are not known.
- In this case the mean can be estimated by finding the **midpoint value** for each class interval and then using the above formula with the midpoint value taken as *x*.
- It can be useful to find the **modal class** for a grouped frequency distribution. This is the class interval with the highest frequency.

Worked example

The grouped frequency table shows the ages of 100 people in the village of Sumton. Calculate an estimate for the mean age and write down the modal class.

Age (A)	0 < A ≤ 20	20 < A ≤ 40	40 < A ≤ 60	60 < A ≤ 80	80 < A ≤ 100
Frequency	12	18	35	28	7

Age (A)	Frequency (f)	Midpoint (x)	fx
0 < A ≤ 20	12	10	120
20 < A ≤ 40	18	30	540
40 < A ≤ 60	35	50	1750
60 < A ≤ 80	28	70	1960
80 < A ≤ 100	7	90	630
Totals	100		5000

$$\bar{x} = \frac{\Sigma fx}{\Sigma f} = \frac{5000}{100} = 50$$

The modal class is 40–60.

Worked example

The frequency diagram shows the time (*t*) it takes 50 employees to get to work in the morning. Estimate the range and the mean of the distribution.

Start by constructing a grouped frequency table.

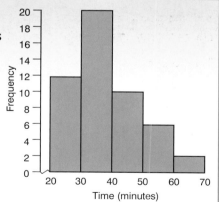

Time (t)	Frequency (f)	Midpoint (x)	fx
20 < t ≤ 30	12	25	300
30 < t ≤ 40	20	35	700
40 < t ≤ 50	10	45	450
50 < t ≤ 60	6	55	330
60 < t ≤ 70	2	65	130
Totals	50		1910

The range is
highest possible time – lowest possible time
= 70 – 20 = 50 minutes

$$\bar{x} = \frac{\Sigma fx}{\Sigma f} = \frac{1910}{50} = 50 = 38.2 \text{ minutes}$$

Worked example

The grouped frequency table shows the marks and levels awarded to two Year 9 classes in their SATs maths test papers.

Level	Level 5	Level 6	Level 7	Level 8
Mark Range	23–29	30–44	45–79	80–120
Class 9AZ	4	10	16	6
Class 9BY	0	16	14	2

a How many pupils are there in each class?
b Estimate the range and mean mark for each class.
c Draw a frequency polygon for each class, on the same diagram.
d Which class obtained the better results? Explain why.

a 36 pupils in Class 9AZ and 32 pupils in Class 9BY.
b Construct a grouped frequency table for each class. The marks are discrete data and so there is no need to put the class intervals into continuous data format. Find the midpoint x by adding the marks at the end of each mark range and dividing the answer by 2.

Class 9AZ

Mark range	Frequency (f)	Midpoint (x)	fx
23–29	4	26	104
30–44	10	37	370
45–79	16	62	992
80–120	6	100	600
Totals	36		2066

Class 9BY

Mark range	Frequency (f)	Midpoint (x)	fx
30–44	16	37	592
45–79	14	62	868
80–120	2	100	200
Totals	32		1660

Range = 120 − 23 = 97 marks

$\bar{x} = \dfrac{\Sigma fx}{\Sigma f} = \dfrac{2066}{36} = 57.4$ marks

Range = 120 − 30 = 90 marks

$\bar{x} = \dfrac{\Sigma fx}{\Sigma f} = \dfrac{1660}{32} = 51.9$ marks

c Remember to plot the points at the midpoints of the class intervals.

d Although the range for 9AZ is wider, showing a greater spread of results, the mean is higher than the mean for 9BY. Class 9AZ therefore obtained slightly better results.

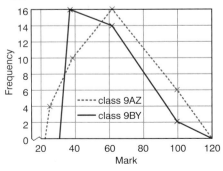

CHECK YOURSELF QUESTIONS

Q1 Josh threw a dice 60 times in an investigation at school. This is his table of results. Calculate the mean score.

Score (x)	Frequency (f)
1	8
2	11
3	9
4	12
5	9
6	11

Q2 The annual wage of 80 people who work at a local supermarket is given in the frequency table below:

Annual salary	£10 000–	£15 000–	£20 000–	£25 000–	£30 000–
Frequency	37	30	8	3	2

  a Calculate an estimate for the mean wage (to 3 s.f.).
  b An estimate for the median wage is £15 500. Which average best reflects the average wage of the employees? Give a reason.

Q3 The frequency diagram shows the life span of 100 'Photon' light bulbs. Calculate an estimate for the mean. Write down the modal class.

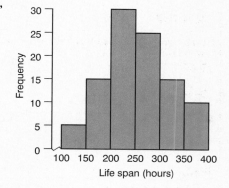

Q4 These are the marks of 50 pupils in the Year 9 French exam.

47	61	38	36	82	74
65	48	40	42	70	63
18	59	53	87	52	25
68	55	32	25	33	54
35	21	70	14	61	80
77	89	40	93	60	82
64	71	58	16	29	57
49	68	68	71	61	90
66	20				

  a Calculate the exact mean for the data.
  b Construct a grouped frequency table for the data, taking equal class intervals 1–20, 21–40, ... , 81–100. Hence calculate an estimate for the mean.
  c Comment on your answers.

Answers are on page 241.

- **You should be able to draw a line of best fit on a scatter diagram by eye.**

SCATTER DIAGRAMS

- Given two sets of data, you can recognise whether there is correlation between them by drawing a scatter diagram.
- You can recognise the degree of correlation by the way the points cluster on the diagram.

DRAWING A LINE OF BEST FIT

- A **line of best fit** is a straight line drawn through the middle of all the points on a scatter diagram.
- The line of best fit should be close to as many points as possible.
- You can draw the line by eye, making sure that there are roughly equal numbers of points on either side of the line and with the line passing through some of the points if possible.
- If the line of best fit is accurate, it will pass through the point representing the mean value for each set of data on the scatter diagram.
- The line should be extended to touch at least one of the axes if possible.
- The line of best fit does not necessarily have to pass through the origin or go through the extreme points.

Worked example

The scatter diagram shows the masses of 15 children against their ages.

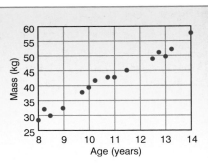

a What does the diagram tell you?

b Draw a line of best fit on the scatter diagram.

c Use the line of best fit to estimate the mass of a child who is 12.

a There is positive correlation.

b The line of best fit must go through the middle of the points.

c The child's mass is about **48 kg**. It can be useful to draw dotted lines on the diagram to help find the mass for any given age.

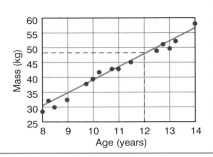

Worked example

The table shows the population (in millions) of a large city over a 10 year period.

Year	1980	1982	1984	1986	1988	1990
Population (m)	3.5	3.3	3.2	2.9	2.8	2.6

a Show the data on a scatter diagram and draw a line of best fit.
b What can you deduce from the diagram?
c Estimate the population of the city in 1985.

a The line of best fit is drawn through the middle of the points.
b The diagram shows negative correlation. The population has been decreasing over the 10 years.

c The population was just less than 3.1 million in 1985.
   The dotted lines help to work out this answer.

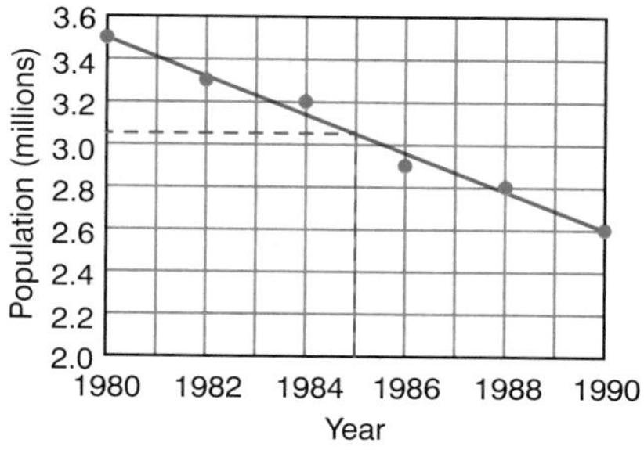

? CHECK YOURSELF QUESTION

Q1 Shaun was carrying out an experiment to find out if there was a relationship between the length of the extension of a spring when different masses were hung from it. He decided to do the experiment six times, using different masses. His results are recorded in the table.

Mass (g)	50	100	150	200	250	300
Extension (cm)	1.7	3.8	5.8	8.2	10.1	11.8

a Calculate the mean for the masses and for the extensions.
b Show the data on a scatter diagram and draw a line of best fit.
c Estimate the length of the extension if a mass of 120 g were hung from the spring.

Answers are on page 241.

What you should already know

- *How to find the probability of an event with equally likely outcomes*
- *How to calculate probability by finding all the equally likely outcomes, using lists or diagrams*

- You should understand relative frequency as an estimate of probability and use it to compare the outcomes of experiments.

RELATIVE FREQUENCY

- It is not always possible to use equally likely outcomes, so sometimes you can only estimate probability.
- You can repeat an experiment to estimate the probability for a particular outcome of an event: each experiment is called a **trial**.
- **Relative frequency** = $\dfrac{\text{the number of trials for the outcome}}{\text{total number of trials}}$
- This gives an estimate for the **theoretical probability**.
- The more trials you conduct, the closer your estimate will be to the theoretical probability.

Worked example

Dana throws a dice 120 times. Her results are given in the table. Use relative frequency to estimate the probability of getting a 6.

Score	1	2	3	4	5	6
Frequency	18	19	20	17	24	22

There are 120 trials. Relative frequency $= \frac{22}{120} = \frac{11}{60}$.
(Theoretical probability $= \frac{1}{6}$)

Worked example

Graham, James, Ruth and Tim want to find the probability that a drawing pin will land point-up. Each of them decides to carry out a different number of trials by dropping a number of pins onto the floor. Their results are shown in the table.

	No. of trials	No. of trials with point up
Graham	100	63
James	120	72
Ruth	200	122
Tim	50	37

a Complete the table to show the relative frequency for each person.

b Whose answer will give a better estimate for the probability of a pin landing point-up? Explain why.

c Meg dropped a box of 288 drawing pins on the floor. Estimate how many of them landed point-up.

a Complete the table.
b Ruth because she conducted more trials.
c Estimated probability for point-up
$= \frac{122}{200} = 0.61$

The number landing point-up
$= 288 \times 0.61 = 175.68$
So approximately 176 would land point-up.

	No. of trials	No. of trials with point up	Relative frequency
Graham	100	63	0.63
James	120	72	0.60
Ruth	200	122	0.61
Tim	50	37	0.74

CHECK YOURSELF QUESTIONS

Q1 A sampling bottle contains 100 black and white balls. [A sampling bottle is a sealed tube containing coloured balls which cannot be seen. After the bottle is shaken, a ball descends into a clear tube at one end.] Samantha wants to find out how many black balls there are in the bottle. She conducts a number of trials and her results are shown in the table. How many black balls did Samantha estimate were in the bottle?

No. of trials	No. of black balls	Relative frequency
10	3	0.30
50	9	0.18
100	24	0.24
200	38	0.19

Q2 A four-sided dice used in a game has one blue, one green, one red and one yellow face. Four people playing the game think that the dice is biased. To check this, they kept a record of the colours each threw during a game. Their results are shown in the table.

	No. of throws	Blue	Green	Red	Yellow
Albert	45	10	15	8	12
Beatrix	60	14	18	12	16
Charles	40	9	11	7	13
Dot	55	13	18	10	14

a Put all their results together and draw a relative frequency table.
Do you think that the dice is biased? Explain why.
b Work out an estimate for the probability of getting each colour.

Q3 Clifford and Derek were conducting a survey to find out the months in which pupils in Year 9 had their birthdays. To illustrate their data, they drew this chart.
a Find the total number of pupils in the survey.
b Draw a relative frequency table to show the data.
c Estimate:
   (i) P(A pupil has a birthday in July)
   (ii) P(A pupil's birthday is not in March).
d There are 30 pupils in Clifford and Derek's form. Estimate how many of them will have a birthday in October.

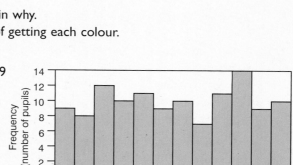

Answers are on page 241.

1 a Look at these cards.

You can see two of the expressions. The third is hidden.

 $3x - 10$ $3x$ **?**

The **mean** value of the expressions is **3x**.

What is the hidden expression?   *1 mark*

b Write a set of three expressions that has a mean value of **4x**.

☐   ☐   ☐   *1 mark*

c What is the mean value of these expressions?

$2x + 3$ $5x - 9$ $5x + 12$

Show your working.
Write your expression as simply as possible.   *2 marks*

2 I have two bags of counters.

Bag A contains
12 red counters and
18 yellow counters.

Bag B contains
10 red counters and
16 yellow counters.

I am going to take one counter at random from either bag A or bag B.

I want to get a **red** counter.
Which bag should I choose?

Show working to explain your answer.   *2 marks*

3 A class collected information about the number of children in each of their families. The information was displayed in a frequency chart, but you cannot see all the information.

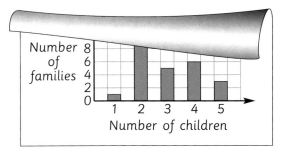

Call the number of families that have **two** children *n*.

a Show that the total number of children in all the families is **55 + 2n**.   *1 mark*

b Write an expression for the **total number of families**.   *1 mark*

c The **mean** number of children per family is 3.
What is the value of *n*?
Show your working.   *2 marks*

4 The goldcrest is Britain's smallest species of bird.

On winter days, a goldcrest must eat enough food to keep it warm at night. During the day, the mass of the bird increases.

The scatter diagram shows the mass of goldcrests at different times during winter days. It also shows the line of best fit.

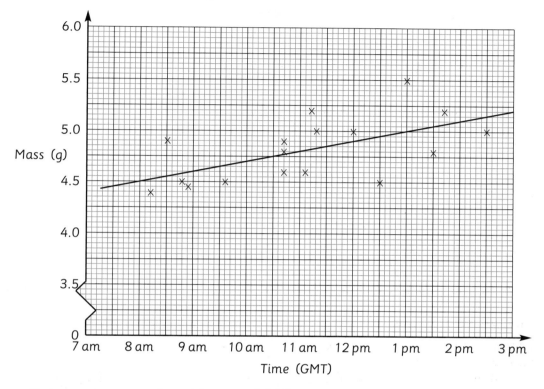

a Estimate the mass of a goldcrest at **11:30 am**. *1 mark*

b Estimate how many grams, on average, the mass of the goldcrest **increases** during **one hour**. *1 mark*

c Which goldcrest represented on the scatter diagram is **least likely** to survive the night if it is cold?

Show your answer by circling the correct point on the scatter diagram, then explain why you chose that point. *1 mark*

5 a From 5th May 2000 to 5th May 2001 a swimming club had the same members.

Complete the table to show information about the ages of these members.

Ages of members	
Mean (5th May 2000)	24 years 3 months
Range (5th May 2000)	4 years 8 months
Mean (5th May 2001)	
Range (5th May 2001)	

1 mark

b The table below shows information about members of a different club.

Ages of members	
Mean	17 years 5 months
Range	2 years 0 months

A new member, aged **18 years 5 months**, is going to join the club. What will happen to the **mean** age of the members?
Tick (✓) the correct statement below.

It will increase by more than a year. ☐

It will increase by exactly a year. ☐

It will increase by less than a year. ☐

It will stay the same. ☐

It is not possible to tell. ☐   *1 mark*

What will happen to the **range** of ages of the members?

It will increase by more than a year. ☐

It will increase by exactly a year. ☐

It will increase by less than a year. ☐

It will stay the same. ☐

It is not possible to tell. ☐   *1 mark*

6 The percentage charts show information about the wing length of adult blackbirds, measured to the nearest millimetre.

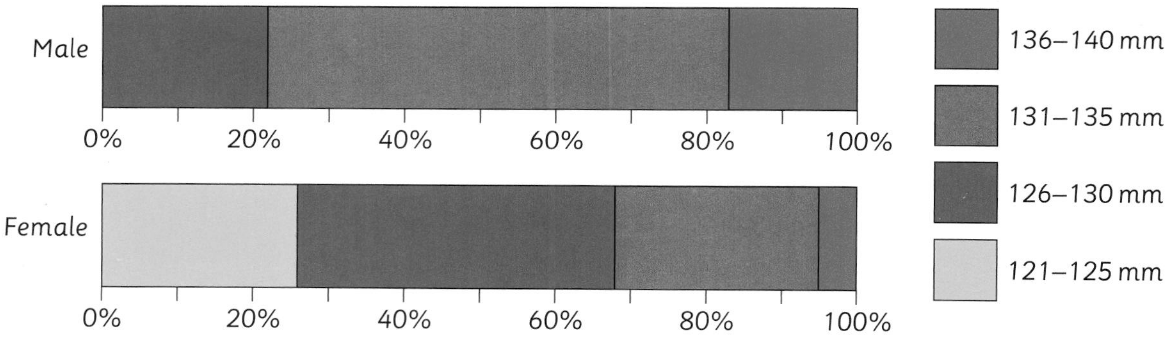

Use the data to decide whether these statements are true or false, or whether there is not enough information to tell.

The smallest male's wing length is larger than the smallest female's wing length.

☐ True   ☐ False   ☐ Not enough information
Explain your answer.   *1 mark*

The biggest male's wing length is larger than the biggest female's wing length.

☐ True   ☐ False   ☐ Not enough information
Explain your answer.   *1 mark*

Answers are on page 253.

LEVEL 8

INTRODUCTION

- A few pupils sit Nationl Test papers that cover level 8. If you have found the work in this book straightforward then you might be able to take the tier 6–8 paper. This is usually something that your teachers decide. You should know what tier paper you will be sitting. If you do not, ask your teacher.
- The following four sections list the National Curriculum descriptors for level 8 in Number, Algebra, Shape, space and measures and Handling data. Each of the descriptors is linked to a past National Test question. The answers to the National Test questions, together with examiner's comments, start on page 253.

LEVEL 8 NUMBER

- You should be able to use powers or roots, with numbers expressed in standard form, to solve problems, checking that the answers are of the correct order of magnitude. (Question 1)
- You should be able to choose fractions or percentages to solve problems involving repeated proportional changes or the calculation of the original quantity given the result of a proportional change. (Questions 2, 3, 4)
- You should be able to evaluate algebraic formulae, substituting fractions, decimals and negative numbers. (Question 5).
- You should be able to calculate one variable, given the others in formulae such as $V = \pi r^2 h$. (Questions 4 and 6)

QUESTIONS

1 Look at the table.

	Earth	Mercury
Mass (kg)	5.98×10^{24}	3.59×10^{23}
Atmospheric pressure (N/m²)		2×10^{-8}

a The atmospheric pressure on Earth is **5.05×10^{12} times** as great as the atmospheric pressure on Mercury .
Calculate the atmospheric pressure on Earth. *1 mark*

b What is the **ratio** of the mass of Earth to the mass of Mercury?
Write your answer in the form $x : 1$. *1 mark*

c The approximate volume, V, of a planet with radius r is given by $\frac{4}{3}\pi r^3$.
Assume the radius of Mercury is 2400 km.
Calculate the volume of Mercury. Give your answer to **1 significant figure, in standard form**. *2 marks*

2 A **10% increase** followed by **another 10% increase** is **not** the same as a total increase of 20%.

What is the total percentage increase? Show your working. *2 marks*

3 A shop had a sale. All prices were reduced by 15%.

A pair of shoes cost **£38.25** in the sale.
What price were the shoes before the sale?
Show your working. *2 marks*

4 In **1995**, the Alpha Company employed 4000 people.

For **each** of the next **2 years**, the number of people employed increased by 10%.

1995	employed 4000 people
1996	employed 10% more people
1997	employed 10% more people

a Tony said:
'Each year, the Alpha company employed another 400 people.'

Tony was wrong. Explain why. *1 mark*

b Circle the calculation below which shows how many people worked for the company in 1997.

$4000 \times 0.1 \times 2$ 4000×0.1^2 $(4000 \times 0.1)^2$

$4000 \times 1.1 \times 2$ 4000×1.1^2 $(4000 \times 1.1)^2$ *1 mark*

c Look at these figures for the Beta Company.

1995	employed n people
1996	employed 20% **fewer** people
1997	employed 10% **more** people

Write an expression using n to show how many people the company employed in **1997**.

Show your working and write your expression as simply as possible. *2 marks*

5 Use the formula $d = \dfrac{m^2 - s^2}{2g}$ to find d when $g = {}^-8.9$, $m = 0$, $s = 27.0$.
Show your working. *? marks*

6 The formula for the volume, V, of a square-based pyramid is
$V = \frac{1}{3}b^2h$

b is the base length, h is the perpendicular height.

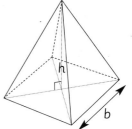

a A square-based pyramid has base length 5 cm and perpendicular height 6 cm.

What is its volume? *1 mark*

b A different square-based pyramid has base length 4 cm. Its volume is 48 cm³.
What is its perpendicular height?

1 mark

c The volume of another square-based pyramid is 25 cm³.
Its perpendicular height is 12 cm.
What is its base length?
Show your working.

2 marks

d The diagram shows a triangular-based pyramid.
The base is an isosceles, right-angled triangle.
The perpendicular height is m.

Write a formula, in terms of m, for the
volume, V, of the pyramid.

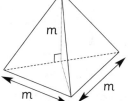

1 mark

LEVEL 8 ALGEBRA

- You should be able to manipulate algebraic formulae, equations
  and expressions, finding common factors and multiplying two
  linear expressions. (Questions 7, 8, 9 and 10)
- You should be able to solve inequalities in two variables.
  (Question 11)
- You should be able to sketch and interpret graphs of linear,
  quadratic, cubic and reciprocal functions, and graphs that model
  real situations. (Question 12)
- You should know that $a^2 - b^2 = (a + b)(a - b)$. (Question 13)

QUESTIONS

7 Equations may have different numbers of solutions.

For example: $x + 2 = 7$ has only one solution, $x = 5$
but $x + 1 + 2 = x + 3$ is true for all values of x.

Tick (✓) the correct box for each algebraic statement below.

	Correct for no values of x	Correct for one value of x	Correct for two values of x	Correct for all values of x
$3x + 7 = 8$				
$3(x + 1) = 3x + 3$				
$x + 3 = x - 3$				
$5 + x = 5 - x$				
$x^2 = 9$				

3 marks

8 The two rectangles below have the **same area**.

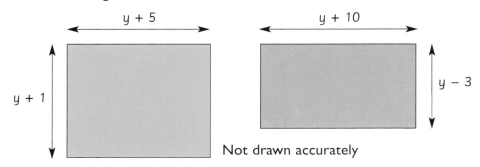

Not drawn accurately

Use an algebraic method to find the value of y.
You must show your working.

4 marks

9 y^2 represents a square number; y is an integer.

a Think about the expression $9 + y^2$.

Explain how you know there are values of y for which this expression
does **not** represent a square number.

1 mark

b Explain why the expression $16y^2$ **must** represent a square number.

1 mark

10 Each year a school has a concert of readings and songs.

In 1999 the concert had 3 readings and 9 songs.
It lasted 120 minutes.

In 2000 the concert had 5 readings and 5 songs.
It lasted 90 minutes.

In 2001 the school plans to have 5 readings and 7 songs.

Use simultaneous equations to estimate how long the concert will last.

Call the time estimated for a reading x minutes, and the time estimated
for a song y minutes.

You must show your working.

4 marks

11 This pattern is formed by straight-line graphs of equations in the first quadrant.

a One region of the pattern can be described
by the inequalities:

$x \leqslant 2, x \geqslant 1, y \geqslant x, y \leqslant 3$

Put an R in the single region of the pattern
that is described.

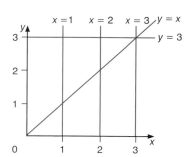

2 marks

b This is another pattern formed by straight-line graphs of equations in the first quadrant.

The shaded region can be described by three inequalities.

Write down these three inequalities.

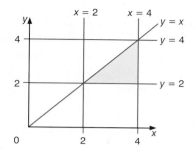

3 marks

12 The diagram shows a sketch of the curve $y = 16 - x^2$.

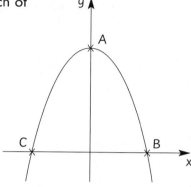

a What are the coordinates of points A, B and C?

2 marks

The curve $y = 16 - x^2$ is reflected in the line $y = 12$.

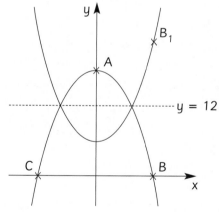

b B$_1$ is the reflection of B.
What are the coordinates of B$_1$?

1 mark

c What is the equation of the new curve?

1 mark

13 a Show that $\dfrac{a^2 - b^2}{a - b}$ simplifies to $a + b$.

1 mark

b Simplify the expression $\dfrac{a^3 b^3}{a^2 b^2}$.

1 mark

c Simplify the expression $\dfrac{a^3 b^2 - a^2 b^3}{a^2 b^2}$.

Show your working.

2 marks

- ,You should understand and be able to use mathematical similarity. (Question 14)
- You should be able to use sine, cosine and tangent in right-angled triangles when solving problems in two dimensions. (Question 15)
- You should be able to distinguish between formulae for perimeter, area and volume, by considering dimensions. (Question 16)
- You should understand congruence. (Question 17)

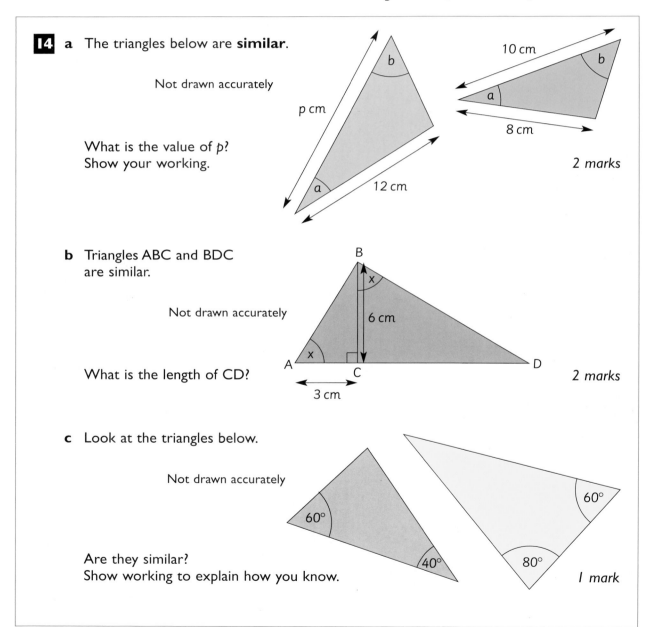

14 **a** The triangles below are **similar**.

Not drawn accurately

What is the value of *p*?
Show your working.

2 marks

b Triangles ABC and BDC are similar.

Not drawn accurately

What is the length of CD?

2 marks

c Look at the triangles below.

Not drawn accurately

Are they similar?
Show working to explain how you know.

1 mark

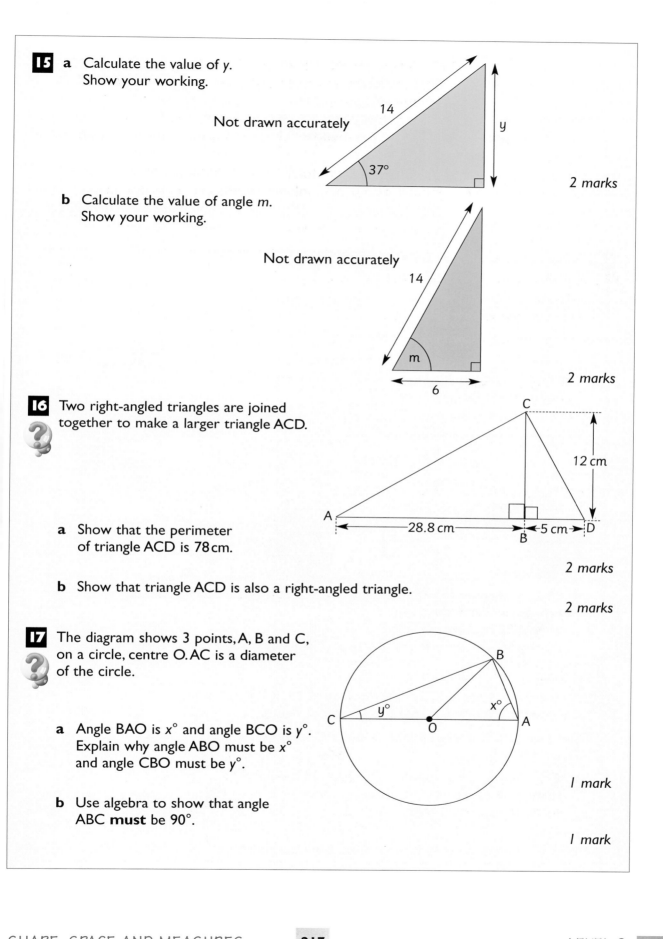

15 a Calculate the value of y.
Show your working.

14

Not drawn accurately

y

37°

2 marks

b Calculate the value of angle m.
Show your working.

Not drawn accurately

14

m

6

2 marks

16 Two right-angled triangles are joined
together to make a larger triangle ACD.

C

12 cm

A

28.8 cm

B

5 cm

D

a Show that the perimeter
of triangle ACD is 78 cm.

2 marks

b Show that triangle ACD is also a right-angled triangle.

2 marks

17 The diagram shows 3 points, A, B and C,
on a circle, centre O. AC is a diameter
of the circle.

B

C

$y°$

O

$x°$

A

a Angle BAO is $x°$ and angle BCO is $y°$.
Explain why angle ABO must be $x°$
and angle CBO must be $y°$.

1 mark

b Use algebra to show that angle
ABC **must** be 90°.

1 mark

- You should be able to interpret and construct cumulative frequency tables and diagrams, using the upper boundary of the class interval, be able to estimate the median and interquartile range and use these to compare distributions and make inferences. (Question 18)
- You should understand when to apply the methods for calculating the probability of a compound event, given the probabilities of either independent events or mutually exclusive events and solve problems using these methods. (Question 19)

18 A teacher asked fifty pupils in Year 9:

How much time did you spend on homework last night?

The results are shown in the table.

Time spent on homework (minutes)	Frequency
$0 \leqslant$ time $\leqslant 30$	6
$30 <$ time $\leqslant 60$	14
$60 <$ time $\leqslant 90$	21
$90 <$ time $\leqslant 120$	9
Total	**50**

a Show that an estimate of the mean time spent on homework is 64.8 minutes.

2 marks

The teacher used the data to draw a cumulative frequency diagram.

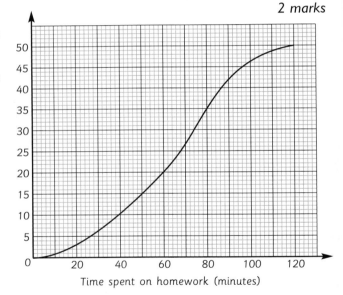

Cumulative frequency

Time spent on homework (minutes)

b Use the diagram to estimate the **median** time pupils spent on their homework. Show on the diagram how you get your answer. *2 marks*

c Use the diagram to estimate how many pupils spent **more than 100 minutes** on their homework. Show how you get your answer. *2 marks*

19 A robot can move N, S, E or W along the lines of a grid. It starts at the point marked ● and moves one step at a time.

For each step, it is **equally likely** that the robot will move **N, S, E or W**.

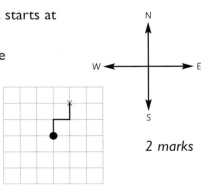

a The robot is going to move 3 steps from the point marked ●. What is the probability that it will move along the path shown? Show your working.

2 marks

b The robot is going to move 3 steps from the point marked ●. What is the probability that it will reach the point marked **X** by **any route**?

2 marks

Answers are on page 253.

LEVELS 4-8 MENTAL ARITHMETIC TEST 2

MENTAL ARITHMETIC TEST 2: LEVELS 4 TO 8

The Questions:

Time: 5 seconds

1 What is eighty-six multiplied by ten?

1	

2 Change one hundred and seventy millimetres into centimetres.

2	cm

3 What is forty-eight divided by six?

3	

4 What is seven point four multiplied by one hundred?

4		7.4

5 Write three hundredths as a decimal number.

5	

6 A line is measured as seven millimetres to the nearest millimetre. What is the minimum length that the line could be?

6	mm

The Questions:

Time: 10 seconds

7 A television programme starts at ten minutes to eight. It lasts twenty-five minutes. At what time does the programme finish?

7	

8 Fifty per cent of a number is forty-five. What is the number?

8	

9 What is half of one hundred and thirty-eight?

9	

10 In a group of seventy-three children, thirty-nine are girls. How many are boys?

10	boys

11 Ten per cent of a number is sixteen. What is the number?

11	

12 Write down the number six and a half million in figures.

12	

13 Write six-tenths as a decimal number.

13	

14 Jean got fifteen out of twenty on a test. What percentage did she get?

14	%

15 Two angles in a triangle are each seventy degrees. What is the size of the third angle?

15	°

16 Huw and Lynn share some money in the ratio of three to four. Huw's share is one hundred and fifty pounds. How much money is Lynn's share?

16	£	3 : 4 £150

17		6.08

17 Multiply six point nought eight by one thousand.

18 Two hundred and one out of two hundred and ninety-eight people said they could swim. Estimate the percentage who could swim.

18	%	

19 How many fourteenths are there in three-sevenths?

19	

20 Look at the inequality on your answer sheet. What is the greatest integer x can be?

20		$x^2 < 144$

21 What is nought point seven divided by nought point nought one?

21		0.7 0.01

The Questions:

Time: 15 seconds

22 What is the cost of five mugs at one pound ninety-nine pence each?

22	£

23 Look at the angle on you answer sheet. Estimate the size of the angle, in degrees.

23	°

24 Each side of a square is twenty-seven centimetres. What is the perimeter of the square?

24	cm

25 Look at the calculation on your answer sheet. What is thirty-two multiplied by twenty-two?

25		$32 \times 44 = 1408$

26 Look at the equation on your answer sheet. If a equals eight, what is b?

26	$b =$	$b = 9a - 18$

27 Forty per cent of a number is sixteen. What is the number?

27		16

28 Look at the calculation on your answer sheet. What is four hundred and forty-eight divided by one point six?

28		$28 \times 16 = 448$

29 A square has a perimeter of twenty-four metres. What is the area of the square?

29	m²

30 Look at your answer sheet. If x equals two y and y equals ten, work out x plus y, all squared.

30		$x = 2y$ $(x + y)^2$

31 The price of a train ticket goes up from five pounds to five pounds and twenty-five pence. What is the percentage increase?

31	%	

32 Look at the calculation on your answer sheet. Write an approximate answer.

32		$\dfrac{80.18 \times 9.89}{1.96}$

Answers are on page 242.

ANSWERS TO CHECK YOURSELF QUESTIONS

LEVEL 4 NUMBER

1 THE FOUR OPERATIONS OF NUMBER (page 3)

A1

×	7	6	3
2	14	12	6
5	35	30	15
10	70	60	30

×	2	5	9
9	18	45	81
4	8	20	36
8	16	40	72

×	3	7	6
4	12	28	24
8	24	56	48
6	18	42	36

×	5	2	7
7	35	14	49
9	45	18	63
3	15	6	21

A2 63 pots

COMMENT This is the multiplication 9 × 7. There is an easy way to remember the 9 times table. Hold up the fingers of both hands, facing you. Count across 7 fingers from the left and put that finger down. There are 6 fingers before the gap and 3 fingers after it. 7 × 9 = 63!

A3 21 centimetres

COMMENT This is short division 147 ÷ 7 or 7)147.

A4 **a** He can catch the 07.45 or the 08.10
b 08.54   **c** 9 minutes

COMMENT Time problems are common in SATs. You are likely to make mistakes if you do these with a calculator as there are not 100 minutes in an hour!

A5
$$\begin{array}{r} 235 \\ -78 \\ \hline 157 \end{array}$$
a 235 −78 = 157   **b** 176 −97 = 79   **c** 506 −358 = 148

COMMENT You will not be expected to show carries and borrows but these make the sum easier for you.

A6 **a** He is wrong: there will be less than 300 when the people get off but the guard has forgotten to count the people who got on.
b 418 − 129 = 289   289 + 58 = 347

COMMENT Keep your explanation short and to the point.

A7 **a** 9   **b** 12   **c** 18   **d** 21
e 24   **f** 16   **g** 24   **h** 28
i 32   **j** 36   **k** 42   **l** 48
m 49   **n** 56   **o** 64

COMMENT You should know the 1, 2, 5 and 10 times tables. Cross them out of the table. Check the questions. If two are the same, such as 3×4 and 4×3, cross one out. This leaves 15 multiplication facts to learn! You have just done the 'special' facts in Question 7. Learn them!

2 MULTIPLYING AND DIVIDING BY 10 AND 100 (page 5)

A1 **a** 370   **b** 6030   **c** 780   **d** 5200
e 30700   **f** 2100   **g** 49   **h** 63
i 9   **j** 43   **k** 6   **l** 40

COMMENT You can multiply or divide whole numbers by 10 and 100 simply by adding or crossing off zeros.

A2 **a** £40   **b** £400

COMMENT This is just multiplying by 10 and 100.

A3 **a** False   **b** True   **c** True   **d** False

COMMENT 6 tens is 6 × 10 = 60 so (a) is false. 600 is 600 units, so (d) is false.

A4 The first set is 40 tens, 400 units and 400. The second set is 40 hundreds, 4 thousands and 4000.

COMMENT In Questions 2 and 3, be careful with the number of zeros at the end of a number.

A5 45p

COMMENT Make £4.50 into 450p before dividing.

A6 **a** 2200 cups of tea   **b** 220 snacks

COMMENT Be careful with the number of zeros. Take 1 off when dividing by 10 and 2 off when dividing by 100.

A7 20 cm

COMMENT Write 20 metres as 2000 centimetres.

A8 **a** 425 or 254 or 245   **b** 524 or 542
c Pick zero: The number is 4520

COMMENT You have to think which card represents the hundreds digit, which is the tens digit and so on.

3 ADDITION AND SUBTRACTION OF DECIMALS (page 7)

A1 **a** 6.87   **b** 3.92   **c** 0.75   **d** 0.92

COMMENT Don't forget to line up the decimal point. After that, just do it like a normal sum.

A2

1.00	1.02	1.20	1.23	1.3

COMMENT Be careful! Do not take 1.20 as bigger than 1.3 because 20 is bigger than 3. Remember that 1.3 can also be written as 1.30. The trick is to add zeros so each number has the same number of decimal places.

A3 3.5 3.48 3.462 3.09 3.089

COMMENT If you add zeros as recommended in question 2, the numbers are 3.46, 3.40, 3.30, 3.08 and 3.06.

A4 **a** 10.69 cm   **b** 0.78 cm

COMMENTS Remember to line up the decimal points.
a The sum is 7.23 + 3.46 | b The sum is 5.15 − 4.37

A5 **a** 3.2 and 5.8 added together are not bigger than 10.4, so they would not fit around a triangle.   **b** 22.1 cm

COMMENT Any two sides of a triangle added together must be bigger than the third side. This is really a shape question, but you may be asked to measure sides of a triangle or another shape.

A6 **a** £63.95   **b** £16.05

COMMENT Take £5 as 5.00 before you line up the point. Four £20 notes is £80, so take this as 80.00.

A7 **a** 2.3 cm   **b** 8.7 cm
    c 6.1 cm   **d** 17.1 cm

COMMENT If you are asked to measure lines in SATs, you can be out by a millimetre and still get the marks for a correct answer.

A8 Part (c) is wrong. 9 is about 10 so the answers should be about 57, 96 and 23. The actual answers will be a bit bigger as 9 is smaller than 10. 62 is too far out.

A9 She will probably have saved enough.
    $1840 \times 10 = 18\,400$ so 1840×11 is a bit bigger than this, but she won't get much change!

4 SIMPLE FRACTIONS, DECIMALS AND PERCENTAGES (page 9)

A1 **a** 20%   **b** 40%   **c** 70%   **d** 90%

COMMENT Most of the percentages you will be asked to estimate will be multiples of 5 or 10.

A2 **a** $\frac{1}{4}$ **b** $\frac{2}{3}$ **c** $\frac{1}{4}$ **d** $\frac{3}{5}$

COMMENT Remember the bottom number (the denominator) will always be 2, 3, 4, 5 or 10.

A3 **a**

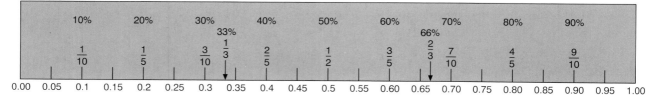

COMMENT The lines could go either way in both answers. You can be a little bit out from the exact answer. Try measuring the shape to see if it divides up exactly.

A4 **a** $\frac{3}{4}$ **b** $\frac{1}{4}$ **c** $\frac{1}{2}$ **d** $\frac{9}{10}$

COMMENT In Questions 1 to 4, there can be some differences in your answers and you will not be expected to give fractions percentages or decimals to greater accuracies than these.

A5 10% 0.10 $\frac{1}{10}$ 25% 0.25 $\frac{1}{4}$

    0.80 $\frac{4}{5}$ 80%   33% 0.33 $\frac{1}{3}$

    50% 0.50 $\frac{1}{2}$ 5% 0.05 $\frac{1}{20}$

COMMENT It is worth learning some of the more common equivalent fractions and decimals. You might find the chart at the bottom of page 14 useful.

A6 **a** £10   **b** £30   **c** £5   **d** £1

COMMENT 10% is the same as dividing by 10.

A7 **a** £1   **b** £100   **c** £50   **d** £10

COMMENT One-third is a basic fraction. It is the only one that you have to learn at this level that doesn't have a simple percentage. It is 33.33333... %. usually we write this as 33% or 33.3%.

A8 **a** Sept − 40%, Oct − 55%, Nov − 65%, Dec − 90%
    b Sept − £12, Oct − £16.50, Nov − £19.50, Dec − £27   **c** 10%

COMMENT Each division is 10% which is £3. Half a division is £1.50

A9 **a** 3   **b** 30   **c** 90   **d** 300

COMMENT Find a quarter then multiply it by 3. This chart may help you to remember some of the equivalent fractions, percentages and decimals:

10%	20%	30%		40%	50%	60%	70%	80%	90%
			33%				66%		
$\frac{1}{10}$	$\frac{1}{5}$	$\frac{3}{10}$	$\frac{1}{3}$	$\frac{2}{5}$	$\frac{1}{2}$	$\frac{3}{5}$	$\frac{2}{3}$ $\frac{7}{10}$	$\frac{4}{5}$	$\frac{9}{10}$

0.00 0.05 0.1 0.15 0.2 0.25 0.3 0.35 0.4 0.45 0.5 0.55 0.60 0.65 0.70 0.75 0.80 0.85 0.90 0.95 1.00

Level 4 Algebra
5 Number patterns (page 15)

A1 **a** Up in 3s   **b** Up in 2s   **c** Up in 3s
d Up by one more each time
e Up by 2 more each time

A2 **a** 18, 21, 24   **b** 11, 13, 15   **c** 20, 23, 26
d 29, 37, 46   **e** 36, 49, 64

COMMENT Don't forget to write down the number pattern and put down the differences.

A3 **a** (i) (ii) (iii) (iv)

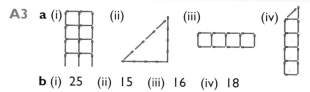

b (i) 25   (ii) 15   (iii) 16   (iv) 18

COMMENT These patterns all go up by a regular amount. Count on twice from the 3rd picture. In SATs you can lose marks if you do diagrams because the exam is trying to test if you can work things out using number patterns.

A4 **a** The ground floor numbers go up by 5, so do the 1st floor, 2nd floor, 3rd floor and 4th floor.
b All the patterns go up by 5.
c Flat 7 will be on the 2nd floor.

COMMENT You can work out part (c) by doing a sketch or by realising that flat 5 will now be on the ground floor and so 5, 6, 7 means that the 7th flat will be on the 2nd floor.

A5 **a**
b The pattern is increasing by 4 more each time.
c The sixth pattern will need 24 marbles.

A6 **a**
b The pattern is increasing by 1 more each time. It goes up 1, then 2, then 3 and so on.
c The sixth pattern will need 21 marbles.

COMMENT Write it out as a number pattern to see how it builds up.

A7 **a**
b The pattern is increasing by 2 more each time. It goes up by 3 then by 5 then by 7 and so on.
c The sixth pattern will need 36 marbles.

COMMENT These are called Square numbers and are dealt with on page 69.

6 Multiples, factors, primes and squares (page 17)

A1 **a** 4, 8, 12, 16, 20   **b** 6, 12, 18, 24, 30
c 9, 18, 27, 36, 45   **d** 11, 22, 33, 44, 55
e 20, 40, 60, 80, 100

COMMENT Remember multiples are the times tables.

A2 **a** {1, 2, 3, 6}   **b** {1, 2, 5, 10}
c {1, 2, 3, 5, 6, 10, 15, 30}
d {1, 2, 3, 6, 9, 18}   **e** {1, 2, 4, 8, 16, 32}

COMMENT Remember factors of a number divide into it exactly.

A3 **a** 2   **b** 31, 37   **c** 2, 3, 5, 7, 11, 13, 17, 19

COMMENT You have to learn the prime numbers. You should only need to learn those below 20.

A4 **a** 17   **b** 18   **c** 5
d 20   **e** 3

COMMENT Only one number fits each description.

A5

	Factors of 15	Prime numbers
Multiples of 5	15	5
Factors of 20	1	2

COMMENT Some numbers fit into more than one box, but there is only one way that all 4 numbers fit into the grid.

A6 **a** 5   **b** Odd
c $1 \times 16 = 16, 2 \times 8 = 16, 4 \times 4 = 16$

COMMENT The rule about every factor having a pair is not true when a number is its own pair. Other numbers that have an odd number of factors like this are 4, 16, 25 and so on. You may have met these before. They are called the square numbers.

A7 12

COMMENT The numbers that fit the first balloon are:
3, 6, 9, 12, 15, 18, 21,...
The numbers that fit the second balloon are:
4, 8, 12, 16, 20, 24, 28,...
The numbers that fit the third balloon are:
11, 12, 13, 14, 15, 16, 17, 18, 19
12 is the only number in all three lists.

7 SIMPLE FORMULAE (page 18)

A1 **a** 4   **b** 6

COMMENT Sums are 7 – 3 and 18 ÷ 3

A2 **a** 2   **b** 25

COMMENT You need to work out the middle step for a double number machine.

A3 **a** 45 ÷ 5 = 9,   **b** 100 ÷ 5 = 20,
9 × 9 = 81,   20 × 9 = 180,
81 + 32 = 113.   180 + 32 = 212.
So the answer is 113°F.   So the answer is 212°F.

COMMENT You might have known the last answer from Science which is why you must show your working.

A4 **a** £14   **b** £8   **c** £10

COMMENT The sums are 4 + 2 × 5, 4 + 2 × 2 and 4 + 2 × 3.

8 COORDINATES (page 20)

A1   A = (2, 1); B = (5, 0); C = (2, 6); D = (4, 4); E = (6, 5); F = (0, 3)

COMMENT Take care to write coordinates properly, for example, don't write them as 2-5 or 2/5. If you keep getting them the wrong way round, learn the rule again.

A2

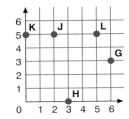

A3 **a** A is (0, 6); B is (5, 1); C is (5, 6)

A4 **a** P is (3, 1); Q is (5, 2); R is (3, 6)
     b S is at (1, 5)

COMMENT Draw the points. They do make a rectangle.

A5 **a** (0, 3)   **b** (5, 2)   **c** (5, 3)

COMMENT Join the black counters to see where to put the other counter. Repeat for the white and grey counters.

A6 **a** A is (1, 1); B is (2, 2); C is (3, 3);
       D is (4, 4); E is (5, 5)
     b All the numbers in each co-ordinate are the same.
     c No, because the numbers are not the same.

COMMENT If you can't spot the pattern, try plotting points to see if they are on the same straight line.

LEVEL 4 SHAPE, SPACE AND MEASURES
9 2-D AND 3-D SHAPES (page 25)

A1 **a** Yes   **b** No   **c** No   **d** Yes

COMMENTS b There would be a hole in this cube.
c There are too many edges joined together; this would be impossible to fold.

A2

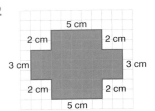

COMMENT Use 1 cm grid paper to draw this net accurately.

A3

Front elevation   Side elevation   Top elevation

COMMENT Put in all the edges that you can see.

A4   The dice has 6 edges, 4 corners and 4 faces.

COMMENT Remember to count the edge and the face at the back that are not seen.

A5

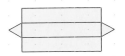

COMMENT The chocolate box is made out of 3 rectangles and 2 equilateral triangles. The sides of the triangles must be the same length as the width of the rectangle. Tabs are not necessary.

10 SYMMETRY (page 27)

A1

COMMENT Use a mirror to check.

A2 **a** order 6   **b** order 4   **c** order 6   **d** order 5

COMMENT Use tracing paper if you are not sure.

A3 **a** and **c**, **b** and **e**, **d** and **f**.

COMMENT First, trace the shapes that you think are the same, then check that you are right.

11 MEASURING INSTRUMENTS AND SCALES (page 28)

A1 **a** 6.8 cm   **b** 3.3 cm   **c** 0.9 cm

COMMENTS **a** Or 68 mm. The units are important.
b The line is in between 3.3 cm and 3.4 cm
so both of these answers would be accepted.
c Or 9 mm. Look at the line to check
your answer. It looks about 1 cm long.

A2 350 ml

COMMENT There are 2 divisions between 0 and 100, so
each division is 50. Remember to put in the units.

A3 45 minutes

COMMENT There are 4 divisions between 0 and 60, so
each division is 15 (60 ÷ 4 = 15).

12 PERIMETER, AREA AND VOLUME (page 30)

A1 **a** Perimeter is 16 cm. Area is 12 cm².
    b Perimeter is 20 cm. Area is 15 cm².

COMMENTS **a** Just count the squares to find the area.
b finding the perimeter, mark the first side you count with
a tick. You can check the area by counting the unshaded
squares. In diagram (b), there are 10 unshaded squares.
Add this number to your answer and you should get the
area of the whole shape: 15 + 10 = 25 cm².

A2 There are a possible number of answers.
    Your answer could be a
    rotation of either of these
    two answers.

COMMENT All you need to do is to find a pair of
numbers which multiply to give 16 (1×16 and 2×8).

A3 The perimeter is 12 cm.

COMMENT First, draw a diagram or a
sketch of the larger diamond shape.
Don't just multiply 9 × 4!

A4 18 m²

COMMENT Each square has an area of 1 m². There are
16 whole squares and 4 half squares. So, the total area
is 16 + 2 = 18 m².

A5 15 m³

COMMENT Count the cubes on each layer:
5 + 4 + 3 + 2 + 1 = 15

LEVEL 4 HANDLING DATA
13 COLLECTING DATA (page 36)

A1 **a**

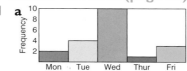

  b You cannot tell from his data.
  c There could have been a school trip or it
     might have been a religious holiday.

COMMENTS **a** Remember to label the axes.
b The chart only shows absences.

A2 **a** Coffee   **b** 130
    c It was possibly a cold or rainy day.

COMMENTS **a** The one with the highest line.
b Add together the heights of all the lines:
35 + 45 + 15 + 25 + 10 = 130
Read the frequency axis carefully. Use your ruler to
draw lines across to the axis.
c This is because of the amount of hot drinks sold.

A3 **a**

Amount	Tally	Frequency
0p–49p	̶H̶H̶ ̶H̶H̶ ‖	12
50p–99p	̶H̶H̶ ‖‖‖	9
£1.00–£1.49	‖	2
£1.50–£1.99	‖‖‖‖	4
£2.00–£2.49	‖‖‖	3
	TOTAL	30

  b

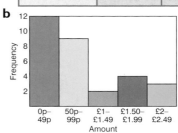

A4

No. of letters	Tally	Frequency
1	̶H̶H̶ ‖‖‖	8
2	̶H̶H̶ ‖‖‖	8
3	̶H̶H̶ ‖	6
4	̶H̶H̶ ̶H̶H̶	10
5	̶H̶H̶	5
6	‖	2
7	̶H̶H̶	5
8	‖‖‖‖	4
9	‖	1

There are **49** words in the extract.

COMMENT Always use a tally column. Add the numbers
in the frequency column to check your total is correct.

14 MODE AND MEDIAN (page 38)

A1 **a** mode = 2 median = 2
     b mode = 9 median = 14
     c mode = 4 median = 5
     d no mode median = 47

COMMENTS Put all the lists in order first.
c There are 8 values; the middle 2 are both 5, so the median is 5.
d There is no mode as all values appear once only. There are 10 values and the middle two are 46 and 48. The median, 47, is halfway between these two.

A2 **a** 6   **b** 25   **c** 5   **d** 18

COMMENT The range is largest value – smallest value.

A3 161 cm

COMMENT To find the median height, remember to first put the boys' heights in numerical order.

A4 **a** 7   **b** 7

COMMENTS a The mode is the most common shoe size, the one with the highest frequency. So the mode is size 7, as 8 pairs were sold, more than any other size.
b The median is the middle value of all 25. List all the sizes sold and find the 13th. Or, from the table, the 13th pair sold is a size 7. It is not 6 – the middle size.

15 LINE GRAPHS (page 40)

A1 **a** High 25°C, low 16°C   **b** 10°C
     c October

COMMENTS Each division on the temperature axis is 2°, so 1° is half a square.
a Highest and lowest points on the graph.
b High: 29°C, low 19°C The difference is 10°C.
c This is the least distance between the 2 lines. The least difference is 6°C in October.

A2 **a** See the graph.

     b No

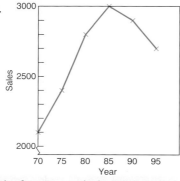

COMMENTS a Notice the frequency axis does not start at 0. The scale would be incredibly small if it did!
b You can only guess.

16 PROBABILITY (page 41)

A1 **a** unlikely   **b** equally likely
     c very unlikely **d** impossible
     e very likely   **f** certain   **g** likely

COMMENTS a There are 4 different suits to choose from.
b There are 3 even and 3 odd numbers.
c There are nearly 14 million different ways of choosing the 6 numbers.
d The world record is 3 minutes 44.39 seconds.
e Most cars on British roads are made in Europe.
f You are doing some now!
g Most of the letters are consonants.

LEVEL 5 NUMBER

1 LONG MULTIPLICATION AND LONG DIVISION (page 46)

A1 **a** 1152   **b** 13 312   **c** 13 032   **d** 8544

COMMENT d As well as the three methods in the examples, you can also use a method that depends on splitting the numbers down into tens and units.

$$
\begin{aligned}
10 \times 178 &= 1780\\
10 \times 178 &= 1780\\
10 \times 178 &= 1780\\
10 \times 178 &= 1780\\
5 \times 178 &= 890\\
1 \times 178 &= 178\\
1 \times 178 &= 178\\
1 \times 178 &= 178\\
\hline
48 \times 178 &= 8544
\end{aligned}
$$

A2 18 crates

COMMENT The problem is 432 ÷ 24.

A3 **a** 58   **b** 33   **c** 34   **d** 31

COMMENT You can also use the standard method, as shown by the following examples.

```
a          5 8          b          3 3
      16 )9 2 8              28 )9 2 4
         8 0                    8 4
         ———                    ———
         1 2 8                    8 4
         1 2 8                    8 4
         ———                    ———
         0 0 0                    0 0
```

A4 26 stamps and 6p change

```
COMMENT        2 6    r 6
           19 )5 0¹²0
```

2 DECIMALS (page 49)

A1
a
$$\begin{array}{r} 2.6 \\ + 5.7 \\ \hline 8.3 \end{array}$$
b
$$\begin{array}{r} 5.3 \\ - 2.8 \\ \hline 2.5 \end{array}$$
c
$$\begin{array}{r} 3.4 \\ \times\ \ 7 \\ \hline 23.8 \end{array}$$
d
$$\begin{array}{r} 1.6 \\ \hline 3)4.8 \end{array}$$

COMMENT Line up the decimal points.

A2
a
$$\begin{array}{r} 3.47 \\ + 6.85 \\ \hline 10.32 \end{array}$$
b
$$\begin{array}{r} 6.53 \\ - 3.86 \\ \hline 2.67 \end{array}$$
c
$$\begin{array}{r} 2.36 \\ \times\ \ \ 8 \\ \hline 18.88 \end{array}$$
d
$$\begin{array}{r} 2.52 \\ \hline 8)20.16 \end{array}$$

COMMENT Line up the decimal points

A3
a
7	5	8	0

b
7	4	8

c
7	5	.	8

COMMENT Make sure you notice the difference between 10 less and 10 times smaller.

A4 The total cost is £39.37:
$$\begin{array}{r} 18.45 \\ 5.60 \\ + 15.32 \\ \hline 39.37 \end{array}$$

A5 There are 2.88 kg of potatoes left:
$$\begin{array}{r} 5.63 \\ - 2.75 \\ \hline 2.88 \end{array}$$

A6 The cost will be 550.8p (or £5.51 to the nearest penny):
$$\begin{array}{r} 61.2 \\ \times\ \ \ 9 \\ \hline 550.8 \end{array}$$

A7 Each monthly instalment is £13.69:
$$\begin{array}{r} 13.69 \\ \hline 9)123.21 \end{array}$$

A8
a $4.6 \times \boxed{10} = 46$

b $4.6 \times 100 = \boxed{460}$

c $4.6 \boxed{\div} 10 = 0.46$

d $4.6 \div \boxed{100} = 0.046$

3 NEGATIVE NUMBERS (page 51)

A1
a In order: $^-6, ^-3, 5$

b In order: $^-6, ^-3, ^-2, ^-1$

c In order: $^-4, ^-1, 3, 7$

COMMENT Put each set of numbers on a number line.

A2 a $-5 > ^-6$ b $^-12 < 6$ c $7 > ^-8$

COMMENT Put each set of numbers on a number line.

A3
a $^+3$ b $^+2$ c $^+6$ d $^-1$
e $^-9$ f $^-5$ g $^-5$ h $^-5$
i $^+7$ j $^-8$ k $^-6$ l $^-8$

COMMENT Remember start at zero and count to the right for plus numbers and to the left for minus numbers. Questions (i) to (l) have the same values with one plus and one minus. These cancel each other out.

A4 In the fifth row, $^-1$ is missing. In the sixth row, $^-2$ and $^-4$ are missing. In the bottom row, $^-3$ and $^-5$ are missing.

COMMENT Both the first and last columns are decreasing by one each time.

A5 a 5250 metres   b 1500 metres
c 500 metres   d 4250 metres

COMMENT You have to work from the base at zero metres.

A6 a $^-14$ b $^-44$ c $^-145$

COMMENT You must be careful about what each division on the scale is worth and which way the scale reads. In (a) each division is 1 unit and the scale reads from right to left. In (b) each division is 2 units and the scale reads from right to left. In (c) each division is 10 units and the scale reads from left to right.

A7 £56.22 − £75.89 = $^-$£19.67.
$^-$£19.67 + £20.00 = £0.33.
So, I have 33p in the bank after Christmas.

COMMENT If you use a calculator then make sure you type the sum in correctly. If you get a little minus sign in your display this means you have put it in the wrong way.

4 FRACTIONAL AND PERCENTAGE PARTS (page 53)

A1 a £32   b £41   c £6   d £3.20
e £0.70 or 70 p   f £3.25   g £1.27
h 7p   i 15 elephants
j $2\frac{1}{2}$, or 2.5 packets of sweets

COMMENT Remember 10% is the same as dividing by 10.

A2 a £64   b £82   c £12   d £6.40
e £1.80   f £8.30   g £3.28   h 12 p
i 50 elephants.   j 9 packets of sweets.

COMMENT To find 20%, find 10% and then double it.

A3 **a** £120   **b** £16   **c** £40   **d** £90
      e £1   **f** £15   **g** £277.50
      h £13.44 **i** £4.55

COMMENT 30% is 3 times 10% etc. 25%, 50% and 75% are $\frac{1}{4}$, $\frac{1}{2}$ and $\frac{3}{4}$, respectively. 1% is the same as dividing by 100.

A4 **a** 200   **b** 120   **c** 30   **d** 40

COMMENT To find $\frac{2}{3}$, first find $\frac{1}{3}$ by dividing by 3 and then double your answer.

A5 **a** 75   **b** 24   **c** 30   **d** 15

COMMENT To find $\frac{3}{4}$, first find $\frac{1}{4}$ by dividing by 4 and then times your answer by 3.

A6 **a** 14   **b** 20   **c** 28   **d** 15

COMMENT Find the single fraction first.

A7 20 square feet.

COMMENT $\frac{1}{7}$ is 10 square feet.

A8 **a** 500 ml   **b** 40 washes

COMMENTS a 25% is $\frac{1}{4}$ which is an extra 100 g

b $\frac{1}{4}$ of 32 is 8.

5 Fractions, ratio and proportion (page 54)
A1 **a** $\frac{2}{3}$ **b** $\frac{3}{7}$ **c** $\frac{1}{3}$

COMMENT The HCFs are 6, 3 and 15 respectively.

A2 For example, $\frac{6}{8}$ or $\frac{9}{12}$ or $\frac{30}{40}$.

COMMENT Multiply the numerator and denominator by the same number.

A3 £1.54

COMMENT Find out the cost of 1 tin, £1.32 ÷ 6 = £0.22, then multiply by 7.

A4 **a** 50 centilitres   **b** 12.5 kilograms

COMMENTS a Each kilogram takes 20 centilitres so $2\frac{1}{2}$
kilograms takes $2\frac{1}{2} \times 20 = 50$ cls.

b Find out how many 10 centilitres there are in $2\frac{1}{2}$ litres
= 250 centilitres. 250 ÷ 20 = 12.5.

A5 £2.00

COMMENT Each mile costs 25p (£1.25 ÷ 5). 8 × 25 = 200 pence.

6 NUMBER PATTERNS, SQUARE NUMBERS AND OPPOSITE OPERATIONS (page 59)
A1 **a** − 7   **b** + 6   **c** ÷ 5   **d** × 9

COMMENT The operation changes, but the number stays the same.

A2 **a** 13   **b** 16   **c** 3   **d** 27

COMMENT Reverse the machines:

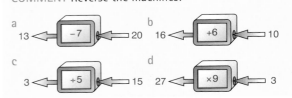

A3 **a** 3   **b** 49

COMMENT Reverse the machines:

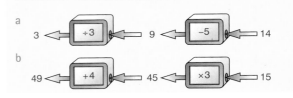

A4 **a** (i) 9 (ii) 81 (iii) 100
    b (i) 6 (ii) 8 (iii) 1

COMMENT To square, times a number by itself. Square root is the opposite.

7 APPROXIMATING AND ROUNDING (page 61)
A1 **a** 2   **b** 17   **c** 10

A2 **a** 40   **b** 50   **c** 70   **d** 80
    e 110   **f** 100   **g** 50   **h** 500

COMMENT Even though (f) and (h) are hundreds, the answers are still to the nearest 10.

A3 **a** 200   **b** 600   **c** 300   **d** 500

A4 **a** 3000   **b** 2000   **c** 1000   **d** 5000

A5 **a** 2400   **b** 7000   **c** 35 000
    d 180 000

A6 **a** 20   **b** 10   **c** 5   **d** 30

A7 **a** 50 × 60 = 3000   **b** 10 × 70 = 700
    c 5 × 70 = 350   **d** 300 × 600 = 180 000

A8 60 + 40 = 100, 30 − 20 = 10
    and 100 ÷ 10 = 10.

8 SIMPLE FORMULAE (page 63)

A1 **a** $n - 3$ **b** $4n + 1$, or $4 \times n + 1$
      c $n \div 3$ or $\frac{n}{3}$ **d** $\frac{n}{2} - 2$

COMMENT In (b), you could put $n \times 4$ but not $n4$.

A2 **a** $\times 7$ **b** $+ 8$ **c** $\times 3$ and $- 9$.

COMMENT The answer to (c) has to be in this order.

A3 **a** Charles is correct.

COMMENT $2n + 4n + n + n = 8n$ $3 - 5 + 7 = +5$
You cannot mix up letters and numbers.

     b $4n + 5$

COMMENT Do the letters separately from the numbers:
$3n - n + 2n = 4n$; $-6 + 7 + 4 = 5$

A4 **a** Because $n + n + n + n = 4n$
      b Because two sides meet and are not on the
         perimeter.
      c $n + n + n + n + n + n = 6n$

COMMENT Think of a number sum:
$3 + 3 + 3 + 3 = 4 \times 3 = 12$.
If it works with numbers, it works with letters.

9 USING FORMULAE AND RULES: COORDINATES IN ALL FOUR QUADRANTS (page 66)

A1 $A = (^-5, 5)$; $B = (^-4, 3)$; $C = (1, 4)$;
    $D = (4, ^-2)$; $E = (^-3, ^-3)$; $F = (^-5, ^-2)$.

A2
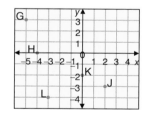

A3 **a** $A = (^-2, 4)$; $B = (3, 4)$; $C = (1, ^-2)$.
    b $D = (^-4, ^-2)$.

COMMENT It might help to draw the parallelogram.

A4 The other co-ordinates are $(0, 3)$; $(^-1, 2)$ and
    $(^-2, 1)$. They make a straight line:

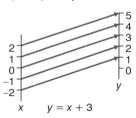
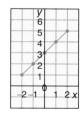

LEVEL 5 SHAPE, SPACE AND MEASURES
10 ANGLES (page 71)

A1 **a** 74   **b** 137

COMMENTS You might have to extend the lines before
you can measure the angles.
 a The base line on the protractor needs to be vertical. It
   is an acute angle.
 b It might help if you turn the page round until one of
   the lines is horizontal. This is an obtuse angle.

A2 **a**   **b**

COMMENT Try drawing angles from a horizontal line
about 5 cm long.

11 SYMMETRY OF 2-D SHAPES (page 73)

A1 **a** 2   **b** 1   **c** 2

COMMENT Look back at the diagrams if you are not sure.

A2 **a** 2   **b** 6   **c** 4

COMMENT Look back at the diagrams if you are not sure.

A3 It has 8 lines of symmetry and
its order of rotational symmetry
is also 8.

12 METRIC AND IMPERIAL UNITS (page 75)

A1 **a** 8320 m   **b** 1.52 m   **c** 4.385 kg   **d** 0.8 g
    e 470 cl   **f** 0.42 l

COMMENTS a $8.32 \times 1000 = 8320$ m
 b $152 \div 100 = 1.52$ m
 c $4385 \div 1000 = 4.385$ kg
 d $800 \div 1000 = 0.8$ g
 e $4.7 \times 100 = 470$ cl
 f $420 \div 1000 = 0.42$ l
 a and e: larger to smaller units, so multiply.
 b, c, d and f: smaller to larger units, so divide.

A2 Yes

COMMENT The mass of the sacks is
$85 \times 50 = 4250$ kg $= 4.25$ tonnes.
The total mass is $4.5 + 4.25 = 8.75$ tonnes.
8.75 is less than (<)10, so it is safe to cross.

A3 **a** 1.8 m   **b** 2250 l   **c** 900 g   **d** 800 m

COMMENTS a 1 foot = 30 cm, 6 feet = 180 cm = 1.8 m
 b $500 \times 4.5 = 2250$ l
 c $2 \times 450 = 900$ g
 d 1 mile = 1.6 km = 1600 m, $\frac{1}{2}$ mile = 800 m

13 Estimating measures (page 76)

A1 Your answers should be close to these:
   a about 2 mm   **b** about 30 g
   c about 300 l **d** about 200 cm
   e about 2–3 kg

COMMENT Remember you can check these afterwards.

A2 About 5 g

COMMENT 2.5 kg = 2.5 × 1000 g = 2500 g
2500 ÷ 500 = 5 g

14 Area (page 78)

A1 35 cm²

COMMENT Use the formula
Area = length × width = 7 x 5 = 35 cm²

A2 4 cm

COMMENT If the area is length × width then
40 = 10 × width.

A3 **a, b** and **c**

COMMENT The areas of the rectangles are 48 cm²,
48 m², 48 cm² and 49 cm² respectively.

A4 2 cm by 8 cm, 1 cm by 16 cm, etc.

COMMENT Any pair of numbers that multiply together
to give 16 will be correct.

A5 The area of rectangle A is 48 cm². The area of
rectangle B is 12 cm². So rectangle A is a quarter of
the area of rectangle B.

COMMENT You must show all the working to justify
your answer.

Level 5 Handling data

15 Mean and range (page 85)

A1 **a** 14 and 8   **b** 149.5 and 27
   c 3.9 and 2.9

COMMENTS a The mean is 112 ÷ 8 = 14.   The range is
   18 – 10 = 8.
b The mean is 897 ÷ 6 = 149.5. The range is 162 – 135
   = 27.
c The mean is 19.5 ÷ 5 = 3.9. The range is 5.4 – 2.5 = 2.9.

A2 3.5 °C and 20 °C.

COMMENT The mean is 42 ÷ 12 = 3.5. Be careful how
you add together the minus numbers and remember to
count 0. The range is 20°C (14 – (⁻6) = 20).

A3 **a** Claire: 1 hour; Sarah: 1 hour
   b Claire: 1 hour; Sarah: $1\frac{3}{4}$ hours
   c Their means are the same. This shows they
      spent the same amount of time on their
      homework over the week. Sarah's range is
      wider than Claire's which shows she is more
      variable on the time she spends.

COMMENTS a Claire's mean is
$$\frac{\frac{1}{2} + \frac{3}{4} + 1\frac{1}{2} + 1\frac{1}{4} + 1}{5} = 1 \text{ hour.}$$
Sarah's mean is
$$\frac{1 + 1 + \frac{3}{4} + 2 + \frac{1}{4}}{5} = 1 \text{ hour.}$$
b Claire's range is $1\frac{1}{2} - \frac{1}{2}$ = 1 hour.
Sarah's range is $2 - \frac{1}{4} = 1\frac{3}{4}$ hours.

16 Pie charts (page 87)

A1 **a** (i) About $\frac{1}{8}$ (ii) About $\frac{1}{3}$
   b No   **c** About 10 million

COMMENTS a (i) About eight of these sectors would fit
   in the chart.
(ii) About three of these sectors would fit in the chart.
   These are only estimates: you will be allowed
   answers that are close to these fractions.
b The pie chart only shows the proportions of the
   population.
c 60÷ 6 = 10. The sector is about $\frac{1}{6}$ of the diagram.

A2 **a** About 20%   **b** (i) £60   (ii) 12%

COMMENTS a An answer between 16% and 24% is
   acceptable.
b (i) 1% of £400 is £4.   15% is £4 × 15 = £60.
   (ii) Use part (i) to help: 1% of £400 is £4, so, £48 is 12%.

A3 **a** 360° ÷ 24 = 15°
   b

Activity	Angle of sector	No. of hours
Sleeping	135°	9
School	105°	7
Meals	30°	2
Watching TV	45°	3
Travelling	15°	1
Youth Club	30°	2

COMMENTS a 1 complete turn = 360°. 1 day = 24 hours.
   1 hour = 360° ÷ 24 = 15°.
b The angles were made easy to measure. Check the total is
   360°. Divide the angles by 15 to get the number of hours.

17 THE PROBABILITY SCALE (page 88)

A1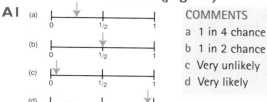

(a), (b), (c), (d) scales from 0 to 1/2 to 1

COMMENTS
a 1 in 4 chance
b 1 in 2 chance
c Very unlikely
d Very likely

18 CALCULATING PROBABILITIES (page 90)

A1 a $\frac{1}{13}$ b $\frac{1}{4}$ c $\frac{2}{13}$

COMMENTS Total number of equally likely outcomes is 52.
a $\frac{4}{52} = \frac{1}{13}$ b $\frac{13}{52} = \frac{1}{4}$ c $\frac{8}{52} = \frac{2}{13}$
Always remember to cancel fractions.

A2 a $\frac{1}{4}$ b $\frac{5}{8}$ c $\frac{1}{2}$

COMMENTS Total number of equally likely outcomes is 8.
a $\frac{2}{8} = \frac{1}{4}$ (There are two 3s). b $\frac{5}{8}$ (Don't include the 2s).
c $\frac{4}{8} = \frac{1}{2}$ (There are four even numbers).

A3 $\frac{2}{7}$

COMMENT There are 49 equally likely outcomes, with 14
favourable outcomes (3, 13, 23, 30, 31, 32, 33, 34, 35, 36,
37, 38, 39, 43). P(at least one 3 on 1st ball) = $\frac{14}{49} = \frac{2}{7}$

A4 a 30% b 60% c 80%

COMMENTS Total number of equally likely outcomes is 100.
a P(blue) = $\frac{30}{100}$ = 30% b P(green or red)= $\frac{60}{100}$ = 60%
c P(not green) = $\frac{80}{100}$ = 80%.
If it's not green then it must be red, blue or yellow.

A5 a $\frac{21}{30}$ b $\frac{1}{10}$ c $\frac{4}{5}$

COMMENTS Total number of equally likely outcomes is 60.
a P(car or van) = $\frac{42}{60} = \frac{21}{30}$ b P(lorry or bus) = $\frac{6}{60} = \frac{1}{10}$
c P(not a motorbike) = $\frac{48}{60} = \frac{4}{5}$ (60 – 12 = 48)

LEVEL 6 NUMBER

1 WORKING WITH DECIMALS (page 99)

A1 a 4 tenths b 6 hundredths
    c 4 hundredths d 2 thousandths

COMMENT You need to learn the column headings.

A2 4.002 4.02 4.022 4.202 4.21

COMMENT Add zeros to give each decimal numbers the
same number of places.

A3 a 0.7 b 0.1 c 0.7 d 2.8

COMMENT Tenths is the first decimal place. Show this
by putting (1 d.p.) after the answer.

A4 a 0.55 b 0.24 c 0.82 d 2.38

COMMENT Put (2 d.p.) after these answers.

A5 a 0.42 b 0.0016 c 0.009 d 0.45
    e 35 f 40 g 360 h 6.3

COMMENT Count the decimal places.

A6 a 60 b 5000 c 2000 d 4000

COMMENT Make (a) 300 ÷ 5 and so on.

A7 a 700 × 0.08 = 56 b 900 ÷ 0.3 = 3000
    c 50 × 0.03 ÷ 0.3 = 1.5 ÷ 0.3 = 5
    d 300 × 0.06 ÷ 0.9 = 18 ÷ 0.9 = 20

COMMENT There can be other answers. They must be
about the same and you must not use a calculator.

2 COMPARING NUMBERS, FRACTIONS AND PERCENTAGES (page 102)

A1 a 1 : 5 b 2 : 5 c 1 : 9 d 3 : 11

COMMENT Cancel by the highest common factor.

A2 a 1 : 5 b 1 : 2.5 c 1 : 5 d 1 : 0.2

COMMENT Divide by the first number.

A3 a $\frac{1}{4}$ b $\frac{2}{5}$ c $\frac{4}{15}$ d $\frac{3}{10}$

COMMENT Write as fractions, then cancel.

A4 The increase is 44 – 32 = 12 cm.
The fraction is $\frac{12}{32} = \frac{3}{8}$

COMMENT The highest common factor (HCF) is 4.

A5 a 33.3% b 60% c 18%

COMMENT The calculation in a, for example,
is 15 ÷ 45 × 100.

A6 a 30 elephants have been killed:
       30 ÷ 150 × 100 = 20%
    b 100% – 20% = 80%

COMMENT In b take the decrease away from 100.

A7 a 16 × 78 ÷ 100 = £12.48
    b 30 × 190 ÷ 100 = 57 pupils
    c 18 × 120 ÷ 100 = £21.60
    d 35 × 200 ÷ 100 = 70
    e 52 × 138 ÷ 100 = £71.76
    f 48 × 59 ÷ 100 = 28.32 = 28 desks

COMMENT You can divide by 100 first and then
multiply. The answer will still be the same.

3 EQUIVALENT FRACTIONS, DECIMALS AND PERCENTAGES (page 105)

A1 **a** 0.67 **b** 0.22 **c** 0.08 **d** 0.175

COMMENT Move digits two places to the right.

A2 **a** 44% **b** 40% **c** 87.5% **d** 66%

COMMENT Move the digits two places to the left.

A3 **a** 75% **b** 20% **c** 28.6% **d** 88.9%

COMMENT **c** and **d** are rounded to one d.p.

A4 **a** $\frac{7}{25}$ **b** $\frac{12}{25}$ **c** $\frac{2}{5}$ **d** $\frac{2}{3}$

COMMENT Write over 100 then cancel.

A5 **a** 0.1 **c** 0.875
  b 0.625 **d** 0.344 (3 d.p.)

A6 **a** $\frac{9}{10}$ **b** $\frac{17}{25}$ **c** $\frac{3}{8}$ **d** $\frac{13}{20}$

COMMENT Write over 10, 100 and so on, then cancel if you can.

A7 **a** 45% **b** 290 g

COMMENT 45% of 100 is 45 so 45% of 200 is 90. You can also multiply 200 by 1.45.

A8 **a** $\frac{1}{5}$ **b** 6 gallons

COMMENT $\frac{1}{5}$ of 5 gallons is 1 gallon.

A9 $\frac{9}{20}$ is 0.45. 170 × 1.45 = 246.5

COMMENT This can be rounded to 246 or 247 fish.

4 SOLVING RATIO PROBLEMS (page 107)

A1 **a** 2 : 3 : 4 **b** 1 : 3 : 5 **c** 2 : 5 : 6 : 7
  d 1 : 2 : 4 **e** 4 : 7 : 9 : 11 **f** 2 : 3 : 7 : 10

COMMENT The factors are 2, 5, 3, 7, 2 and 6.

A2 **a** 5 : 2 : 1 **b** 2 : 1 : 1

COMMENT **a** The ratio is 15 : 6 : 3. Factor 3. In **b** The new ratio is 12 : 6 : 6. Factor 6.

A3 **a** £16 : £12 **b** £3 : £9 : £18
  c £55 : £65

COMMENT Add the 'shares' and divide.

A4 1000 hardback books

COMMENT 2 + 5 = 7 shares. 1400 ÷ 7 = 200.
200 × 5 = 1000.

A5 560 fiction books

COMMENT Start by dividing by 5 this time.

5 TRIAL AND IMPROVEMENT (page 108)

In each case do a table like the one in the example. Don't forget to check the halfway value between the estimates with one decimal place.

A1 2.6 **A2** 4.4 **A3** 3.4

6 ADDING AND SUBTRACTING FRACTIONS (page 110)

A1 **a** $\frac{11}{12}$ **b** $\frac{13}{24}$ **c** $\frac{17}{15} = 1\frac{2}{15}$

COMMENTS **a** The new denominator is 12. $\frac{8}{12} + \frac{3}{12} = \frac{11}{12}$

b The new denominator is 24. $\frac{4}{24} + \frac{9}{24} = \frac{13}{24}$

c The new denominator is 15. $\frac{6}{15} + \frac{11}{15} = \frac{17}{15}$
This answer can be turned into a mixed number.

A2 **a** $\frac{1}{2}$ **b** $\frac{7}{20}$ **c** $\frac{11}{18}$

COMMENTS **a** The new denominator is 6. $\frac{4}{6} - \frac{1}{6} = \frac{3}{6} = \frac{1}{2}$
This answer will cancel down.

b The new denominator is 20. $\frac{12}{20} - \frac{5}{20} = \frac{7}{20}$

c The new denominator is 18. $\frac{14}{18} - \frac{3}{18} = \frac{11}{18}$

LEVEL 6 ALGEBRA

7 FINDING THE NTH TERM (page 116)

A1 **a** $3n$ **b** $2n - 1$ **c** $3n - 1$ **d** $6n - 4$

COMMENT Look for difference and compare the pattern to the times tables. In **a** the pattern is the same as the 3 times table.

A2 **a** (i) $5n$ (ii) $3n$ (iii) $3n + 1$ (iv) $3n + 3$
  b (i) $m = 5n$ (ii) $m = 3n$ (iii) $m = 3n + 1$
  (iv) $m = 3n + 3$

COMMENT For each example write out a table.
For example, for **a** (i): Pattern: 1 2 3 4 5
                Matches: 5 10 15 20 25
There are other answers, for example, (iv) could be $m = 3(n + 1)$.

A3 **a** It goes up in 5s and $5 \times 1 - 4 = 1$ and so on.
  b Row B is $5n - 3$, Row C is $5n - 2$, Row D is
  $5n - 1$ and Row E is $5n$. **c** $25n - 10$

COMMENT This pattern goes up by 25 each time. If you add all the rules for rows A, B, C, D and E you get:
$5n - 4 + 5n - 3 + 5n - 2 + 5n - 1 + 5n$
This adds up to $25n - 10$.

8 LINEAR EQUATIONS (page 119)

A1 **a** 19 **b** 8 **c** 40 **d** ⁻1

> COMMENT Check your answers!

A2 I started with 8.

> COMMENT 8 × 3 = 24, then 24 – 5 = 19.

A3 **a** $a = 3$ **b** $b = 25$ **c** $c = 32$

> COMMENT Do not forget to check!

A4 **a** $2y + 7 = 27$ **b** $2y = 20 \ (- 7)$
$y = 10 \ (\div 2)$

> COMMENT Check: 2 × 10 + 7 = 27 ✓

A5 **a** $c = 13$ **b** $e = 3$ **c** $d = 5$ **d** $f = 9$

> COMMENT Remember to 'get rid' of the smallest letter term.
> In **a** subtract c, in **b** add $4e$, in **c** subtract $3d$, in **d** subtract f.

A6 **a** $3 × 1 - 4 = 4 × 1 - 5 = -1$
  b $b = 7$ **c** $b = 3$
  d Alex and Cath: if $3b - 4 = 3b + 2$, no value of
  b will work.

> COMMENTS **b** The equation is $4b - 5 = 3b + 2$.
> **c** The equation is $4b - 5 = b + 4$.
> **d** Try to find a number. You can't!

9 MAPPINGS AND GRAPHS (page 122)

A1 Coordinate pairs are
(⁻2, ⁻3), (⁻1, 0), (0, 3),
(1, 6), (2, 9).

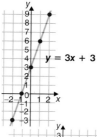

A2 Coordinate pairs are
(⁻6, ⁻3), (⁻3, ⁻2), (0, ⁻1),
(3, 0), (6, 1).

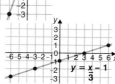

> COMMENT Choose multiples of 3 as this avoids fractions.

A3 **a** 2 **b** ⁻2 **c** $\frac{1}{3}$

> COMMENT **a** and **b** have the same steepness but **b** has a
> negative gradient.

A4

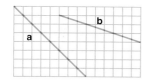

> COMMENT **a** is 1 across 1 down. **b** is 3 across 1 down.

10 DRAWING LINEAR GRAPHS (page 126)

A1 **a** $y = -\frac{1}{2}x + 1$ **b** $y = 2x$ **c** $y = 3x + 2$

> COMMENT In (b) the intercept is at the origin so c = 0.

A2 **a** Points are (⁻3, ⁻4), (0, ⁻3), (3, ⁻2)
  b Points are (⁻1, ⁻6), (0, ⁻4), (1, ⁻2), (2, 0)

> COMMENT There are other answers but the ones given
> are sensible ones. Only three of the points in **b** are
> actually needed to draw the graph.

Graphs for Questions
2, 3 and 4:

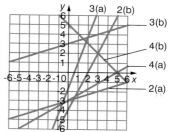

> COMMENTS **a** By cover-
> up $x = 5$, $y = -3$ **b** By
> cover-up $x = 5$, $y = 5$

Graphs for Questions
5 and 6:

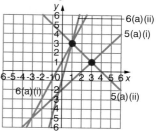

A5 Lines meet at
(3, 1).

A6 Lines meet at
(1, 3).

LEVEL 6 SHAPE, SPACE AND MEASURES

11 ISOMETRIC DRAWINGS (page 131)

A1

> COMMENT Draw the face
> BCGF first, then the vertical
> edges 3 units high.

12 GEOMETRIC PROPERTIES OF SHAPES (page 135)

A1 **a** 78° **b** 58° **c** 30°
  d 40°, 80° and 120°

> COMMENT **a** Angles in a triangle = 180°.
> $a = 180° - (47° + 55°) = 78°$
> **b** For an isosceles triangle, base angles are equal.
> $b = 180° - (61° + 61°) = 58°$
> **c** In first triangle, the 3rd angle = $180° - (56° + 64°)$
> = 60°; in second triangle, angles are c, 90° and 60°
> (opposite angle). So, $c = 180° - (90° + 60°) = 30°$
> **d** Angles in a quadrilateral = 360°
> $d + 2d + 3d + 120° = 360°$
> $6d + 120° = 360°$
> $6d = 240°$
> so $d = 40°$

A2 **a** 900° **b** 290°

> COMMENT a Use $S = 180°$ $(n - 2)°$ with $n = 7$.
> $S = 180° \times 5 = 900°$
> b The two missing interior angles are 120° and 40°.
> So, $x + 120° + 40° + 90° + 140° + 140° + 80° = 900°$,
> $x + 610° = 900°$, $x = 290°$.

A3 **a** 87° **b** 63°

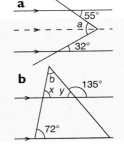

> COMMENTA a Draw another
> parallel line; a is the sum
> of the two alternate angles.
> b $x = 72°$ (corresponding angle);
> $y = 45°$ (angles on line);
> $b = 180° - (72° + 45°) = 63°$
> (angles in a triangle).

13 TRANSFORMATION GEOMETRY (page 138)

A1   START
   FORWARD 60
   RIGHT TURN 90
   FORWARD 30
   RIGHT TURN 90
   FORWARD 20
   LEFT TURN 90
   FORWARD 50
   RIGHT TURN 90
   FORWARD 40
   RIGHT TURN 90
   FORWARD 80

A2

> COMMENT Remember to use
> tracing paper. Put the tracing
> paper over the T and the point A
> and use a pencil point to hold the
> tracing paper at A. Now rotate
> through 90° anticlockwise.

A3

> COMMENT
> Remember to use
> tracing paper.

A4   A' (0, 2),
   B' (4, ⁻2),
   C' (⁻4, ⁻2).

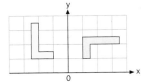

COMMENT **Multiply
the numbers in each
coordinate pair by 2 and
then plot these new coordinates.**

A5

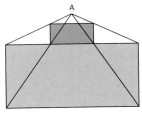

Diagram not to scale

> COMMENT Join A to the
> four vertices of the
> rectangle. Measure these
> rays and multiply these
> lengths by 3. Draw these
> new rays from A and join
> to get the enlarged
> rectangle.

14 PERIMETER, AREA AND VOLUME FORMULAE (page 141)

A1   **a** 240 cm² **b** 60 m² **c** 14.58 cm²
   d 480 mm²

> COMMENTS a Area of rectangle = $12 \times 16 = 192$ cm²
> Height of triangle = $24 - 16 = 8$ cm
> Area of triangle = $\frac{1}{2} \times 12 \times 8 = 48$ cm²
> Total area = $192 + 48 = 240$ cm²
> b Area of rectangle = $10 \times 8 = 80$ m²
> Area of triangle = $\frac{1}{2} \times 10 \times 4 = 20$ m²
> Area of shape = $80 - 20 = 60$ m²
> c $A = bh = 5.4 \times 2.7$. Ignore slant height
> d $A = \frac{1}{2}(a + b)h = \frac{1}{2}(30 + 18) \times 20$
> $= 480$ mm²

A2   **a** 8000 m² **b** 4000 m²

> COMMENTS a Length of field = $120 - 20 = 100$ m
> Width of field = $100 - 20 = 80$ m
> Area of field = $100 \times 80 = 8000$ m²
> b Area of whole complex = $120 \times 100 = 12\,000$ m²
> Area for spectators = $12\,000 - 8000 = 4000$ m²

A3   3.75 m²

> COMMENT The side is a trapezium.
> $A = \frac{1}{2}(a + b)h = \frac{1}{2}(3 + 2) \times 1.5 = 3.75$ m²

A4   **a** $c = 75.4$ cm and $A = 452.4$ cm²
   b $c = 8.2$ m and $A = 5.3$ m²

> COMMENT Using calculator value for π:
> a $r = 12$, $c = 2\pi r = 2 \times \pi \times 12 = 75.4$
> $A = \pi r^2 = \pi \times 144 = 452.4$
> b $r = 1.3$, $c = 2\pi r = 2 \times \pi \times 1.3 = 8.2$
> $A = \pi r^2 = \pi \times 1.3^2 = 5.3$

A5   397.1 cm²

> COMMENT Area of triangle = $\frac{1}{2} \times 20 \times 24 = 240$
> Area of semicircle = $\frac{1}{2}\pi r^2 = \frac{1}{2} \times \pi \times 10^2$
> $= 157.1$ (1d.p.)
> Total area = $240 + 157.1 = 397.1$ cm²

15 FREQUENCY DIAGRAMS (page 146)

A1 a

Time (t mins)	Frequency
$0 < t \leqslant 2$	6
$2 < t \leqslant 4$	8
$4 < t \leqslant 6$	6
$6 < t \leqslant 8$	5
$8 < t \leqslant 10$	2
$10 < t \leqslant 12$	3

b

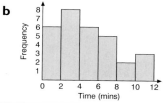

COMMENT a Check that the frequencies add up to 30.
b Notice the numbers on the time axis are the boundaries of the class intervals.

A2 a

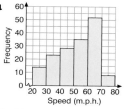

b 160

c No. You do not know the speed of each vehicle from the grouped frequency table. At level 7 you will learn how to estimate this.

COMMENT a Use 2 mm graph paper so that you can plot the frequencies accurately.
b Add together all the frequencies.

A3 a

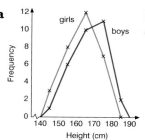

b 160 to 170 cm
c The boys are generally taller than the girls.

COMMENT a The points are plotted in the middle of the class intervals. Use a different type or colour of line for boys and girls.
b 22 is the highest frequency for the boys and girls added together. The most common height must be given as an interval.

16 DRAWING PIE CHARTS (page 147)

A1

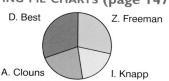

COMMENT The table shows how to calculate the angles.

Candidate	Frequency	Calculation	Angle
Z. Freeman	10	$\frac{10}{36} \times 360 = 100$	100°
I. Knapp	7	$\frac{7}{36} \times 360 = 70$	70°
A. Clouns	8	$\frac{8}{36} \times 360 = 80$	80°
D. Best	11	$\frac{11}{36} \times 360 = 110$	110°
Totals	36		360°

When drawing angles, you are allowed to be up to 2° out. It is not necessary to write the angles on the pie chart but you must label each sector.

A2

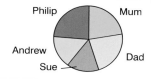

COMMENT The table shows how to calculate the angles.

Person	Amount	Calculation	Angle
Mum	£11.00	$\frac{11}{50} \times 360 = 79.2$	79°
Dad	£11.50	$\frac{11.5}{50} \times 360 = 82.8$	83°
Sue	£7.50	$\frac{7.5}{50} \times 360 = 54$	54°
Andrew	£8.00	$\frac{8}{50} \times 360 = 57.6$	58°
Philip	£12.00	$\frac{12}{50} \times 360 = 86.4$	86°
Totals	£50.00		360°

To make it easier to draw the pie chart, the angles have been rounded to the nearest degree.

17 SCATTER DIAGRAMS (page 149)

A1 a There is positive correlation. **b** No

COMMENT a The taller you are, the more you are likely to weigh.
b Going across from the y–axis at 62, the points close by are for the shorter people.

A2 a There is a negative correlation.
b In warmer weather people drink fewer hot drinks.

COMMENT a As the temperature increases the number of hot drinks sold decreases.

b Or in cooler weather people buy more hot drinks.

A3 a

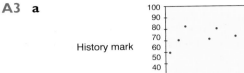

b There is no obvious correlation.

COMMENT a Use 2 mm graph paper to make it easier to plot the points.

b Someone who is good at French is not necessarily good or bad at History.

18 PROBABILITY AND COMBINED EVENTS (page 152)

A1 a IR, IO. IN, RI, RO, RN, OI, OR, ON, NI, NR, NO   b $\frac{1}{3}$

COMMENT a He cannot choose the same letter twice because he keeps the first letter.

b There are 12 equally likely outcomes.
P(two-letter word)= $\frac{4}{12}$ = $\frac{1}{3}$ (IN, OR, ON, NO)

A2 a Barbara and Ian; Barbara and Linda; Barbara and Mike; Ian and Linda; Ian and Mike; Linda and Mike   b $\frac{2}{3}$

COMMENT a No names can be the same and the order of the names does not matter.

b There are 6 equally likely outcomes.
P(a boy and a girl) = $\frac{4}{6}$ = $\frac{2}{3}$

A3

COMMENT There are 12 possible outcomes. You could also show the outcomes on the diagram as H1, H2, H3 etc.

A4 a

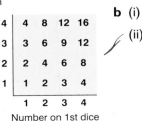

b (i) $\frac{3}{4}$
(ii) $\frac{1}{4}$

COMMENT a It is easier to put the scores rather than Xs on the sample space diagram.

b There are 16 equally likely outcomes.
(i) P(even) = $\frac{12}{16}$ = $\frac{3}{4}$
(ii) P(odd) = 1 − $\frac{3}{4}$ = $\frac{1}{4}$ (mutually exclusive events)

LEVEL 7 NUMBER

1 ROUNDING TO SIGNIFICANT FIGURES AND ESTIMATING (page 158)

A1 a 3   b 4   c 4   d 2

COMMENT Count all the digits except zero. Only count zero if it is between other digits.

A2 a 1   b 3   c 4   d 3

COMMENT You might have said 2 for the answer to d. You should count the last zero.

A3 a 200   b 4000   c 3000   d 0.08

A4 a 250   b 2400   c 2300   d 0.084

A5 a 2460   b 2420   c 2290   d 0.0843

A6 a 35–50   b 35–40   c 360–600 d 6–10

COMMENT Answers can be within a range.

A7 About 4 per pound so about 40 stamps

COMMENT 24 is about 25. This is not 1 sf but it is a nice number to work with, particularly with pounds.

A8 A litre is about 80p so about £40. (50 × 80)

A9 a 6 × 30 = 180 minutes = 3 hours
b Probably over as 30 is 4 miles longer

COMMENT She might not run at the same pace in a marathon, so you could say under. Either would be accepted as long as your reasoning was correct.

2 MULTIPLYING BY NUMBERS BETWEEN 0 AND 1 (page 160)

A1 a n^2, and $n \div 0.5$ b $0.5n$, $\sqrt{n}$ and $\frac{1}{n}$
c $\sqrt{n}$, $n \div 0.5$ and $\frac{1}{n}$ d $0.5n$ and n^2

COMMENT a and b Just substitute numbers into each expression.

c and d Use your calculator to work these out.

A2 a $n \div 0.5$ b $0.5n$

COMMENT Squaring (n^2) , square root ($\sqrt{n}$) and reciprocal ($\frac{1}{n}$) depend on whether n is greater than 1 or less than 1.

A3

	$n > 1$	$n < 1$	$n = 1$
n^3	Always $> n$	Always $< n$	Always $= n$
$\sqrt{n}$	Always $< n$	Always $> n$	Always $= n$
$\frac{1}{n}$	Always $< n$	Always $> n$	Always $= n$

COMMENT Work a few out on a calculator.

3 USING A CALCULATOR EFFICIENTLY (page 163)
A1 **a** $5 + 5 \otimes 3 = 20$ **b** $8 + 6 \div 2 = 11$
c $3 + 4^{②} = 19$ **d** $(3 \oplus 4)^2 = 49$
e $2 \times 5^{②} = 50$ **f** $4 \otimes 3 - 6 = 6$

COMMENT Use BODMAS to decide which to do first.

A2 **a** $4 + 4 \times (4 \div 4) = 8$
b $4 \div (4 + 4) + 4 = 4.5$
c $(4 + 4) \div (4 + 4) = 1$
d $(4 + 4 + 4) \div 4 = 3$

COMMENT Try brackets in different places until it works.

A3 **a** square, $\div, \times, +, -$. Answer is 35.
b $+$ in (), $-$ in (), square, $\div$. Answer is 36.

COMMENT Check by typing the sums into your calculator 'as they read'.

A4 **a** 21.8   **b** 24.7

COMMENT Either put a bracket around everything on top and bottom or press equals to work out top row. **b** may need nested brackets on top.

A5 **a** 3.84   **b** 80.1

COMMENT In **a** put 3.2+1.8 into the memory. In **b** put 98.5 – 18.5 into the memory and do

8	+	MR	x²	=	÷	MR	=

A6 37.2

4 PROPORTIONAL CHANGES (page 165)
A1 **a** £150   **b** £250   **c** £260   **d** 65 kg

COMMENT Find 1% in each case, then 100%, for example, for a divide by 40, multiply by 100.

A2 250 pupils

COMMENT Sum is $16 \div 6.4 \times 100$.

A3 £230

COMMENT This time you have to include the original so divide by 103.2 first.

A4 50 trees

COMMENT Find 100% which is 250 then do 20% of 250.

A5 Yes. The final cost is £960

COMMENT This is not really a reverse percentage. 20% increase on £1000 gives £1200, and a 20% decrease of £1200 gives £960.

A6 **a** £270.40 **b** £2621.59

COMMENT This is best done using decimals. In **a** multiply by 1.04 twice and in **b** multiply by 1.07 four times.

A7 **a** (i) 27 cm (ii) 49.21 cm **b** 6 weeks

COMMENT The decimal is 1.35.

A8 **a** (i) £9600 (ii) £4915.20
b 7 years (Between 6 and 7 years)

COMMENT The decimal for this sum is 0.8 because it is a 20% decrease.

A9 £4140.56

COMMENT As the number of years is so big you would probably lose count so do the sum 1000×1.07^{21} as each year is 1.07 times the value of the last year.

LEVEL 7 ALGEBRA
5 FINDING THE NTH TERM WHEN THE RULE IS QUADRATIC (page 171)
A1 **a** $n(n + 2)$ **b** $n(n + 1)$
c $(n - 1)(n + 1)$ **d** $2n(n + 1)$

COMMENTS a is $1 \times 3, 2 \times 4, 3 \times 5, 4 \times 6, 5 \times 7, ...$
b is $1 \times 2, 2 \times 3, 3 \times 4, 4 \times 5, 5 \times 6, ...$
c is $0 \times 2, 1 \times 3, 2 \times 4, 3 \times 5, 4 \times 6, ...$
d is $2 \times 2, 4 \times 3, 6 \times 4, 8 \times 5, 10 \times 6, ...$

A2 **a** Second difference is 3.
b 8, 22, 42, 68, 100, 138
c $1 \times 8, 2 \times 11, 3 \times 14, 4 \times 17, 5 \times 20, 6 \times 23$
d $3n + 5$
e $\frac{1}{2}n(3n + 5)$

COMMENT The trick of multiplying by 2 sometimes works. You will usually be given a big hint when to use it. Don't forget to divide by 2 for the final answer.

A3 **a** $\frac{1}{2}n(n + 3)$ **b** $\frac{1}{2}(n + 1)(n + 6)$

COMMENTS a The doubled series is: $1 \times 4, 2 \times 5, 3 \times 6, 4 \times 7, ...$
b The doubled series is: $2 \times 7, 3 \times 8, 4 \times 9, 5 \times 10, ...$

A4 $2n(n + 1)$

COMMENT Same as 1d.

6 SOLVING SIMULTANEOUS EQUATIONS BY ALGEBRA (page 173)

A1   **a** $x = 10, y = 2$ **b** $x = 2, y = {}^-1$
      c $x = 3, y = 2$ **d** $a = {}^-1, b = 2$

COMMENT In **a** use equation 2 minus equation 1. In **b** 1 minus 2. In **c** 1 add 2 and in **d** 2 minus 1 or 1 minus 2.

A2   **a** $x = 3, y = 1$ **b** $x = 2, y = {}^-1$
      c $x = 5, y = 2$ **d** $a = 7, b = {}^-8$

COMMENT In **a** multiply 1 by 2 and add. In **b** multiply 2 by 3 and add. In **c** multiply 2 by 2 and add or multiply 2 by 3 and subtract. In **d** multiply 1 by 5 and subtract.

A3   **a** $x = 3, y = {}^-1$ **b** $x = 2, y = {}^-1$
      c $x = 5, y = 3$ **d** $a = 6, b = {}^-4$

COMMENT In every case you can balance the xs by multiplying an equation by the coefficient of x in the other equation. For example, in **a** multiply equation 1 by 3 and equation 2 by 5.

A4   **a** $2t + 7d = 1310$ **b** $d = 150, t = 130$
        $3t + 4d = 990$

COMMENT Multiply 1 by 3, 2 by 2.
$$6t + 21d = 3930$$
$$6t + 8d = 1980$$
$$13d = 1950$$

A5   The Hills pay £3.00. Tea costs 60p and buns are 90p.

COMMENT $3t + 5s = 630$
         $4t + 3s = 510$

A6 $6x + 48y = 138$
     $5x + 22y = 70$
     $3x + 35y = £96.50$

COMMENT You should find that $x = £3.00$ and $y = £2.50$.

7 USING GRAPHS TO SOLVE SIMULTANEOUS EQUATIONS (page 175)

A1   **a** $x = 3, y = 2$ **b** $x = 3, y = 2$

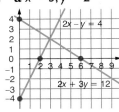
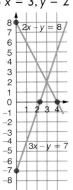

COMMENT **a** Draw both lines by the cover-up rule and don't forget to check.

b The first is not easy to draw by the cover-up rule as the x-value is a fraction $2\frac{1}{3}$. So you must check the answer.

A2   **a**

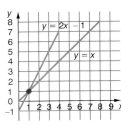

x	0	1	-2
y	-1	1	3

b $x = 1, y = 1$

COMMENT You can use the gradient-intercept method to draw the second graph.

A3 $x = -1,$
      $y = -1$

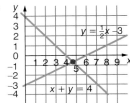

COMMENT For the first line use the gradient-intercept method. For the second line use the cover-up method.

A4   **a**

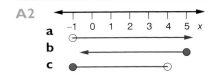

b $x = 4.7, y = -0.7$
Check:
$4 \times 4.7 - 3 = -0.65$
(almost 0.7)
$4.7 + {-0.7} = 4$
(spot on)

COMMENT You can be a bit out as you would not be expected to read a graph to more than 1 decimal place. (The actual answer is $4\frac{2}{3}, -\frac{2}{3}$).

8 SOLVING INEQUALITIES (page 177)

A1   **a** $^-1, 0, 1, 2, 3, 4$ **b** $0, 1, 2, 3, 4, 5$
      c $^-3, ^-2, ^-1, 0, 1, 2, 3, 4$

COMMENT You must understand the difference between strict inequalities and inclusive inequalities.

A2

COMMENT Remember open circles are strict inequalities.

A3   **a** $x \leqslant 3$ **b** $x > 1$ **c** $-3 \leqslant x < 5$

A4   **a** $x < 13$ **b** $x \geqslant 8$

COMMENT Solve these just like you solve an equation, e.g. in **b** $x = 2 \times 4 = 8$

A5 **a** $x \leqslant {}^-9$ **b** $x \geqslant 2$

COMMENT Move the smallest x-term over the inequality, eg in **b** $3x - 2 \geqslant 20 - 8x$, $11x - 2 \geqslant 20$, $11x \geqslant 22$

A6 **a** $x > {}^-6$ **b** $x \geqslant {}^-16$

COMMENT These have a minus x-term so need to have the signs changed at some stage.

A7 When a negative number is squared the answer is positive.

COMMENT Don't forget that all squares are positive. You will probably not get a square at level 7.

A8 **a** ${}^-4, {}^-3, {}^-2, {}^-1, 0, 1, 2$ **b** 16

COMMENT Squaring a negative gives a positive.

9 EXPANDING BRACKETS (page 178)
A1 **a** $x^2 + 8x + 15$ **b** $x^2 + 9x + 18$
  c $x^2 + 8x + 16$

A2 **a** $x^2 + 4x - 5$ **b** $x^2 - 3x - 10$
  c $x^2 - 9$

A3 **a** $x^2 - 5x + 4$ **b** $x^2 - 11x + 30$
  c $x^2 - 6x + 9$

LEVEL 7 SHAPE, SPACE AND MEASURES
10 PYTHAGORAS' THEOREM (page 183)
A1 **a** 11.66 cm **b** 5.65 m **c** 7.07 cm

COMMENTS

a x is the hypotenuse.
$$x^2 = 10^2 + 6^2$$
$$= 136$$
$$x = \sqrt{136}$$
$$x = 11.66 \text{ (2 d.p.)}$$

c z is the hypotenuse.
$$z^2 = 5^2 + 5^2$$
$$= 50$$
$$z = \sqrt{50}$$
$$z = 7.07 \text{ (2 d.p.)}$$

b y is a short side.
$$y^2 = 8.1^2 - 5.8^2$$
$$= 31.97$$
$$y = \sqrt{31.97}$$
$$y = 5.65 \text{ (2 d.p.)}$$

A2 87 cm

COMMENT AC is the hypotenuse in the triangle ACD.
Let AC = x.
$$x^2 = 80^2 + 35^2$$
$$= 7625$$
$$x = \sqrt{7625}$$
$$x = 87 \text{ (2 s.f.)}$$

A3 **a** 15 cm **b** 90 cm^2

COMMENTS a The perpendicular bisects YZ.
Draw a sensible diagram:
h is a short side.
$$h^2 = 16^2 - 6^2$$
$$= 220$$
$$h = \sqrt{220}$$
$$h = 14.8 \text{ cm}$$
$$= 15 \text{ cm to nearest cm}$$
b $A = \frac{1}{2}bh = \frac{1}{2} \times 12 \times 15 = 90$ cm^2

11 AREAS OF COMPOUND SHAPES AND VOLUMES OF PRISMS (page 186)
A1 **a** 75 cm^2 **b** 7.5 m^2 **c** 615 cm^2 **d** 3.2 m^2

COMMENTS a Use symmetry to help. The two trapezia have the same area. The height of each one is 3 cm.
The area of each trapezium = $\frac{1}{2}(10 + 3) \times 3 = 19\frac{1}{2}$.
So the area of both is 39 cm^2.
Area of rectangle = 36
Total area = 39 + 36 = 75 cm^2
b Area = product of diagonals $\div$ 2 = 15 $\div$ 2 = 7.5 m^2
c Area of trapezium = $\frac{1}{2}(20 + 42) \times 25 = 775$
Area of rectangle = 20 $\times$ 8 = 160
Area of shape = 775 $-$ 160 = 615 cm^2
d Area of square = 2.4 $\times$ 2.4 = 5.76
Radius of circle = 0.9
Area of circle = $\pi \times 0.9^2 = 2.545$
Area of shape = 5.76 $-$ 2.545
$$= 3.2 \text{ m}^2 \text{ (1 d.p.)}$$

A2 3.24 m^3

COMMENT Area of triangle = $\frac{1}{2} \times 1.2 \times 1.8 = 1.08$
Volume of tent = 1.08 $\times$ 3 = 3.24 m^3

A3 12 m

COMMENT The side of the pool is a trapezium.
Area of trapezium = $\frac{1}{2}(1 + 2) \times 50 = 75$
Volume of the pool = $Ax = 75x$
$$75x = 900$$
$$x = 900 \div 75 = 12$$

12 LOCI (page 188)
A1

A ——————————————— B

COMMENT The line AB is the required locus. It is parallel to the other two lines and is exactly halfway between them.

A2 a   **b**

 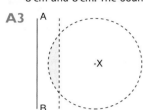

COMMENTS a All points lie on a circle which has a radius of 3 cm.
b All points lie in the region between two circles with radii 3 cm and 5 cm. The boundary lines are not included.

A3
COMMENT The diagram must be accurately drawn. The boundary lines should be dotted. All the points to the left of the dotted line are less than 2 m from AB and the points inside the circle are less than 4 m from X. The shaded region satisfies both conditions.

A4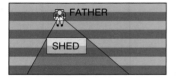

COMMENT The shaded region shows the area where Liam cannot be seen. The boundary lines should be included. Notice that it is not just the area directly behind the shed.

13 ACCURACY OF MEASUREMENT AND COMPOUND MEASURES (page 191)
A1 $405 \text{ miles} \leqslant d < 415 \text{ miles}$

COMMENT Since the number is rounded to the nearest 10 miles, half a unit is 5 miles.

A2 $69.5 \text{ cl} \leqslant V < 70.5 \text{ cl}$

A3 1.6 m/s

COMMENT Use the formula $s = \frac{d}{t}$.
Change 4 minutes 10 seconds to seconds to give 250 seconds. $d = 400$ m and $t = 250$ s, so $s = 400 \div 250 = 1.6$ m/s.

A4 16 070 400 000 miles

COMMENT Use the formula $d = st$. Change 1 day into seconds. 1 day = $60 \times 60 \times 24 = 86\,400$ s.
$d = 186\,000 \times 86\,400 = 16\,070\,400\,000$ miles. (Your calculator may not show this answer, but remember that you can ignore the zeros before you multiply.)

A5 5.79 kg

COMMENT Use the formula $M = DV$.
$M = 19.3 \times 300 = 5790$ g = 5.79 kg

A6 2.7 g/cm^3

COMMENT Use the formula $D = \frac{M}{V}$.
Find the volume of the sheet in cm^3.
Length = 10 m = 1000 cm
Width = 45 cm
Thickness = 0.08 mm = 0.008 cm
So volume of sheet = $1000 \times 45 \times 0.008$
$\qquad\qquad\qquad = 360 \text{ cm}^3$
$D = 972 \div 360 = 2.7 \text{ g/cm}^3$

14 ENLARGEMENT BY A FRACTIONAL SCALE FACTOR (page 193)
A1 **a** Enlargement scale factor $\frac{1}{3}$ about (0, 0).

   b Enlargement scale factor $\frac{1}{2}$ about (4, 0)

COMMENTS a Count the squares from the origin.
b Join equivalent corners with 'rays' to see that they all pass through (4, 0).

A2

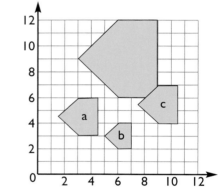

LEVEL 7 HANDLING DATA
15 DESIGNING QUESTIONNAIRES (page 199)
A1 **a** How often do you go to restaurants in a month?
Never ☐ once ☐ 2 or 3 times ☐
more than 3 times ☐
What type of restaurant do you prefer?
English / Chinese / Indian / Italian / French / Other
   b Did you do your Maths homework last night?
Yes ☐ No ☐
How long do you usually spend on the homework?
up to 30 mins ☐ 30 mins to 1 hour ☐
more than 1 hour ☐

COMMENT For time intervals, all possible values should be covered and with no overlap.

A2 Questionnaire for Year 9 pupils.
1 Which form are you in?
9A ☐ 9B ☐ 9C ☐ 9D ☐ 9E ☐ 9F ☐
2 Would you like to go on a Year 9 visit?
Yes ☐ No ☐ Don't know ☐
3 Which day would you prefer for the visit?
Mon ☐ Tue ☐ Wed ☐ Thu ☐ Fri ☐ Sat ☐ Sun ☐
4 If you had the choice, where would you like to go?
Blackpool ☐ London ☐ Theme park ☐
Outdoor pursuit centre ☐ Other ☐
5 How much are you prepared to spend?
less than £5 ☐ £5 –£10 ☐ more than £10 ☐

COMMENT For price intervals, all possible values should be covered and with no overlap.

16 FINDING AVERAGES FOR GROUPED DATA
(page 203)

A1 $\bar{x} = \frac{\Sigma fx}{\Sigma f}$

$= \frac{216}{60} = 3.6$

COMMENT Remember it is usual to give the mean to 1 dp.

Score (x)	Frequency (f)	fx
1	8	8
2	11	22
3	9	27
4	12	48
5	9	45
6	11	66
Totals	60	216

A2 a

Annual salary	Frequency (f)	Midpoint (x)	fx
£10 000–	37	12 500	462 500
£15 000–	30	17 500	525 000
£20 000–	8	22 500	180 000
£25 000–	3	27 500	82 500
£30 000–	2	32 500	65 000
Totals	80		1 315 000

$\bar{x} = \frac{\Sigma fx}{\Sigma f} = \frac{1\,315\,000}{80} = £16\,400$ (to 3 sf)

b The median. It does not take into account the few high wages which inflate the mean.

COMMENT Take the last interval to be £30 000 – £35 000.

A3 $\bar{x} = \frac{\Sigma fx}{\Sigma f} = \frac{255.00}{100} = 255$ hours
The modal class is 200–250 hours.

COMMENT

Lifespan (t hours)	Frequency (f)	Midpoint (x)	fx
100<t≤150	5	125	625
150<t≤200	15	175	2625
200<t≤250	30	225	6750
250<t≤300	25	275	6875
300<t≤350	15	325	4875
250<t≤400	10	375	3750
Totals	100		25 500

The modal class is the one with the highest frequency.

A4 a $\bar{x} = \frac{2737}{50} = 54.7$ marks (1 dp)

b $\bar{x} = \frac{\Sigma fx}{\Sigma f} = \frac{2725}{50} = 54.5$ marks

c The estimate for the mean is very close to the exact mean. It is much quicker to find the estimate.

COMMENT Notice that the midpoint of the class intervals uses $\frac{1}{2}$ marks. The grouped frequency table is:

Marks	Frequency (f)	Midpoint (x)	fx
1–20	4	10.5	42
21–40	11	30.5	335.5
41–60	12	50.5	606
61–80	17	70.5	1198.5
81–100	6	90.5	543
Totals	50		2725

An easy way of finding the midpoint is to add together the two end points of the interval and divide by 2.

17 LINES OF BEST FIT (page 205)

A1 a Mean for the masses = 175 g
Mean for the extensions = 6.9 cm

b

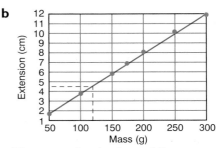

c The extension is about 4.5 cm

COMMENTS a For masses: mean = 1050 ÷ 6 = 175
For extensions: mean = 41.4 ÷ 6 = 6.9
b Remember to plot the point for the means. Use 2 mm graph paper to make your answers more accurate. The diagram shows positive correlation.
c Draw on the dotted lines to help.

18 RELATIVE FREQUENCY AND PROBABILITY (page 207)

A1 19 or 20

COMMENT Use the data with the most trials. Estimated probability for getting a black ball = 0.19. Estimated number of black balls = 0.19 × 100 = 19. Since this is an estimate, an answer of 20 is acceptable.

A2 a

	Total no. of trials	No. of trials for each colour	Relative frequency
Blue	200	46	0.23
Green	200	62	0.31
Red	200	37	0.185
Yellow	200	55	0.275

Yes. The relative frequencies should all be about the same.

b P(blue) = 0.23   P(green) = 0.31
    P(red) = 0.185   P(yellow) = 0.275

COMMENT b Check that the answers add up to 1.

A3 a 120

b

Month	Number of pupils	Relative frequency (to 3dp)
Jan	9	0.075
Feb	8	0.067
Mar	12	0.1
Apr	10	0.083
May	11	0.092
Jun	9	0.075
Jul	10	0.083
Aug	7	0.058
Sep	11	0.092
Oct	14	0.117
Nov	9	0.075
Dec	10	0.083

c (i) 0.083
    (ii) 0.9
d 4

COMMENTS a the frequencies: 9 + 8 + 12 + 10 + 11 + 9 + 10 + 7 + 11 + 14 + 9 + 10
b relative frequency = Number in month ÷ 120
c (i) Read the value from the table.
   (ii) 1 − 0.1 = 0.9
d 30 × 0.117 = 3.51, so four pupils will have birthdays in October.

ANSWERS TO MENTAL ARITHMETIC TESTS
MENTAL ARITHMETIC TEST 1 (page 95)

1	3006	2	87	3	580
4	25	5	7	6	13
7	470	8	64	9	9
10	760	11	19	12	8.7–8.9 inc.
13	7.15	14	36	15	120
16	81	17	34	18	8
19	5903	20	17	21	130
22	4 500 000	23	0.8	24	53
25	9.95	26	2404	27	6
28	16–24 inc.				

MENTAL ARITHEMTIC TEST 2 (page 219)

1	860	2	17	3	8
4	740	5	0.03	6	6.5
7	8.15	8	90	9	69
10	34	11	160	12	6 500 000
13	0.6	14	75	15	40
16	200	17	6080	18	65–70 inc.
19	6	20	11	21	70
22	£9.95	23	140–160 inc.	24	108
25	704	26	54	27	40
28	280	29	36	30	900
31	5	32	380–420 inc.		

ANSWERS TO TEST QUESTIONS WITH EXAMINER'S COMMENTS

LEVEL 4 NUMBER (page 10)

A1   **a** 27   **b** 7   **c** 100   **d** 10

COMMENTS **a** You do not have to work out 38 + 17, if you see that 28 is ten less than 38 so just add 10 to 17.
b Because this is a subtraction problem you take 10 off both numbers to keep the sides balanced.
c You can probably see that $40 \times 10 = 400$ so that the answer is 4×100.
d Again, it is easy to see that $7000 \div 100 = 70$ (cancel two zeros), so the answer is $700 \div 10$.

A2   **a** <   **b** >   **c** >

COMMENTS **a** When working with directed numbers, think of a number line. $^-7$ is to the left of $^-2$ so it is the smaller number.
b $3 - 2 = 1$ which is to the right of $^-5$ on the number line so it is bigger.
c $5 - 5 = 0$ which is to the right of $4 - 6 = {}^-2$.

$$^-8\ ^-7\ ^-6\ ^-5\ ^-4\ ^-3\ ^-2\ ^-1\ 0\ 1\ 2\ 3\ 4\ 5\ 6\ 7\ 8$$

A3   **a** 21 years   **b** 1989   **c** 1995

COMMENTS **a** From 2001 to 2010 is 9 years. Add this to 12.
b Subtract 12 from 2001.
c James will be 6 years old in 2001. Subtract 6 from 2001.

A4   £5.65

COMMENTS Before 6 pm it will cost them £11.15. After 6 pm it will cost them £16.80.

A5   **a** 54, 108
     b For example $108 \div 4 = 27$ or $54 \div 2 = 27$

COMMENTS **a** 50% is a half so double 27. Just multiply 27 by 4, which you should be able to do mentally. $4 \times 25 = 100$, $4 \times 2 = 8$, $100 + 8 = 108$.
b Any combination that works will be correct but you should use the clues from part (a).

A6   **a** 5°C   **b** 11°C

COMMENTS **a** You can use the thermometer to start at $^-2°$ and count up 7 places.
b You can mark 3 and $^-8$ on the thermometer and count the divisions between them.

A7   75p

COMMENT This question tests if you can find information from a diagram. You have to realise that there are five lots of 8 minutes in 40 minutes. Then calculate 5×15.

A8   **a** $5 + 2 = 10 - 3$ **b** $12 - 3 = 3 \times 3$
     c $2 + 1 = 9 \div 3$ **d** $6 - 6 = 7 - 7$
                        $6 \div 6 = 7 \div 7$

COMMENT In this question you just have to try various combinations of the signs until you find one that works.

A9   **a** 1.2 m   **b** 1.15 m   **c** 170 cm

COMMENTS **a** You need to realise that this is an addition problem: $0.9 + 0.3$.
b This is a subtraction problem: $1.45 - 0.3$.
c There are 100 cm in 1 metre, so $1.7 \times 100 = 170$.

A10   **a** $4000 \rightarrow 3751$ **b** $1500 \rightarrow 1537$ **c** $1600 \rightarrow 1573$

COMMENT You need to find the combination of cards that gives the number closest to the given number.

A11   **a** 58 coaches   **b** £24 360   **c** £8.12

COMMENTS **a** This is a division problem. Use a calculator to work out $3000 \div 52 = 57.69...$. Remember that you cannot have a decimal part of a coach, so 58 coaches are needed.
b This is a multiplication problem: 58×420.
c This is a division problem: $24\,360 \div 3000$

A12   1.2 kg

COMMENTS Read the total mass from the scale. Two small tins weigh $5 - 2.6 = 2.4$ kg. One weighs half this.

A13   £26.89

COMMENTS **a** Ben pays $24 \times £8.62 = £206.88$. Subtract £179.99 from this. You must show your working. If you make just one small error and write down a wrong answer you will get no marks.

LEVEL 4 ALGEBRA (page 21)

A1   **a** (8, 8)   **b** (40, 40)
     c Because all the ● are at corners with even-numbered coordinates.
     d (4, 3), (6, 5), (8, 7)   **e** (14, 13)   **f** 10

COMMENTS **a** Look for a pattern. On tile 1 the ● is at (2, 2). On tile 2 it is at (4, 4), on tile 3 it is at (6, 6).
b You should realise that the coordinate numbers are double the tile number each time.
d Read the first two of these from the graph. For the third one, note that both values go up by 2 each time.
e You need to spot that the x-value is twice the tile number and the y-value is one less than this.
f This is a reverse of the pattern in part (e). The tile number is half the x-value.

A2 **a** (5, 2)   **b** (2, 1)

COMMENTS a Mark the point on the diagram.
b D has the same *x*-coordinate as the point A and the same *y*-coordinate as the point C.

A3 **a** Add 12, multiply by 3, multiply by 2 then add 6 (or multiply by 1.5).
b Divide by 2.

COMMENTS b This rule has to work for both examples.

A4 **a** Exact: 77 °F, approximate: 80 °F
b Exact: 32 °F, approximate: 30 °F
c Exact: $10 \times 1.8 = 18$, $18 + 32 = 50$ °F, approximate: $2 \times 10 = 20$, $20 + 30 = 50$ °F

COMMENTS a Use your calculator to work out exactly $25 \times 1.8 + 32$. Find the approximate value mentally or use your calculator to work out $25 \times 2 + 30$.
b Remember that anything multiplied by zero is zero.
c You need to show the calculation to get the marks.

A5 **a** 51 minutes   **b** 245 minutes   **c** 56 minutes

COMMENTS a You need to put the value of 3 into the formula for the microwave oven. $12 \times 3 + 15 = 51$
b This time put the value of 7 into the formula for an electric oven. $30 \times 7 + 35 = 245$
c Microwave: $12 \times 2 + 15 = 39$ minutes. Electric oven: $30 \times 2 + 35 = 95$ minutes. Then subtract: $95 - 39 = 56$.

A6 **a** 1 group of 16, 2 groups of 8, 4 groups of 4, 8 groups of 2, 16 groups of 1
b 1, 2, 3, 4, 6, 12

COMMENTS a These are the factors of 16.
b Factors go together in pairs, 1×12, 2×6, 3×4.

A7 **a** More classes in Y9 and Y8 $\rightarrow 4 - 3$
How many pupils altogether in Y8 and Y9 $\rightarrow (3 \times 27) + (4 \times 25)$
There are more pupils in Y9 than Y8 $\rightarrow (4 \times 25) - (3 \times 27)$
b How many pupils are there in Y9?

COMMENT Match the story in words and in numbers.

LEVEL 4 SHAPE, SPACE AND MEASURES (page 31)
A1 **a** Most on Tuesday, least on Friday.
b 0.25 cm   **c** 1.5 cm, 15 mm

COMMENTS a You have to know that 0.8 is the largest decimal and 0.05 is the smallest decimal in the list.
b This is a subtraction, $0.5 - 0.25$.
c The first part is an addition, $0.2 + 0.8 + 0.5$. For the second part, remember that there are 10 mm in 1 cm.

A2 **a** The shape is a quadrilateral. The shape is a kite.
b (5, 7)   **c** Cross at (7, 5)   **d** Cross at (7, 1)

COMMENTS a Make sure you know the properties of all the quadrilaterals – square, rectangle, rhombus, parallelogram, kite and trapezium.
b Remember to go across first then up.
c You can draw the mirror line which is the line $y = x$, or use tracing paper to help.
d The rotation is a quarter-turn about (3, 3) in a clockwise direction. You can use tracing paper to help you.

A3 **a** Acute   **b** No. The angles are the same size.

COMMENTS a You should know that acute angles are between 0° and 90°, obtuse angles are between 90° and 180° and reflex angles are bigger than 180°.
b The value of the angle is not affected by the length of its arms or sides. You can use tracing paper to check.

A4 **a** No. The triangle has four small triangles and the hexagon has six small triangles.
b Yes. Both perimeters are 6 units.

A5 **a** 90°   **b** 30°   **c** 150°   **d** 1 hour

COMMENTS a You can see from the picture that the angle is a right angle.
b Each hour has an angle of 30°.   c This is 5×30.
d The minute hand does a full turn (360°) in an hour.

A6 **a** Area 5 cm², perimeter 12 cm
b For example a 3 cm $\times$ 2 cm rectangle
c For example, 10 cm for a 3×2 rectangle
d 7 cm²
e The diagonal across a 1×1 square is longer than 1 cm.

COMMENTS a You can work both of these out by counting squares and sides.
b There are many answers, any shape that covers six squares will be correct.
c The answer will depend on your shapes.
d You can do this by counting squares. There are 5 full squares and four half squares.
e There are four lines like this and four lines that are 1 cm long, so the perimeter is over 8 cm.

A7 **a** Yes   **b** Fourth shape

COMMENTS a Each piece has seven whole squares and two half squares, so each is 8 cm².
b You can use a piece of tracing paper, trace the shape and turn it over.

Level 4 Handling data (page 42)

A1 a Spinner A **b** It doesn't matter.
  c Three sectors with a 4 and two sectors with a 3

COMMENTS **a** 1 has a bigger angle on spinner A than on spinner B. You can see that the angle is larger, or you can quote the probabilities.
P(1) on spinner A = $\frac{1}{5}$, P(1) on spinner B = $\frac{1}{6}$.
b Both spinners have the same chance. The size of the spinner doesn't matter. It is the size of the angles that matter. The angles are all the same and each spinner has P(3) = $\frac{1}{6}$.
c To make 4 more likely you need to fill in more than two sectors. To make the chance of a 3 equal to the chance of a 2 you need to fill in two sectors,

A2 10 black and 10 white

COMMENT If there are equal chances of getting a black or a white then there must be the same number of each colour in the bag. 20 ÷ 2 = 10.

A3 a The chance depends on how many of each colour there are in the bag.
  b 3   **c** 5, 6, 7 or 8 tokens

COMMENTS **a** You can quote the probabilities, P(gold) = $\frac{4}{5}$ and P(silver) = $\frac{1}{5}$.
b The numbers of each colour must be equal.
c The number of gold must be higher than the number of silver. In fact, there does not have to be any silver tokens at all.

A4 a Year 7 – eat a school dinner
    Year 8 – eat a school dinner
    Year 9 – eat a packed lunch
  b 12

COMMENTS **a** You have to see which of the shaded bars for each year group is tallest.
b You can work out how many are in each year (be careful of scales). In Year 8 there are 36 + 26 + 42 = 106, In Year 9 there are 36 + 28 + 30 = 94. 106 − 94 = 12.

A5 1, 3, 5, 7, 9

COMMENTS The 'clues' for this are in the question. Each card is different. It is impossible for it to be even, so it must be odd. It is certain to be less than 10. There are only five odd numbers less than 10.

Level 5 Number (page 55)

A1 a $^-1 + 4 = 3$ or $^-3 + 6 = 3$
  b $0 + ^-1 = ^-1$ or $^-5 + 4 = ^-1$ or $^-7 + 6 = ^-1$ or $^-3 + 2 = ^-1$
  c $^-4$ **d** $^-7 + ^-5 + ^-3 = ^-15$

COMMENT When you are working with directed numbers, you will find a number line useful. Start counting at zero. Count to the right for positive numbers and to the left for negative numbers.

A2 a £4.50   **b** £45   **c** 35%   **d** £5

COMMENT In this question you can use the table to help you or you can just work out the answers.
a 10% of £30 is £3 and 5% is £1.50.
b From the table you can see that £2.25 (5%) and £4.50 (10%) have a total of £6.75 (15%).
c From the table 5% of £10 is 50p so £3.50 = 7 × 50p = 7 × 5% = 35%.
d From the table 50p is 5% of £10, so 25p must be 5% of £5.

A3 a 12 168   **b** 13

COMMENTS **a** This is a long multiplication problem. You can use any method you are happy with. The two most common methods are the standard column method and the box method.
b This is long division. The best way to do this is by 'chunking' or repeated subtraction.

A4 a

  b $\frac{2}{12} = \frac{1}{6}$, $\frac{1}{2} = \frac{12}{24}$, $\frac{1}{4} = \frac{6}{24}$

COMMENTS **a** The line is divided into 12 sections. So $\frac{1}{3}$ is 4 sections and $\frac{5}{6}$ is 10 sections.
b To find equivalent fractions multiply or divide both top and bottom by the same number, so for example, in the first question divide 2 and 12 by 6. This is also called cancelling down.

A5 a $\frac{1}{3}$ **b** 40%   **c** Shape C

COMMENTS **a** There are 2 whole squares shaded out of 6 squares, which is $\frac{2}{6}$. This needs to be cancelled down.
b 4 squares out of 10 squares are shaded. 4 out of 10 is 40%.
c Shape C has 25% shaded but shape D has less than 25% shaded.

A6 a 1 : 3   **b** 2 : 3
  c For example, 1 more carton of orange

COMMENTS a A ratio compares like quantities. In this case there is 1 carton to every 3 cartons.

b The ratio this time is $1 : 1\frac{1}{2}$, which can be doubled to get rid of the fractions.

c Any combination that works will be correct. For example, 1 more carton of apple juice and 3 more cartons of orange. You need to end up with half as much apple as orange.

A7 £2.12, £12.25

COMMENTS You can work the first part out on a calculator as $8 \times 26.5 \div 100 = 2.12$.
An alternative way to do the second part to use a multiplier, so calculate $0.125 \times 98 = £12.25$.

A8 a 600 ml **b** 50 ml **c** No

COMMENTS a The ratio is $1 : 4$ so you need four times as much water as screenwash.

b The ratio is $1 : 9$ so you need nine times as much water as screenwash.

c A ratio of $1 : 4$ means that the screenwash makes up one-fifth of the total mixture and the water four-fifths.

LEVEL 5 ALGEBRA (page 67)
A1 $7 + 5t, 3b + 17$

COMMENTS You can also write the first part as $5t + 7$. Collect like terms. $2t + 3t = 5t$. You cannot do anything with the 7.
For the second part, $b + 2b = 3b$ and $7 + 10 = 17$.

A2 3 ... 1200 ... Maria ... 6 ... Kay ... $1\frac{1}{2}$ ...

COMMENTS You need to read off the values from the axes, reading across or down from the points on the graph.

A3 Ann and Ben have a combined age of 69.
Ben is twice as old as Cindy.
The mean of the three ages is 28.

COMMENTS You need to make up a word story to match the letter story. Those given are examples, other answers are possible. You could use the information to say what the ages are, Ann is 39 and Cindy is 15.

A4 a The number of grey tiles
b 1 black and 36 grey **c** 20 **d** $1 + 6N$
e Any picture that has 1 black tile at the centre and 4 arms going off.

COMMENTS b You should spot that there is always 1 black tile and the number of grey tiles is 3 times the pattern number.

c Take away the 1 black tile and divide by 3.

A5 a $6 + 5y$ and $5y + 6$
b Yes, because there could be 10 sweets in each packet.

COMMENTS a Each packet has y mints so 5 packs have $5y$ mints plus 6 single mints.

b You can show how to solve the equation.
$5y + 6 = 56, 5y = 10, y = 10$

A6 a £48, £72
b Graph goes through $(0, 0)$ and $(30, 72)$.
c £50, £64
d Graph goes through $(0, 22)$ and $(30, 64)$.
e 22 swims

COMMENTS a Multiply the number of swims by £2.40.
c This time the calculation is £22 + swims × £1.40.
e Read the point on the 'swims' axis where the graphs cross.

LEVEL 5 SHAPE, SPACE AND MEASURES (page 79)
A1

		Number of lines of symmetry			
		0	1	2	3
Order of	1	E	F		
	2	B		C	
	3	D			A

COMMENT Use tracing paper to work with symmetry.

A2 a $5, 5, 7, 4 + 3$ or $5, 5, 6, 4 + 2$
b For example, $8, 6 + 2, 7, 4 + 3$
c $5 + 5, 6 + 4, 7 + 3, 8 + 2$

COMMENTS In this question you have to find combinations of rods that make the required shapes.
b There are seven other possible combinations.
c Each side must be 10 cm long.

A3

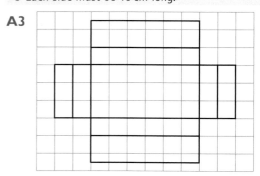

COMMENT The base is given so you have to build on this. The two ends have two tabs that are 3 cm by 1 cm. The sides each have one tab that is 6 cm by 1 cm and one tab that is 6 cm by $1\frac{1}{2}$ cm.

A4 a 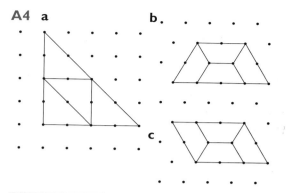 **b.**

c.

COMMENT You will find it helpful to trace the shapes onto tracing paper.

A5 a 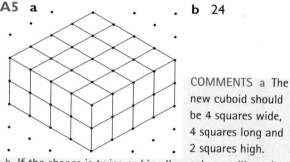 **b** 24

COMMENTS a The new cuboid should be 4 squares wide, 4 squares long and 2 squares high.

b If the shapes is twice as big all round you will need $2 \times 2 \times 2 = 8$ times as many. So $8 \times$ the 3 original cubes = 24 cubes.

A6 a **b** 90° **c**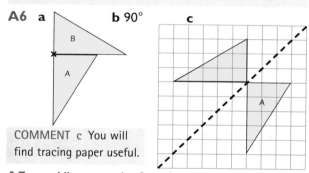

COMMENT c You will find tracing paper useful.

A7 a All except the 2 cm by 4 cm rectangle
b 40 cm

COMMENTS a Remember that the area of a rectangle is width × breadth.

b If the area is 100 cm² then the side must be 10 cm. This means that the perimeter is 4×10 cm = 40 cm.

A8 8 kilometres

COMMENT You need to know some conversions from imperial (British) units to metric (European) units. These are 2.2 pounds weight ≈ 1 kilogram, 5 miles ≈ 8 kilometres, 1 inch ≈ 2.54 centimetres, 1 litre ≈ 1.75 pints.

A9 a Accurate drawing
b 5.5–5.7 cm **c** 110–114 metres

COMMENTS a You need to make an accurate drawing with an angle of 80° at the left-hand end of the line and an angle of 30° at the right-hand end of the line.
b Use a ruler to measure the line.
c Multiply the answer in **b** by 20 and change the units to metres.

A10 a 14.1 ounces **b** 225 grams **c** 35 ounces

COMMENTS a You can read the answer from the scale.
b You have to estimate the answer so your answer can be slightly out.
c 200 grams is about 7 ounces so 1000 grams ≈ 5 × 200 grams.

LEVEL 5 HANDLING DATA (page 91)
A1 a September
b May, June, October, November and December
c January, February, December

COMMENTS a Look for the narrowest bar.
b Look for the bars that are the same width as June.
c You can use a ruler to compare the maximum temperatures which are at the right-hand side of the bars.

A2 a $\frac{1}{2}$ **b** heads, tails; tails, heads; tails, tails
c $\frac{1}{4}$ **d** $\frac{1}{2}$

COMMENTS a A coin can only land two ways, head or tail.
c You can use the table to get this answer. The outcome of two tails occurs one way out of a possible four. Remember to write probabilities as fractions.
d The probability does not change. The coin does not have a memory.

A3 a Q
c Angle A is 38°, angle B is 135°.

COMMENTS a You can use a protractor but it is obvious that angle Q is the only one that is near 120°.
b Don't forget to put an arc in and label the angle.
c Angle A was the most frequently-chosen angle. Even though 45° is the most frequent angle, the majority of measurements are around 135°. Students read the wrong scale on the protractor.

A4 a P(4) = $\frac{1}{4}$, P(even) = 1
b Two sectors marked with 4s, Two sectors marked with any other even numbers and two sectors marked with any odd numbers.

COMMENTS a Two out of eight sectors are marked 4. The outcome of picking an even number is certain as all the numbers are even.

b If $P(4) = \frac{1}{3}$, then there must be two sectors marked with a 4.

A5 **a** 28   **b** Not possible to tell   **c** Month B

COMMENTS a Add up the total of the tops of the bars. $(20 + 6 + 2)$

b There is no indication of how many days are represented.

c There is a greater proportion of days with more than 8 hours in month B and a greater proportion of days with less than 4 hours in month A.

A6 **a** Plain, P(cheese) = $\frac{1}{10}$ **b** $\frac{1}{8}$
 c Plain 7, vinegar 3, chicken 2, cheese 0

COMMENTS a There are ten bags altogether and five of them are plain. One bag out of ten is cheese flavour.

b There are eight bags left and one of these is cheese flavour.

c Make each fraction into a fraction with a denominator of 12 or multiply 12 by each probability.

A7 Because there are not equal numbers of pupils teachers and canteen staff. There will be more pupils.

A8 **a** P(A) = $\frac{1}{4}$, P(C or D) = $\frac{1}{2}$
 b P(A) = 0, P(C or D) = $\frac{2}{3}$

COMMENTS a There is only one card out of four that Zoe needs. There are two cards out of four that Paul needs. This cancels to $\frac{1}{2}$.

b This is an impossible event. There are two chances in three of Paul getting his card.

A9 **a** 6   **b** 2

COMMENTS a As there are only four numbers the median falls between 5 and 7.

b The three numbers are 6, 6 and ?. John doesn't take size 6 so, if the range is 4, he must take a 2 or 10. You are told he doesn't take a 10.

A10 The average is 39.9

COMMENT Add up the four values which gives 159.6 km and divide by 4 to get the mean.

LEVEL 6 NUMBER (page 111)

A1 **a** $\frac{7}{16}$ **b** £60

COMMENTS a All the fractions needs to have the same denominator. $\frac{1}{4} = \frac{4}{16}$, $\frac{1}{8} = \frac{2}{16}$

b $\frac{3}{16} = \frac{6}{32}$, so the answer is $6 \times £10$.

A2 **a** 5 and $^-3$ **b** $^-5$ and $^+3$ **c** $^-4$ and $^-2$ **d** $^-5$

COMMENTS a First consider the numbers that will multiply to give an answer of $^-15$, then decide which pair add to $^+2$.

c Remember that $- \times - = +$.

d Squares can also have a negative root.

A3 Calculate the area of each part of the diagram. The red squares have areas 81 cm² and 9 cm² which is a total of 90 cm². The yellow rectangles each have an area of 27 cm² which is a total of 54 cm². The ratio of red to yellow is 90 : 54 which can be cancelled on both sides by 18.

A4 104 lambs

COMMENTS 30% of 80 is 24. This means that 24 sheep had two lambs and 56 had one lamb.

A5 For example, $^-2 - ^-7 = 5$ and $^-7 - ^-2 = ^-5$

COMMENTS Any combination of negative numbers that work will do. Remember that two minus signs together make a plus.

A6 **a** 78%   **b** 88.6%   **c** Privet

COMMENTS a The calculation is $650 \div 833 \times 100$. The answer is rounded.

b The calculation is $2437.5 \div 2751.15 \times 100$. The answer is rounded.

c Divide the takings by the number of plants to get the cost of each plant. Beech cost £1.70 each and Privet cost £1.30 each.

A7 **a** 643 + 521 and 534 + 216   **b** 356 − 241

COMMENTS There are other possible answers, these are suggestions.

a The only way to do this is by trial and improvement. There are some clues. As the total in the first is over 1100 the first digits must be 6 and 5 and as the last digit in the answer is 4 the last two digits must be 1 and 3. In the second problem the last two digits must be 6 and 4 as it must add to 10.

b Again look for clues. Only 6 and 1 have a difference of 5 so these must be the last two digits.

A8 49 cans

COMMENTS The total amount of money in the machine is $50 \times 31 + 20 \times 2 + 10 \times 41 + 5 \times 59 = 2695$p. Divide this by 55.

A9 24-photo size film, £5.30

COMMENTS Using the 24-photo size, it will take $360 \div 24 = 15$ rolls of film.
This costs $15 \times 2.15 + 15 \times 0.99 + 15 \times 0.60 =$ £56.10.
Using the 36-photo size, it will take $360 \div 36 = 10$ rolls.
This costs $10 \times 2.65 + 10 \times 2.89 + 10 \times 60 =$ £61.40.
You must show all your working on this type of question.

Level 6 Algebra (page 127)

A1 a 100, 80, 32; 252 cm; $18 \times 14 = 252$
  b $n^2, 2n, 6$

COMMENTS a The total of each side is 18 and 14 so the answer to 18×14 is the total.
b The principal is the same but this time the answers are algebraic expressions rather than numbers.

A2 E, A, C, D, B

COMMENTS You need to know that lines of the form $y = a$ are parallel to the x-axis, lines of the form $x = a$ are parallel to the y-axis and that the line $y = x$ is the line that goes through the points $(0, 0)$, $(2, 2)$, ... The other two lines can be identified by the intercept on the y-axis, which is the number on its own at the end of the equation.

A3 $7 + 5t, 3d + 17, 4d + 3, 4m$

COMMENTS You have to collect together like terms. For the third part, this is $3d + d = 4d$ and $5 - 2 = 3$. For part d the $^-(^-m)$ is equivalent to ^+m.

A4 a 2   b $\frac{1}{2}$

COMMENTS a You have to collect all the letter terms on one side of the equals sign and all the number terms on the other side. This gives $6 = 3k$.
b As above, to give $6y = 3$, so $y = 3 \div 6$.

A5 a 23, 20, 33 b 3   c 2.5

COMMENTS a Replace the variable x by 5, so the first part is $2 \times 5 + 13 = 23$.
b This is a straightforward linear equation. $2y = 6$.
c Collect letter terms on one side and the numbers on the other side. This gives $4y = 10$, $y = 10 \div 4$.

A6 $2n + 4, n + 2, n$

COMMENT The missing terms are $n + n + 4$, $(2n + 4) \div 4$, $n + 2 - 2$.

A7 a Ground and 12   b 60 seconds
  c A line from $(80, 22)$ to $(125, 0)$

COMMENTS a The floors where the lift stopped are the places on the graph where it levels out.
b Add all the times when the lift is not stationary. This is from 0 to 20 seconds, 30 to 55 seconds and 60 to 75 seconds.

A8 a $a + 2b = 8, d - 2c = ^-3$
  b $14c - 7d = 21$ or $3a + 6b - 2c + d = 21$

COMMENTS a The first equation is found by dividing the first expression by 3. The second is found by changing the sign of the second expression.
b The first solution is found by multiplying the second expression by 7. The second is the first expression minus the second expression, but be careful with $^-(^-d) = ^+d$.

A9 I was walking at a steady speed.

COMMENT The graph shows that the distance covered is the same for each unit of time.

A10

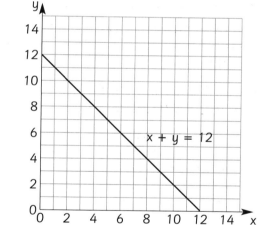

Level 6 Shape, Space and Measures (page 142)

A1 a Either of the two angles between the apex of the top triangle and the horizontal line across the top.   b 50°

COMMENT b The bottom triangle is isosceles so the two angles are equal. $180° - 80° = 100°$, $100° \div 2 = 50°$.

A2 a 706.9 cm² b 19 cm

COMMENTS a The calculation is $\pi \times 15^2$. The answer is rounded.   b The calculation is $120 \div 2\pi$.

A3 a The quadrilateral can be divided into two triangles each of which has an angle sum of 180°.   b 540°   c 900°

COMMENTS **b** A pentagon can be divided into three triangles. **c** A heptagon can be divided into five triangles.

A4 a 157.1 cm **b** 137 m

COMMENTS **a** The calculation is $C = \pi d = \pi \times 50$.
b The calculation is $87 \times 157 = 13\,665$ cm. Divide this by 100 to convert it to metres and then round.

A5 a 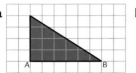 **b**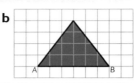

COMMENTS The base of the triangle is 6 cm so the height must be 4 cm². Any triangle with a height of 4 cm will do in part **a**. In part **b** the apex of the triangle must be over the centre of the base line.

A6 a 60 cm³ **b** 6 cm

COMMENTS **a** The volume of a cuboid is the product of the three sides. **b** $2 \times 5 \times x = 60$

A7. 10°

COMMENT
The values of the angles are marked on the diagram.

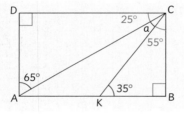

A8 a A, B, C

COMMENT Work out the area of each square. A is given as 36 cm², B has an area of $36 \times 36 = 1296$ cm². C has a side of 9, which means an area of 81 cm².

LEVEL 6 HANDLING DATA (page 153)
A1 a 30%, $\frac{3}{10}$, $\frac{6}{20}$, 0.3 **b** $\frac{9}{20}$, 45%

COMMENTS **a** All of these values are equivalent.
b There are 9 counters that are not red, out of the total of 20.

A2 a $\frac{4}{5}$ **b** 4 **c** 8 **d** 7

COMMENTS **a** P(black) = 1 – P(red)
b To make P(red) = $\frac{1}{5}$, there must be at least four black cubes.
c If there are at least two red cubes there must be at least eight black cubes.
d If P(green) = $\frac{3}{5}$ there must be 12 green cubes. The smallest number of blue cubes is 1.

A3 a The higher the horse the greater the mass.
b 590 kg **c** 167 cm
d The scatter diagram would have positive correlation but the crosses should be below the line shown.

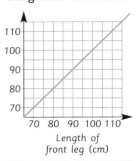

COMMENT **b** Be careful with the scales. Make sure you show the lines on the graph to show how you got your answer.

A4 5, 5, 14

COMMENT If the mode is 5 there must be two fives. If the mean is 8 the total of the three cards must be 24.

A5 a 36° and 324° **b** Not possible to tell.

COMMENTS **a** 6 out of 60 is $\frac{1}{10}$. $\frac{1}{10}$ of 360 is 36°.
b All or none of the pupils who wear glasses could be girls or boys.

A6 a 50% **b** 54% **c** No

COMMENTS **a** This is the size of the bar. Subtract: 82% – 32%.
b This is the sum of the other bars: 47% + 7%.
c There is no data about how many mice there were in each survey.

A7 a The sample is too small. People may not admit to dropping litter.
b People may not necessarily drop litter outside the shop. The sample will not be random.

COMMENTS **a** Questions in surveys should be unbiased and samples should be large enough to give valid results.
b Surveys should use a random sample of people and take place where a valid sample can be obtained.

A8 Ben, Ann, Carl, Donna; Ben, Ann, Donna, Eric; Ben, Carl, Donna, Eric

COMMENTS Ben must go and the only option without Donna and Eric is Ann, Carla and Donna.

A9 a 6 points **b** 1 and 5 **c** 1, 3, 5

COMMENTS **a** Paula's total is 24 over four games.
b The total must be 6 and the difference (range) must be 4.
c The total must be 9 and the difference must be 4.

A1 **a** largest 3^4, $9^2 = 3^4$ **b** 2^5 and 2^7

COMMENTS a 3^4 is $3 \times 3 \times 3 \times 3 = 81$. $9 = 3^2$,
so $(3^2)^2 = 3^4$
b Any odd power of 2 cannot be a square number. Only
even powers of numbers or odd powers of square
numbers are square numbers.

A2 **a** 8   **b** 16   **c** 6   **d** 30

COMMENTS a Rounding numbers to sensible values so
that you can do the calculation gives $72 \div 9$.
b The rounding is 32×0.5.
c The numbers should be rounded to 8, 22 and 5 which
gives $30 \div 5$.
d Round to $(30 \times 24) \div (6 \times 4)$ then cancel to 5×6.

A3 **a** $0.1 \times 0.05 = 0.005$ **b** $10 \div 0.1 = 100$

COMMENTS a Choose the lowest two cards.
b Dividing by 0.1 is the same as multiplying by 10.

A4 **a** $2n$ **b** $\dfrac{2}{n}$ **c** n^2

COMMENTS In this question choose any value and work
out (or estimate) the values of each expression.
c Remember that the square of a negative value is positive.

A5 **a** 13 403.076 92   **b** 13 000

COMMENTS a First work out how many feet there are
in 33 miles, as this is how far the ship travels in 1
hour. Then divide by 13.
b Two significant figures means the nearest number that
has two non-zero digits.

A6 **a** $k = 3$, $m = 6$ **b** 16 384

COMMENTS a You need to be careful with powers.
Write them out in full to check if necessary.
b This is half of 2^{14}, so divide 32 768 by 2.

A7 **a** 92.5 m   **b** 49.5 m   **c** 11 times

COMMENTS a 92.5 would round to 93 m.
b The least distance covered in one circuit is $2 \times (92.5 +
49.5) = 284$ m. This is then divided into 3 km = 3000 m.

A8 **a** 51.8%
    b In 1998 the percentage is 72% which is a
    bigger proportion than 51.8%.

COMMENT a The calculation is $6.16 \div 11.89 \times 100$.

A9 **a** 70×1.09 For example: What is 90% of 70?
    b 0.86

COMMENTS a 1.09 is the multiplier equivalent to an
increase of 9%.
70×0.9 is 90% of 70.
70×1.9 is 190% (a 90% increase) of 70.
70×0.09 is 9% of 70.
b 0.86 is the multiplier that represents a 14% decrease.

LEVEL 7 ALGEBRA (page 179)

A1 **a** $\dfrac{n}{2n + 1}$ **b** $\dfrac{2}{5}$, $\dfrac{3}{10}$, $\dfrac{4}{17}$, ….

COMMENTS a The numerators are just the counting
numbers 1, 2, 3, 4, 5, … and the denominators are the
series 3, 5, 7, 9, 11, … .
b You have to substitute 2, 3 and 4 into the expression.

A2 **a** Choose two points on the line, say $(4, 0)$
    and $(0, 8)$, and substitute them into the
    equation. $2 \times 4 + 0 = 8$ and $2 \times 0 + 8 = 8$.
    If both points obey the equation then the
    equation must be correct.
  b $x + y = 8$ **c**
  d $(1.5, 4)$

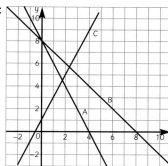

COMMENTS b All points on the line obey this rule.
d $3y = 6x + 3$ Multiply **1** by 3 to balance.
$3y = 4x + 6$
$0 = 2x - 3$ Subtract to eliminate y.
$x = 1.5$ Solve the equation to find x.
$y = 2 \times 1.5 + 1 = 4$ Substitute to find y.

A3 **a** 1.5   **b** $^-16$

COMMENTS a Collect terms on each side to get $4y = 6$.
b Expand the bracket to get $3y - 12$ and then collect
terms to get $2y = ^-32$.

A4 **a** $5(2y + 4)$ and $2(5y + 10)$
    b $12(y + 24)$ **c** $7(y + 2)$
    d $2y^2(3y - 1)$

COMMENTS a Multiply out the brackets.
b When you expand this bracket you get $12y + 288$.
c Take out the common factor, 7, from each term.
d Take out the common factors 2 and y^2.

A5 **a** 2*m*: even, m^2: odd, $3m - 1$: even,
$(m - 1)(m + 1)$: even

b Not possible to tell.

COMMENTS **a** Try the expressions out with an odd
number such as 3.
b If $m = 3$ the answer is 2, which is even.
If $m = 5$ the answer is 3, which is odd.

A6 **a** $y = x^2$ **b** $x = {}^-5$ **c** $y = x^2$
d $x + y = 10$ and $y = 2x + 1$
e (1, 3) and ($^-3, ^-5$)

COMMENTS **a** Try the values in each equation to see if
it is true.
b The *y*-axis has the equation $y = 0$.
c Any graphs that include terms that are powers ($\neq 1$)
of *x* are not straight.
d Try the values out, $3 + 7 = 10$ and $7 = 2 \times 3 + 1$.
e Draw the graph and find the point of intersection.

A7 **a** First box ticked **b** Second box ticked

COMMENTS **a** Subtracting two from any even number
gives an even number, so the number inside the
brackets is even. Squaring an even number gives an
even number.
b An even number minus 1 is odd. An even number plus
1 is odd. So the number in each set of brackets is odd.
Multiplying two odd numbers gives an odd number.

A8 $f = \dfrac{p}{2} - e$

COMMENTS First, divide each side by 2 to get
$\dfrac{p}{2} = e + f$, then subtract *e*. An alternative answer is $\dfrac{p - 2e}{2}$.

A9 **a** 350 kph **b** The gradient of the line is greater.
c See graph.

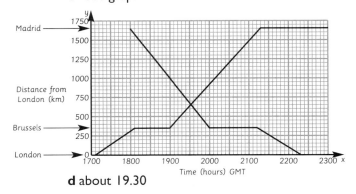

d about 19.30

COMMENTS **a** The plane travels 350 km in 1 hour.
b The steeper the line on a distance–time graph the
greater the speed.
c Make sure you get the times correct on the axis. Each
division represents 6 minutes.

LEVEL 7 SHAPE, SPACE AND MEASURES (page 194)
A1 **a** $10^2 = 8^2 + 6^2$ **b** 168 cm³ **c** 120 cm³

COMMENTS **a** To show that a triangle is right-angled
when you know all the sides, use Pythagoras'
theorem.
b The cross-section is a right-angled triangle with an
area of 24 cm².
c The volume of a prism is cross-sectional area × height.

A2 **a** 50°

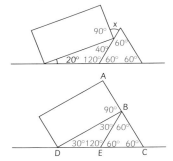

b Angles EBD
and BDE are
both 30° so
the triangle
must be
isosceles.

COMMENTS **a** The angles are marked on the diagram.
You will probably find 60° and 120° first. Then use
the sum of angles in a triangle to find 40°. The
rectangle has a corner of 90° so, as the angles on a
straight line are 180°. The missing angle must be 50°.
b The angles are marked on the diagram. As BDE has
two angles (30°) the same it must be isosceles.

A3

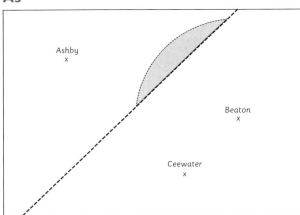

COMMENTS Draw the perpendicular bisector of the line
between Ashby and Ceewater, and a circle of radius
4.5 cm around Beaton. The required area is between the
bisector and the circle.

A4 The ramp is too high.

COMMENTS The easiest way to do this is to use
Pythagoras' theorem to work out the height of the ramp.
(Height)² = $10^2 - 9.85^2 = 2.9775$.
$\sqrt{2.9775} = 1.73$ (2 d.p.)

A5

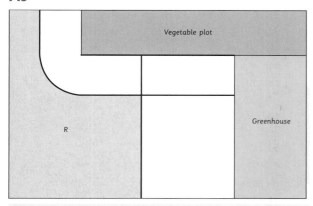

COMMENTS The region that is more than 8 metres from the vegetable plot must be at least 2 cm from the edge of the vegetable plot. The boundary is a line 2 cm from the edge, but where it goes round the corner it is an arc of radius 2 cm.

The region that is more than 18 m from the greenhouse is the region more than 4.5 cm from the edge of the greenhouse in the drawing. This is just a straight line as there are no corners to worry about. The region R is the bit where both the other regions overlap.

A6   a   20.8087 cm   b 9.797 96 cm

COMMENTS a This is a straightforward Pythagoras problem to find the hypotenuse. $17^2 + 12^2 = 433$. Then take the square root of the answer.

b This is a straightforward problem, using Pythagoras' theorem to find a short side. $11^2 - 5^2 = 96$ Then take the square root to find the answer.

A7   21.5%

COMMENT The area of the circle is $\pi r^2 = \pi \times 9 = 28.2743\,cm^2$. The area of the square is $36\,cm^2$. The percentage is $(36 - 28.27) \div 36 \times 100$.

LEVEL 7 HANDLING DATA (page 208)
A1   a $3x + 10$
    b Any three cards with a total of $12x$, e.g. $4x - 5, 4x, 4x + 5$. c $4x + 2$

COMMENTS a If the mean of the three cards is $3x$ then the total of all three cards must be $3 \times 3x = 9x$. The total of the two cards shown is $6x - 10$.

c The total of the cards is $12x + 6$. The mean is $(12x + 6) \div 3$.

A3   a The total of children is $1 \times 1 + 2 \times n + 3 \times 5 + 4 \times 6 + 5 \times 3 = 55 + 2n$.
    b $15 + n$ c $n = 10$

COMMENTS a You cannot see the top of the bar for two children but if there are n families this must represent $2 \times n$ children.

b The total of all the bars is $1 + n + 5 + 6 + 3$.

c If the mean is three then $(55 + 2n) \div (15 + n) = 3$. This is a difficult equation to solve.
$55 + 2n = 3 \times (15 + n)$, so $55 + 2n = 45 + 3n$, $10 = n$.

A2   Bag A

COMMENT There are several ways to do this question. The most straightforward way is to work out the probability of picking a red ball from each bag.
P(Red from A) = $\frac{12}{30}$ = 0.4, P(Red from B) = $\frac{10}{26}$ = 0.385 (3 d.p.)

A4   a 4.85 g   b 0.1 g   c Bird at (12.30, 4.5)

COMMENTS a You need to draw a line from 11.30 am up to the line of best fit and then across to the side axis.

b This can be read off anywhere along the graph. For example at 8.00 am the mass is 4.5 grams and at 9.00 am it is 4.6 grams.

c Even if the mass increases at the normal rate it will still be 0.45 grams below the line of best fit.

A5   a Mean 25 years 3 months, range 4 years 8 months
    b The mean will increase by less than 1 year.
    c It is not possible to tell.

COMMENTS a The mean will increase by 1 year but the range of ages will stay the same.

b There is more than 1 member and the age of the new member is greater than the mean.

c The youngest member will be less than 18 years 5 months but the oldest member may be older than 18 years 5 months already.

A6   True.   Not enough information.

COMMENT There are no male wing lengths in the range 121–125 mm. Both male and female have some birds in the range 136–140 mm and it is not possible to tell the greatest value in this range.

LEVEL 8 NUMBER (page 211)
A1   a 101 000   b 17 : 1   c 6×10^{10}

COMMENTS a This is a calculator paper so you should use your calculator to work this out. You should know which button to press to enter the power of 10. It is marked E, EE or EXP on most calculators.

b The ratio of masses is $5.98 \times 10^{24} : 3.58 \times 10^{23}$. To put it into the form $n : 1$, divide by the last number. This gives 16.657 381 62 : 1. The answer is rounded, but you could leave it as a decimal.

c Substitute the numbers into the formula. The answer is 5.79×10^{10}, which has to be rounded appropriately.

A2 21%

COMMENTS Using percentage multipliers, an increase of 10% corresponds to a factor of 1.1, so $1.1^2 = 1.21$. Alternatively, start with 100 and work out the final answer, which will be 121.

A3 £45

COMMENTS £38.25 represents 85%, so 1% is £38.25 ÷ 85 = £0.45, giving 100% as £45.

A4
a In 1996 they employed 400 more people but in 1997 they employed 10% of 4400 = 440 more people.

b 4000×1.1^2 c $0.88n$

COMMENTS a This is compound interest. The second increase is based on the new figure, not the original figure.

b An increase of 10% involves a multiplier of 1.1. The first increase is 4000×1.1 and the second increase is $4000 \times 1.1 \times 1.1$.

c A decrease of 20% involves a multiplier of 0.80. An increase of 10% involves a multiplier of 1.1, so you find the overall answer by using a multiplier of 0.8 × 1.1 or 0.88.

A5 $d = 40.96$ or 41.0 (3 s.f.)

COMMENTS The sum is $^-(27^2) \div (2 \times ^-8.9)$. The accuracy should not be to more that 4 s.f. as the numbers in the sum are given to 3 s.f. at most. (You can assume that 27.0 is rounded to 3 s.f.)

A6
a $50 \, cm^3$ b $9 \, cm$ c $2.5 \, cm$ d $\frac{m^3}{6}$

COMMENTS a Substitute the numbers into the formula $\frac{1}{2} \times 5 \times 5 \times 6^2$.

b The base has area of $16 \, cm^2$. 48 ÷ 16 = 3. Multiply this by 3.

c You need to solve the equation $\frac{1}{3} \times 12 \times b^2 = 25$.

d Substituting in the formula gives $\frac{1}{3} \times \frac{1}{2} \times m \times m \times m$. The $\frac{1}{2}$ is needed because the volume is half of a regular square-based pyramid.

A7 $3x + 7 = 8$ is correct for one value of x ($x = \frac{1}{3}$). $3(x + 1) = 3x + 3$ is an identity and is correct for all values of x. $x + 3 = x - 3$ is not correct for any value of x, as it leads to the impossible statement $3 = ^-3$. $5 + x = 5 - x$ is correct for one value of x ($x = 0$). $x^2 = 9$ is correct for two values of x ($x = 3, x = ^-3$).

A8 35

COMMENT The equation is $(y + 1)(y + 5) = (y + 10)(y - 3)$ which expands to $y^2 + 6y - 5 = y^2 + 7y - 30$ and this simplifies to $y = 35$.

A9
a If y was 2 then $9 + y^2 = 9 + 4 = 13$, which is not a square number.

b $16 \times y^2 = 4 \times 4 \times y \times y = 4y \times 4y = (4y)^2$, so it is always a square number.

A10 112 minutes

COMMENT Set up two simultaneous equations: $3x + 9y = 120, 5x + 5y = 90$ and then solve them.

A11
a
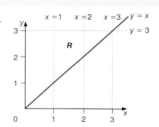
b $x \leqslant 4, y \geqslant 2, y \leqslant x$

COMMENTS a To find an inequality, find the boundary line and then decide which side of the line is represented by the inequality. The boundary line is the line you get when you replace the inequality sign by an equals sign. The region is where x is greater than 1 but less than 2, y is greater than x and less than 3. Only the region marked obeys all four inequalities.

b The region where x is less than 4 and y is more than 2 but less than x. There are other inequalities, for example, $x \geqslant 2$ but these wouldn't really be of any use in describing it as the line $x = 2$ is not a boundary.

A12
a A(0, 16), B(4, 0), C($^-$4, 0)   b (4, 24)
c $y = x^2 + 8$

COMMENTS a The intercept on the y-axis is the constant term 16. The intercepts on the x-axis are the solutions to the equation $y^2 = 16$.

b The x-coordinate stays the same but the y-coordinate was 12 below the line, so is now 12 above the line.

c The curve is $y = x^2 + c$ because of the reflection, and the intercept on the y-axis is 8.

A13 **a** $a^2 - b^2 = (a - b)(a + b)$ **b** ab
c $a - b$

COMMENTS a The $(a - b)$ terms cancel out. $a^2 - b^2$ is called the difference of two squares.
b a^2 and b^2 cancel from the top and bottom.
c The top line factorises to $a^2b^2(a - b)$ then the a^2b^2 cancels in the top and bottom.

LEVEL 8 SHAPE, SPACE AND MEASURES (page 216)
A14 **a** 15 cm   **b** 12 cm
c Yes, all angles are the same.

COMMENTS a The scale factor is 1.5.
b In triangle ACB, the sides are in the ratio $3:6$, which is $1:2$, so in triangle BCD the sides are in the ratio $6:12$.

A15 **a** 8.43   **b** 64.6°

COMMENTS a The calculation is $14 \times \sin 37°$.
b The calculation is $\cos^{-1}(6 \div 14)$.

A16 a CD = 13 and AC = $\sqrt{28.8^2 + 12^2}$ = 31.2
     Perimeter is $31.2 + 28.8 + 5 + 13 = 78$ cm
b $13^2 + 31.2^2 = 1142.44$ and $33.8^2 = 1142.44$

COMMENTS a You should recognise a 5, 12, 13 triangle. The numbers 5, 12, 13 are called a Pythagorean triple. Use Pythagoras' theorem to find AC and then add all the perimeter values together.
b As the sides of the triangle obey Pythagoras' theorem the triangle must be right-angled.

A17 **a** Triangle ABO is isosceles so angle
     ABO = angle BAO = x.
     Triangle CBO is also isosceles so
     angle CBO = angle OCB = y.
b In triangle ABC, the sum of the angles is
     $x + x + y + y = 180°$
     Hence $2x + 2y = 180$
     $2(x + y) = 180°$, $x + y = 90°$
     Therefore angle ABC = $x + y = 90°$

LEVEL 8 HANDLING DATA (page 218)

A18 **a** Taking the midpoints of the ranges,
     $(15 \times 6 + 4.5 \times 14 + 75 \times 21 + 105 \times 9)$
     $\div 50 = 64.8$
b 68 minutes   **c** 4 pupils

COMMENTS a The calculation is $(15 \times 6 + 45 \times 14 + 75 \times 21 + 105 \times 9) \div 50$. The frequencies are multiplied by the mid-value of each bar and the total is divided by the total frequency.
b This can be read from the graph, starting at 25 on the cumulative frequency axis, across to the graph line and down to the time axis.
c This can be calculated from the graph. Start at 100 minutes on the time axis, move up to the graph line and across to the cumulative frequency axis to find 46 pupils. Then $50 - 46 = 4$ pupils.

A19 **a** $\frac{1}{64}$ **b** $\frac{3}{64}$

COMMENTS a The probability each time is $\frac{1}{4}$, so after three moves the probability is $\frac{1}{4} \times \frac{1}{4} \times \frac{1}{4}$.
b There are three routes that the robot can take.

Index

Index

William Collins' dream of knowledge for all began with the publication of his first book in 1819. A self-educated mill worker, he not only enriched millions of lives, but also founded a flourishing publishing house. Today, staying true to this spirit, Collins books are packed with inspiration, innovation and practical expertise. They place you at the centre of a world of possibility and give you exactly what you need to explore it.

Collins. Do more.

Published by Collins
An imprint of HarperCollins*Publishers*
77 – 85 Fulham Palace Road
Hammersmith
London
W6 8JB

Browse the complete Collins catalogue at
www.collinseducation.com

©HarperCollins*Publishers* Limited 2005

First published 2001
This new edition published 2005

10 9 8 7 6 5 4 3 2 1

ISBN-13 978 0 00 721243 9
ISBN-10 0 00 721243 7

Kevin Evans and Keith Gordon assert the moral right to be identified as the authors of this work.

British Library Cataloguing in Publication Data
A Catalogue record for this publication is available from the British Library

Edited by Kathryn Senior and Joan Miller
Production by Katie Butler
Series design by Sally Boothroyd
Book design by Ann Paganuzzi and Wendi Watson
Index compiled by Joan Dearnley
Printed and bound by Printing Express, Hong Kong

Acknowledgements
The Authors and Publishers are grateful to QCA (SCAA) for permission to reproduce past Test questions: pp. 10–12, 21–23, 31–32, 42–43, 55–56, 67–69, 79–82, 91–94, 111–113, 127–130, 142–144, 153–156, 166–168, 179–181, 194–196, 208–218.

Illustrations
Gill Bishop, Harvey Collins, Richard Deverell, Jerry Fowler, Gecko Ltd, Ian Law, Ann Paganuzzi, Dave Poole, Carl Thorney and Tony Warne

Every effort has been made to contact the holders of copyright material but, if any have been inadvertently overlooked, the Publishers will be pleased to make the necessary arrangements at the first opportunity

You might also like to visit
www.harpercollins.co.uk
The book lover's website